W9-CNI-269

AMERICAN FOLK LEGEND

PUBLISHED UNDER THE AUSPICES OF THE
CENTER FOR THE STUDY OF COMPARATIVE
FOLKLORE AND MYTHOLOGY, UNIVERSITY
OF CALIFORNIA, LOS ANGELES

American Folk Legend
A Symposium

edited, with a preface, by WAYLAND D. HAND

UNIVERSITY OF CALIFORNIA PRESS
Berkeley   Los Angeles   London

UCLA CENTER FOR THE STUDY OF
COMPARATIVE FOLKLORE AND MYTHOLOGY

Publications: II

University of California Press
Berkeley and Los Angeles, California

University of California Press, Ltd.
London, England

California Library Reprint Series Edition, 1979
ISBN: 0-520-03836-3
Library of Congress Catalog Card Number: 79-145785
Series design by David Pauly
Printed in the United States of America

1 2 3 4 5 6 7 8 9

Preface

Folk legendry has long been neglected in American folklore scholarship, just as this field has lagged well behind other disciplines within folklore in Europe and elsewhere. As one who in 1959 had a part in stimulating the International Society for Folk-Narrative Research to take up legend study as part of its proper concerns, and as a delegate to two international conferences on folk legend (Antwerp, 1962; Budapest, 1963), I had long cherished the notion of a conference devoted specifically to the problems of American Folk Legend. This opportunity came when the Center for the Study of Comparative Folklore and Mythology at UCLA was empowered by the University to call the UCLA Conference on American Folk Legend. This conference was held June 19 to 22, 1969. Eleven delegates from the United States and Canada participated in the conference in addition to four staff members of the guest institution. Austin E. Fife and Byrd Howell Granger, two well-known American legend scholars were invited to the conference, but were unable to attend.

The proceedings of the conference are published herewith. As editor, I have made only minimal editorial changes, leaving the conferees to speak freely for themselves. Since my article on the "Status of European and American Legend Study" is within easy reach,* and since the proceedings of the conference have exceeded the length originally planned, I have not yielded to the temptation to write a formal Introduction. For historical perspective, the reader

---

* *Current Anthropology*, 6 (1965), 439–446. This has been translated into German: "Der Stand der europäischen und amerikanischen Sagenforschung," in Leander Petzold, ed., *Vergleichende Sagenforschung*, Wege der Forschung, Band CLII (Darmstadt, 1969), 402–430.

is referred to the paper of Richard M. Dorson; matters of definition, classification, structure, and style are taken up in the presenta-
tions of Robert A. Georges; Linda Dégh, Herbert Halpert, Wayland D. Hand, and Barre Toelken; socio-psychological values are
to be found, among other places, in the papers of Horace P. Beck,
Jan Brunvand, Alan Dundes, and Albert B. Friedman; Don Yoder
treats certain aspects of saints' legends in the Pennsylvania German
country; D. K. Wilgus and Lynwood Montell show legendary and
balladic treatments of the same historical event, and Stanley L.
Robe and Américo Paredes survey Hispanic and Latin American
legendary materials.

If the conference proved anything, it was the fact that American
legend studies are still in their infancy. Needed, it is apparent, are
well-annotated collections of legends from all parts of the country,
surveys of various legend genres, and finding-lists to reveal the un-
tapped legend stores. From the basic field data, then naturally will
follow thematic and formal studies. In short, I believe that once
legends are located and arrayed in full and logical groupings much
uncertainty concerning them will be dispelled. If only a tithe of the
energy and interest that has gone into the systematic study of folk
song and ballad, or even into folktale study, in this country, had
been expended on the study of American legendry, there would
be no need to puzzle over what most workers would regard as the
ABC's of American legend study.

Because of the wide-ranging subject matter of papers given at the
Conference, a general bibliography has not been attempted. Rather,
full bibliographical entries, including names of publishers, are
given in the footnotes to each article.

I hope I shall be forgiven for having preempted the Preface to
make a plea for the vigorous prosecution of an almost forgotten
field. If the UCLA Conference on American Folk Legend can have
stimulated field collecting in any way, furthered the searching of
published materials, or even prevailed upon individual scholars to
chart specific areas of inquiry, then the efforts we have expended
shall have been amply repaid.

It is my pleasant task here to thank Vice-Chancellor Foster H.
Sherwood for having underwritten the conference, Robert A.
Georges and Stanley L. Robe for helping to plan it, and Jeanette
Rimola for having worked out the physical arrangements for the
conference with the staff of Rieber Hall, where the conference was
held.

WAYLAND D. HAND

Contents

Abbreviations

CFQ	*California Folklore Quarterly* (See *Western Folklore*)
FA	*Folklore Americas*
FS	Folklore Studies
HF	*Hoosier Folklore Bulletin*
IF	*Indiana Folklore*
JAF	*Journal of American Folklore*
JFI	*Journal of the Folklore Institute*
JOFS	*Journal of the Ohio Folklore Society*
KFQ	*Keystone Folklore Quarterly*
KFR	*Kentucky Folklore Record*
MAFS	Memoirs of the American Folklore Society
MF	*Mississippi Folklore*
MWF	*Midwest Folklore*
NCF	*North Carolina Folklore*
NEF	*Northeast Folklore*
NMFR	*New Mexico Folklore Record*
NWF	*Northwest Folklore*
NYFQ	*New York Folklore Quarterly*
PF	*Pennsylvania Folklife*
PTFS	*Publications of the Texas Folklore Society*
SFQ	*Southern Folklore Quarterly*
TFSB	*Tennessee Folklore Society Bulletin*
WF	*Western Folklore*
WVF	*West Virginia Folklore*

The General Concept of Legend: Some Assumptions to be Reexamined and Reassessed

ROBERT A. GEORGES, *University of California, Los Angeles*

The convening of this conference is certainly an auspicious event. The impressive roster of participants and the diversity of topics for discussion suggest that during these four days, we will all become better informed about a multitude of subjects. Moreover, in the process, many of us will be encouraged to continue to pursue certain lines of inquiry that we have found to be promising, while others of us will be motivated to explore alternative approaches and to experiment with new analytical techniques that some of our colleagues here have found to be fruitful. The need for periodic reinforcement and the desire to share and learn about new ideas are the principal reasons why meetings are held and why so many people attend and participate in them. But there is also a potential danger in a conference that promises to be as wide-ranging as this one—a danger that we may be unable to see the forest because of the trees. For as we are exposed to legends of Mormons and Mexicans, saints and heroes, modern mythmakers and modern society, we may well become so engrossed in, fascinated by, and intrigued with the content of the data which is presented to us that we will tend to forget—or perhaps even find it convenient to ignore—the principal objectives of a conference on so specific a topic as American folk legend.

These objectives, it seems to me, should be, first, to determine, discuss, and assess the validity of the general concept and individual conceptions of legend, and, second, to discuss and attempt to de-

termine (1) whether there should be—and, indeed, whether there
can be—an index of American folk legends; (2) what the motivations are for wanting such an index; (3) whether such motivations
are justified; and (4) what contributions the compilation of an
index of American folk legends—and ultimately, apparently, of an
international index of legend types [1]—might make to the advancement of knowledge. Because of my sincere conviction that these
objectives should remain foremost in our deliberations, and because of my fear that we might be tempted to forget or ignore them
as we become increasingly exposed to specific kinds of data, I have
chosen to devote the time at my disposal this morning to a discussion of the general concept and individual conceptions of legend.
For unless or until we are satisfied that the term *legend* has some
common meaning for us, then questions relating to the possible
need and reasons for compiling *indexes* of legends, and speculations
concerning the potential contributions that such indexes might
make to the advancement of knowledge, are really meaningless, if
not completely irrelevant.

I should like to begin, then, by raising the question that is basic
to the topic that I have chosen to discuss and that should be of
primary concern to every participant in this conference: what does
the term *legend* mean? One way to begin to answer this question, of
course, would be for me to ask each of you to write a *definition* of
legend. Then I could collect them, compare and contrast them,
present the results to the group, and we could devote the remainder
of this meeting to a discussion and interpretation of the findings.
Such a procedure could be very instructive; but most of you would
resent, justifiably, my making such a request; and many of you
would insist that the results of such a survey would undoubtedly
be similar to those that Francis Lee Utley obtained several years
ago when he analyzed the twenty-one definitions of *folklore* that
were printed in volume I of *Funk and Wagnalls Standard Diction-*

---

[1] The compilation of legend indexes is one of the long-range goals of the
International Society for Folk-Narrative Research. In his article "Status of
European and American Legend Study," *Current Anthropology*, vol. 6, no. 4
(1965), Wayland D. Hand notes that at its Budapest meeting in 1963, the
society established a Folk Legend Committee, which had as one of its objectives
"to draw up a listing of main categories under which legends might be classified
internationally" (p. 444). Linda Dégh reports that in recent years, "the International Society for Folk-Narrative Research placed the indexing of national
and international folk-legend material on its schedule" ("Processes of Legend
Formation," in *IV International Congress for Folk-Narrative Research in Athens:
Lectures and Reports,* ed. Georgios A. Megas, [Athens, 1965], pp. 77–78).

ary of Folklore, Mythology and Legend.[2] We would find, you might feel, the same thing that Utley found: that there would be many similarities in the content of the individual definitions and that there would be many differences as well. All that we would be able to conclude from such a survey, if such were to be the case, is that each individual has his *own* definition—and hence, his own *conception*—of legend; and these conclusions would simply confirm, once again, what it is that Roger Welsch has recently asserted is so commendable and satisfying about contemporary American folkloristics: that it is to their great credit that folklorists are aware of the fact that definitions are always relative and that those who would attempt to get folklorists to reach some consensus concerning definitions are really doing a great disservice to their chosen field of study.[3]

But the results of a survey of *legend* definitions would probably be quite different from the results that Utley obtained following his scrutiny of a corpus of definitions of *folklore*. For we would find, I think, that there would be some striking consistencies in our corpus of definitions. If this were, indeed, to be the case, then it would be possible for us to abstract from the individual definitions those parts that were most consistent and hence most significant statistically. And once we had isolated these consistent parts, then we could scrutinize them and attempt to determine from our examination of them whether or not there might be some general concept that underlies and is implicit in individual conceptions of legend as they are revealed in a corpus of definitions. If we discovered, as I think we would, that there *is*, in fact, such a general concept, and if we could characterize that concept, then we could also analyze it and attempt to assess its validity.

It is not my intention to conduct this type of survey here this morning, for I have no desire to do so and no right to impose upon you in such a way. But I would like to engage in a bit of intelligent speculation and suggest what I think we might discover if such a survey *were*, indeed, to be conducted among the members of this (or any other) group of folklorists. I ask you, therefore, to bear with

---

[2] The results of Utley's survey are presented in his article "Folk Literature: An Operational Definition," *JAF*, 74 (1961), 193–206. The article has been reprinted in *The Study of Folklore*, ed. Alan Dundes (Englewood Cliffs, N. J.: Prentice-Hall, 1965), pp. 7–24.

[3] See Roger L. Welsch, "A Note on Definitions," *JAF*, 81 (1968), 262–264. For a reply to Welsch's comments, see Richard Bauman, "Towards a Behavioral Theory of Folklore: A Reply to Roger Welsch," *JAF*, 82 (1969), 167–170.

me for the remainder of the time that has been allotted to me, in
the hope that what might at first seem to you to be nothing more
than simplistic strategy will ultimately reveal a good deal about
our conference topic and also, perhaps, about ourselves.

If we had before us a corpus of definitions of legend written by
the people in this room, I think that the assertion that we could
expect to find to be made most consistently would be the assertion
that a legend is *a story or narrative*. Some definers might qualify
this somewhat by noting that legends are *traditional* stories or narratives, others might insist that legends are always *prose* narratives,
and still others might assert that legends can be in *either* poetry
or prose. But most definitions would simply indicate that a legend
is a story or narrative and let it go at that.

A second assertion that I think we could expect to find to be recurrent in our corpus of definitions is the assertion that a legend
is a story or narrative that is *set in the recent or historical past*.
Some definers might find it convenient to contrast *legend* with *myth*
in order to suggest the relative remoteness from the present of the
setting of each in terms of a time continuum; but most would
probably be content to communicate the notion that a legend is a
story or narrative that recounts something that is over and done
with.

A third assertion that would probably recur in our corpus of
definitions is that a legend is a story or narrative that is *believed to
be true by those who tell it and by those to whom it is told*. The
words "believed to be true" would be left unqualified or unexplained in the majority of definitions, for it would be assumed that
their meaning was obvious. In some instances, however, the definers might explain *why* a legend is "believed to be true" by adding
that it is concerned with an *actual* person, place, event, or phenomenon, or with a person, place, event, or phenomenon that
purportedly exists or is presumed to have existed at some earlier
time. But whether or not such an explanation were included, the
important thing to the definers would be to transmit the notion
that those who tell and listen to legends find what they tell and
hear to be *credible;* and the reason *why* they find what they tell and
hear to be credible is, presumably, because it concerns *something*
that is in some way familiar—and hence, in some way also "real"—
to them.

With the exception of these three kinds of assertions, I do not
think that we would find anything else that we could consider to be
statistically significant. Some definers might note that legends con-

tain "traditional motifs" or "elements found in other forms of folklore," but such statements would probably occur only infrequently because they do not have much meaning. Others might assert that legends "are closely bound up with belief"; but this would merely constitute a redundancy, and the majority of definers would probably not include it for that reason. There would undoubtedly be a large number and variety of what we might call *"may*-clauses": "the legend *may* involve divine or semidivine beings; it *may* be concerned with supernatural or preternatural phenomena; it *may* be sacred or semisacred; it *may* be told in the first person as an actual account of a personal experience; it *may* provide some explanation for, or account for the origins of, some perceivable phenomenon, action, or state," and so forth. If such *"may*-clauses" were included at all, they would probably be presented as characteristics of specific "subtypes" or "subgenres" of legend. But even if one or more of these *"may*-clauses" were to appear with some noticeable statistical frequency, we would have to disqualify it/ them from our survey, for if one or more of these *may* constitute a characteristic of legend, then it also *may not,* thus making such assertions relative and indicating that the characteristics that they communicate are *optional,* not *obligatory,* and hence, not essential to *any* definition. It seems reasonable to assume, then, that we would discover only three kinds of recurrent assertions, but ones that would recur with such consistency and frequency that they would have to be regarded as extremely significant. And on the basis of these three kinds of assertions, we could construct a general definition of legend which might be expressed in this way: *A legend is a story or narrative, set in the recent or historical past, that is believed to be true by those by whom and to whom it is communicated.*

Such a definition would not surprise any of us, of course. It specifies what most people apparently conceive to be the principal characteristics of legend. Moreover, these characteristics have been reiterated in print since the beginnings of serious scholarship.[4] This definition is, in essence, the kind of definition that one finds in the

4 One finds *legend* characterized in such a way in such works as George Laurence Gomme, *Folklore as an Historical Science* (London: Methuen, 1908), p. 129; Sir James George Frazer, *Apollodorus* (London: W. Heinemann; New York, G. P. Putnam, 1921), pp. xxvii–xxxi; W. R. Halliday, *Indo-European Folk-Tales and Greek Legend* (Cambridge: Cambridge University Press, 1933), pp. 1–12; Hippolyte Delehaye, *The Legends of the Saints,* trans. Donald Attwater (New York: Fordham University Press, 1962), pp. 3–48 *passim;* and most other "standard" historical and descriptive works on legend and general works on **folklore.**

most recent introductory textbooks; [5] and it is certainly the kind
of definition that those who teach folklore courses present *to*—and
hence, perpetuate *through*—their students. It has a long history in
tradition; and it seems to provide a fairly precise and concise verbalization of the general *concept* that is, and always has been, implicit in the writings of legend scholars, not only in the United
States, but throughout the rest of the world as well.[6] There is
past precedent, then, for such a definition; and the general *concept*
that is implicit in the definition appears to constitute the very
foundation of legend research.

There is, certainly, nothing wrong with following past precedent,
nor is there, in most instances, any defensible reason for not trying
to build upon the conceptual foundations that were laid down by
one's predecessors. Most of us feel that the scholar's responsibility
is to learn from and contribute to a *cumulative* body of knowledge;
so scholars attempt to master what is already known and add to it
in whatever ways they can. But all of us are also aware of the fact
that inquiry is an ongoing process. New data become available
constantly, and theoretical commitments and research methods
change frequently. Therefore, as we are exposed to new data and
as we find it necessary to modify our theoretical commitments and
research methods, we also have a responsibility to reexamine and
reassess the conceptual foundations upon which we have been building. As long as we are convinced that these foundations are sound,
then we have no reason to alter our basic objectives or to discard
any concepts that make our field of inquiry meaningful. But if, at
some point in time, the soundness of these foundations appears to
be questionable for some reason, then we must attempt to discover
why our suspicions have been aroused and whether they are justified. For if we have uncertainties about the concepts upon which
we base our work, then these uncertainties will be readily apparent
in any work that we produce.

For some time now, I have had the feeling that students of legend

---

[5] See, for example, Kenneth W. Clarke and Mary W. Clarke, *Introducing
Folklore* (New York: Holt, Rinehart and Winston, 1963), pp. 24–25; and Jan
Harold Brunvand, *The Study of American Folklore: An Introduction* (New
York: W. W. Norton, 1968), pp. 87–99.

[6] The general concept and characterization of legend that is prevalent in the
Americas and Asia, as well as in other parts of the world, is derived, ultimately,
from the work of nineteenth-century European scholars, as are most of the
basic concepts that persist in folkloristics throughout the world. In his article
"The American Concept of Folklore," *JFI,* 3 (1966), 226–249, Alan Dundes discusses the "European inheritance" to which American folklorists have committed themselves and criticizes those who blindly follow past precedent.

are exceptionally uneasy about the work that they produce. This uneasiness is implicit, in a general way, in most discussions of the subject; but it has become increasingly apparent to me in the printed pronouncements, pleas, and proposals that have appeared in the scholarly literature during the current decade. Frequent apologies and justifications for the shortcomings of published works on legend, rationalizations for the inadequacy of field data and the insufficient number of national legend collections, and inconsistencies in and uncertainties about terminology and criteria for subclassification are all symptomatic of a kind of insecurity that such uneasiness has the potential to create.[7]

At first, I was very perplexed by this apparent uneasiness, for I had always been struck by what appeared to me to be a remarkable consistency in legend studies. Legend is broadly defined and generally characterized in much the same way in most of the studies with which I am familiar; and the interpretations of legend texts are, for the most part, much more conventional and much more consistent than the interpretations of so-called myth and *Märchen* texts. It seemed to me that, if anything, this kind of consistency had to be indicative of the relative security that investigators enjoy when they have a clear concept of the phenomenon that they have chosen to study, and when their periodic reexaminations and reassessments of the concepts with which they work have reinforced their conviction that they are, indeed, building on sound foundations.

Eventually, however, it occurred to me that I must be wrong and

---

[7] The reports by Hand and Dégh (see n. 1 above) concerning the discussions of legend at recent meetings of the International Society for Folk-Narrative Research clearly indicate the growing uneasiness of legend scholars concerning existing scholarship on the subject. Dégh, for instance, makes the following comments: "The main disagreement between representatives of the many countries involved lay in their different conceptions of what is a folk-legend, and the kind of topics, and the verbal frames belonging to this genre. Vague categories and groups might be attempted, based on earlier attempts, but this would not be of much help. *Until we know what we want to systematize, until we have a common understanding as to what we mean by legend, it will be impossible to establish an international catalogue*" (p. 78; my italics). Commenting on the available legend data, Hand notes: "Finding adequate and representative collections of legends, as a basis for creation of national legend indices, and other kinds of scholarly apparatus for legend study is a problem legend scholars everywhere must face." Hand exemplifies this point by noting that in countries such as Hungary and Bulgaria, existing "stocks of legendry" are regarded as "deficient" and that "remedial field work" is now being conducted. "Likewise, in America," Hand asserts, "workers must create an entirely new corpus of material because there are few scientifically usable collections of folk legends" (p. 440).

that the consistency that I had found to be so commendable might really be the source of the uneasiness that I was convinced I had detected. I reexamined, therefore, what I considered to be a representative sample of legend studies and perused once again a large number of discussions of the nature and characteristics of legend that had been published over the years. The results of these endeavors led me to conclude that the general concept that underlies and is implicit in the individual, but strikingly consistent, definitions, characterizations, collections, and discussions of legend could not help but be the potential cause of considerable anxiety. And if, in fact, my conclusions were valid, then I was convinced that it was, indeed, a serious matter. For if those individuals who work with legends have, either consciously or unconsciously, any uncertainties about the general concept upon which they base their work, then the soundness of the very foundations of legend scholarship is questionable.

The thesis of this paper is that the general concept of legend that underlies and is implicit in definitions, characterizations, collections, and discussions of the subject *is*, indeed, unsound. In order to substantiate this thesis, I should like to return to that general definition that, as I indicated earlier in this presentation, I feel we could expect to be able to derive and construct from a corpus of definitions that could have been compiled had I asked each of you to write a definition of the term. That general definition, you will recall, was expressed as follows: *A legend is a story or narrative, set in the recent or historical past, that is believed to be true by those by whom and to whom it is communicated.* Let us examine each of the three assertions that is made in the definition, consider its meaning, and assess its validity and usefulness.

The first assertion in our definition is that a legend is *a story or narrative.* On the surface, this does not appear to be objectionable. On the one hand, it enables us to differentiate legends from other *kinds* of expression; and on the other hand, it enables us to conceive of legends as being related to other *forms* of expression. In general works on folklore, this is the principal criterion for differentiating legend from song, music, dance, custom, and fixed linguistic expressions; and it provides the primary justification for relating legend *to*, and considering it in conjunction *with*, myths and Märchen. But what does it *mean?* Does it mean that legends contain what students of literature call *plots?* Does it mean that legends have clearly marked *introductions and conclusions* that enable one to differentiate them readily and easily from all other *kinds* of expression within continua of communication?

I think that the answer to each of these questions would have to be ambivalent. Most of us would probably be willing to agree that the majority of expressions that are identified as *legends* contain what could be loosely called, in literary parlance, *plots*. For example, if we were to take the legend of "How Barney Beal Awed the Bully of Peak's Island" which Richard M. Dorson has presented in several of his publications,[8] we would be inclined to agree that it seems to exhibit the general characteristics of what we could call a *plot*. It involves a series of incidents, set in a specific locale and presented in a logical time sequence, that builds to a kind of climax as the interactions of Barney and the bully intensify. But I think that we would also be inclined to feel that the plot of Dorson's legend text, like the plots of most legend texts with which we are familiar, does not completely fulfill our expectations of what a plot should *be* or what a plot should *do*. To put it another way, I think that while most of us would be willing to say that those expressions that we identify as legends contain what we conceive, in a general way, to be *plots*, we would, at the same time, be inclined to want to qualify our statement; and we would find it difficult to determine *why* or *how*. Moreover, the more we reflected on the matter, the more uneasy we would probably become. For we would think of many legends that do not seem to have *plots* at all. In his recent book *The Study of American Folklore*, for instance, Jan H. Brunvand includes "place-name stories" in his discussion of "local legends"; and one of the "stories" that he presents to exemplify what he apparently conceives to be this "subtype" or "subgenre" of "local legends" is the following: *"Emida* is said to be derived from the names of three early settlers, *E*ast, *Mi*ller, and *Da*wson, but other informants point out that 'it's a "dime" spelled backwards, and that's about what it's worth!' "[9] Brunvand is not alone, of course, in considering such expressions to be "stories," and, more specifically, "legends"; but certainly none of us would want to insist that such "legends" have *plots*. The assertion that a legend is a story or narrative, then, cannot mean that a legend must always

---

8 "How Barney Beal Awed the Bully of Peak's Island" is presented in *Buying the Wind*, ed. Richard M. Dorson (Chicago: University of Chicago Press, 1964), pp. 49–51, and, more recently, in Richard M. Dorson, "Legends and Tall Tales," in *Our Living Traditions: An Introduction to American Folklore*, ed. Tristram Potter Coffin (New York and London: Basic Books, 1968), pp. 156–157.

9 Brunvand, *Study of American Folklore*, p. 97.

have a plot—at least not in the sense in which the word *plot* is usually used by students of literature. It *might* contain something *like* a plot, but it frequently contains nothing that is *plotlike* at all.[10]

Then does the assertion that a legend is a story or narrative mean that it has a clearly marked introduction and conclusion that enable one to differentiate it readily and easily from all other *kinds* of expression within continua of communication? Most fieldworkers who have recorded what they identify as *legends* and all perceptive readers of legend texts are aware of the fact that legends are not introduced by such recurrent opening formulas as "Once upon a time," nor are they concluded with statements such as "And they lived well, but we live even better." Conventional linguistic markers, small in number and predictable in kind, do not constitute a principal characteristic of what most people call *legends*. There are, not infrequently, linguistic *clues* that what one is hearing or reading will, once it has been fully communicated, turn out to be something that one would call a *legend*. Words and expressions such as "once," "one time," "years ago," "they used to say that," "some people think that," "let me tell you about something that happened right here," and "there are lots of stories about that, but the *true* story is" suggest that what is conceived to be a legend might be in the process of being generated; and statements such as "now, that's true," "I really believe that," "I saw it with my own eyes," "the fellow who told me about that saw it with his own eyes," "that's the story they tell," and "I don't know about it, but that's what they say" frequently reinforce the listener's or reader's notion that what has gone before can be regarded as a legend. But while such words or expressions may constitute *clues* that a legend is about to be, or has just been, generated or recounted, they cannot be called conventional formulas or markers. They may or may not occur, and they may or may not precede or follow what are conceived to be legends at all. The assertion that a legend is a story or narrative, then, cannot mean that legends have clearly marked introductions and conclusions that enable one to differentiate them readily and

---

10 In his article "Status of European and American Legend Study" (see n. 1), Hand asserts: "Why more scholars have not been attracted to legendry is easy to see, apart from the wider literary and aesthetic appeal of folk tales and related folk narrative forms. For the systematizer, *folk legends seem endless in bulk and variety, and they are often so short and formless as to defy classification* (p. 439; my italics). I infer from Hand's statements—and from many others like them—that it is probably their awareness of the lack of fully developed plots (in the literary sense of the term) in their data that motivates legend scholars to make such assertions.

easily from all other *kinds* of expression within continua of communication.

Could the assertion that a legend is a story or narrative have some *other* meaning? It could, of course; but just *what* that other meaning might be would depend upon the *concept* of *story or narrative* to which one is committed. But few people bother to define the terms *story* or *narrative;* and when these terms *are* defined, the definitions range from the very vague and imprecise (e.g., "a story is an account of incidents or events") to the all-encompassing (e.g., "a narrative is a story, long or short, of past, present, or future, factual or imagined, told for any purpose, with or without much detail").[11] So the assertion that a legend is a story or narrative does not really *mean* very much in our definition unless the terms *story* or *narrative* mean something specific to us. And if, as I suspect to be the case, most folklorists conceive of story or narrative in the literary sense as something that contains what can be called a *plot* and/or something that has a clearly marked introduction and conclusion that enable one to differentiate it readily and easily—as one can presumably do with *all* story or narrative *forms*—from other *kinds* of expression within continua of communication, then the assertion that a legend is a story or narrative turns out to be a *relative* assertion. For if a legend has and yet does not have what we could call a *plot,* and if it has and yet does not have readily recognizable and easily distinguishable markers, then a legend *is,* and at the same time it *is not,* a story or narrative.[12]

Let us turn next to a consideration of the second assertion in our general definition: a legend is *set in the recent or historical past.* Once again, there seems to be nothing objectionable in this asser-

---

11 The two definitions cited here come from widely used desk dictionaries—the first from *Webster's Seventh New Collegiate Dictionary* (Springfield, Mass.: G. & C. Merriam, 1963), the second from *The American College Dictionary* (New York: Random House, 1964).

12 In her essay "Processes of Legend Formation" (see n. 1), Dégh makes the following remarks: "The silent observer can hardly notice who started and who ended the story, and it is even hard to tell how to separate the individual legends from each other, where one ends and the other begins, as there is no clear dividing line between them—as Friedrich Ranke has suggested. The transcripts of my tapes containing legends recorded in social gatherings look like drama texts, separated into roles" (p. 86). Dégh continues: "The legend certainly has an easily recognizable *frame,* an *introduction* and a *conclusion,* but not in the sense as that of a tale. They serve to strengthen the credit of the coming story. The importance of the coming message makes the detailed preliminaries indispensable [*sic*]. In this genre, which is marked by inconsistency of form, I cannot tell the sequence of elements in the introduction, but I certainly can tell what belongs to it" (p. 86; Dégh's italics). My observations on this point are essentially in agreement with those made by Dégh.

tion. As I suggested earlier, what most people who make it probably mean by it—and what it probably means to most people who are exposed to it—is that a legend recounts something that is over and done with. Certainly this notion can be substantiated very easily. Legends *do* communicate information about the past, and those who tell what we conceive to be legends code what they want to communicate in ways that clearly indicate the pastness of what they wish to relate to others. But is this really what we *mean* this assertion to mean? Or is it too specific and precise to be really *meaningful?* In one respect, I think it is. For while what we call *legends* can be said to be *set* in the past, the pastness of their setting may not be conceived to be *recent* or *historical* at all. On the one hand, legends are frequently conceived to be *remote* or *antihistorical* rather than *recent* or *historical;* and on the other hand, they are often conceived to be both past *and present* (and perhaps even *future*) at the same time. Let me try to explain this seemingly enigmatic statement by referring to some specific examples.

In his book *The Folktale,* Stith Thompson discusses an explanation that is sometimes given for the existence of superior and inferior social classes, downtrodden races, monkeys, and peoples of the underworld. The explanation is familiar to most of you, I am sure, but this is the way Thompson presents it:

> The interest in Paradise Lost and in Adam and Eve generally ceases after they are expelled from the garden, but there have been preserved some traditions which give us a last glimpse of the first mother. She has so many children that she is ashamed when God pays her a visit. She hides some of them, and thus they fail to receive the blessing which God gives to all those who are in sight.[13]

Thompson presents this description in his discussion of "Legends and Traditions," under the subheading "Mythological Legends." We can assume, from his placement and discussion of it, that Thompson would call anything that involved the same agents and communicated the same content a *legend.* So would most other folklorists. Now this legend is certainly set in the *past.* But is that past *recent* or *remote, historical* or *antihistorical?* The answer, of course, is that it could be *any* of these. Whether we regard it as recent or remote depends upon our sense of *time,* and whether we consider it to be historical or antihistorical depends upon our sense of *history.* And both are always relative so far as *people* are concerned. The time during which Eve lived is considered to be in the *recent past* by some, in the *remote past* by others, and *never* by

---

[13] Stith Thompson, *The Folktale* (New York: Dryden Press, 1946), p. 236.

still others; and the historical or antihistorical character of the past depends upon whether or not one regards Eve and/or God as "historical personages." Moreover, while this legend relates an incident that is set in the past, some people undoubtedly regard it as being relevant to the *present* (and perhaps to the *future* as well) if they consider the phenomena that it is intended to account for as being *of* the present and *in* the present as well as *from* the past. In such instances, the legend itself might be conceived by some people to be more *of* the present and *concerned with* the present than *of* the past and *concerned with* the past.

This is true not only for the so-called mythological legends, but also of many so-called religious legends, saints' legends, aetiological legends, local legends, and historical legends as well. In fact, it could be true of *anything* that we might call a legend. Furthermore, this relativity in degree and kind of pastness is not an *insignificant* point, it does not result from any *hair-splitting*, and it is not intended to *deceive* anyone by *semantic subterfuge*. I am quite certain that it is the conscious or unconscious awareness of this relativity that motivates many students of legend to note that "one man's legend is another man's myth" or "what is a legend in one time and place may be a myth in another time and place and a *Märchen* in yet another time and place." [14]

This is such an important point, I feel, that I would like to present a second example, this one from my own field data. It was communicated to me by the teen-age daughter of Greek immigrants who lives in Tarpon Springs, Florida, and it goes as follows:

> The Turks had come on the shore of the island of Kerkira. And they went up to the church and pulled out all the eyes of the icons. And when they went back to leave, their boat was frozen. They couldn't leave. And today my grandmother even sees it. They go someplace near the water on the mountain near the church, and you can see it about noon; you can still see the ship there frozen in the water. [15]

---

14 This point concerning the relativity of generic distinctions among "folk-narratives" is made so frequently by writers on the subject that I am certain it is readily familiar. Among the investigators who place the greatest amount of emphasis on this relativity, however, are the following: Stith Thompson, "Myths and Folktales," in *Myth: A Symposium,* ed. Thomas A. Sebeok (Bloomington: Indiana University Press, 1958), pp. 104–110; William Bascom, "The Forms of Folklore: Prose Narratives," *JAF,* 78 (1965), 3–20; C. Scott Littleton, "A Two-Dimensional Scheme for the Classification of Narratives," *JAF,* 78 (1965), 21–27; J. A. K. Thomson, *The Art of the Logos* (London: Allen & Unwin, 1935); and Halliday, *Indo-European Folk-Tales.*

15 This account was recorded in the summer of 1962. The principal motifs are D471.3, "Transformation: ship to stone"; and E535.3, "Ghost ship."

At the time that I recorded this, I considered it to be a legend. I still do; and I think that most folklorists would be inclined to identify it as such, too. It is, certainly, set in the past. The incidents that are related are over and done with. But is the past that is involved a *recent* past or a *remote* past; or does it really matter? And is it the *historical* past or the *antihistorical* past; or does it really matter? Finally, is it *of* the past and *in* the past, *of* the present and *in* the present, *of* the future and *in* the future; or does it really matter? The answers to all of these questions depend upon the answerer. Most of us would probably *infer* that it is set in the *recent,* as opposed to the *remote,* past; but we would be hard pressed if we were asked to explain *why,* and we would probably have to admit that it doesn't *really* matter. Similarly, most of us would probably *infer* that it is set in the *historical,* not the *antihistorical,* past, but only because we know that *Turks* and *churches* and *icons* and *ships* (and, if we know our geography, *Kerkira* as well) all exist; and once again, we would probably have to admit that it doesn't *really* matter. What most of us *would* undoubtedly *have* to admit, however, is that for the person who communicated it to me, the legend is not only *of* the past and *in* the past, but also *of* the present and *in* the present; and we probably would be motivated to assert, on the basis of the closing statements made by the informant, that what she communicated to me is really more *present* (and perhaps *future* as well) for her than it is *past.* For the ship can *still be seen,* and, indeed, it *is* still seen by someone who is very *real to* her and by someone who is very much *of the present for* her—her grandmother. And that really *does* matter.[16]

---

[16] This "presentness" of the past is nowhere better described and discussed than in A. R. Radcliffe-Brown, *The Andaman Islanders* (Cambridge: Cambridge University Press, 1922), chap. VI, "The Interpretation of Andamanese Customs and Beliefs: Myths and Legends," pp. 376–405. Two brief quotations provide some notion of the insights that Radcliffe-Brown had into this "presentness" of the past: (1) "The legends of the Andamanese, then, as I understand them, set out to give an account of how the order of the world came into existence. *But the Andaman Islander has no interest in any part of it except in so far as it affects his own life.* He is interested in the procession of the seasons or the alternation of day and night, or the phases of the moon, *only in so far as these things have effects upon the community.* In other words he is interested in natural phenomena only in so far as such phenomena are *really parts of the social order.*" (2) "The thesis of this chapter has been that the legends are the expression of social values of objects of different kinds. By the social value of an object is meant *the way in which it affects the life of the society,* and therefore, since every one is interested in the welfare of the society to which he belongs, *the way in which it affects the social sentiments of the individual.* The system of social values of a society obviously depends upon the manner in which the society is constituted, and therefore the legends can only be understood by constant reference to the mode of life of the Andamanese." (Italics mine.)

Thus, the assertion that a legend is set in the recent or historical past is an assertion that is too specific and yet too imprecise at the same time. For while a legend is *set* in the past, that past may be conceived to be *either* recent *or* remote and *either* historical *or* antihistorical; and while a legend is set in the *past,* it might really be conceived to be *in* and *of* the *present* (and perhaps the *future* as well). Like the first assertion, then, this one, too, is relative.

The third assertion in our general definition is that a legend is *believed to be true by those by whom and to whom it is communicated. Here,* many of you might insist, is the real crux of the matter. And once again, this does not appear, *at first,* to be objectionable. For as I indicated earlier, it communicates the notion that those who tell and listen to legends find what they tell and hear to be *credible;* and no one would deny the fact that there is always *something* familiar or "real"—and hence something *credible*—about legends.

But a number of problems arise as a result of this assertion, and all of them stem from the words "believed to be true." For these words seem to call into question the whole notion of credibility by suggesting that legends might not be credible at all. Are legends, indeed, true, or are they not?

"The point is irrelevant," it might be argued, "because it doesn't really matter whether legends are true or whether they are not. The important thing is that they *are true* as far as those who tell and hear them are concerned."

"But if this is the case, then why not say that legends *are* true and let it go at that?"

"Because," it might be said, "legends do not *have* to be true."

"Then can they be either *true* or *false?*"

"Yes," the answer might be, "they can be either true or false."

"Then do tellers and hearers of legends sometimes judge what they tell and hear to be false?"

"W-e-l-l, yes; I guess you could say that," might be the response. "But legends are *usually* believed to be true by those who tell and listen to them."

"But if that is the case, then how does a student of legend know when a legend that he is concerned with is believed to be true and when it is believed to be false by its tellers or listeners?"

"If he is in the *field,*" the response might be, "he can *ask.*"

"But wouldn't such an inquiry make the informants uneasy?"

"Well, it could," might be the answer. "But if the fieldworker *felt* that such an inquiry might make the informants uneasy, then he could try to infer from observation and context whether or not the tellers believe that their legends are true."

"What would he observe and what would he expect to find in the context that would enable him to determine whether or not a particular legend was believed to be true?

The general demeanor of the informants, their movements and expressions, the ways in which they tell and react to what they hear," might be the reply.

"But how does a student of legend who is not in the field determine whether the legends with which he works are believed to be true by those from whom others have recorded them?"

"He can listen to the fieldworker's tapes or read what the collector has to say about the circumstances or the context in which the legends were recorded," the answer might be.

"But what would he do if he had only the *texts* of the legends?"

"Then he would have to infer from them," the reply might be, "whether or not the legends might have been believed to be true."

"And how would he draw his inferences and make a judgment?"

"On the basis of the content of the texts," would be the response.

"Then it is the student of legend who must ultimately make the decision?"

"W-e-l-l, yes," we would expect to be told.

"And does he, too, believe that legends are true?"

"Of course not!" would be the reply. "He knows that legends are *not* true."

"How does he know?"

At this point, I think it wise to bring our imaginary dialogue to a close!

The points of the dialogue, however, are obvious: *do* we know, *how* do we know, and how can we be *certain* that we are correct? More important, perhaps, are these questions: how often do students of legend try to find out; and when they do, do they eliminate from their corpus those data that they have inferred or discovered are *not* believed to be true by tellers or listeners, or do such data *remain* in the corpus despite such inferences or discoveries? Let me quote for you once again some data from my own fieldwork. This was communicated to me by a native American man whose parents emigrated to the United States from Greece. He has never been to the homeland of his ancestors, but he interacts daily with Greek-Americans in the community in which he lives—Tarpon Springs, Florida. These are his words:

> There is an island called Zakynthos where they have a lot of earthquakes. Well, now, this would be in the line of superstition, but in

this particular case, it's an exception. I would say that it wouldn't be so much a superstition as quite a fact and a reality, because what they would call a superstition connected with it would only prove that there must be something to it. The people there are very profane speakers. Every other word is—they use vile language. *Everybody* there uses dirty speech. They curse somebody's mother, somebody's brother. And they're always cursing the saints, see. *God forgive me for saying it, but that's what they do.* Like some Greek cursing words about *Panaghia,* our holy saint. Well, now, to them it's very ordinary. And it's so in a few other places, too, but mainly in Zakynthos. And that's why they have earthquakes take place and destroy them all and kill them. Because even in the midst of those earthquakes, they use profane language. . . . They continue to do it. Maybe some people try to help themselves. But, you know, cursing becomes a *habit.* And at times you do it not intending any *harm* to anyone. But whether it's a habit or intentionally done, it's still, I think, a *sin.* So I actually do believe—or rather, I *hope* that those things *do* happen, because they are *sins* of that sort. I remember a few years ago, they had those earthquakes. That was the first thing every Greek right here said. "Oh, serves them right. They ought to curb their tongues." [17]

Is this a legend? I think that most students of folklore would call it one. Some would describe it as an "aetiological legend" and assert that it is told to explain why there are frequent earthquakes on the island of Zakynthos. Others might call it a "place legend" or a "local legend." But I feel quite certain that most folklorists would call it a legend and conceive of it as a legend of *some* kind. Does the teller *believe* that what he is communicating is true? The answer to this could be *yes* or it could be *no,* depending upon how one interprets what my informant had to say. Equally convincing arguments could be presented for either answer, and each answer would be "correct" in its own way. But to me, the only *meaningful* answer would have to be an ambivalent one; and I was the field-worker.

I could, if there were more time, present many other examples to show why the assertion that legends are believed to be true by those by whom and to whom they are communicated is, like the other two assertions in our general definition, a relative one. But let me cite just three short examples. Most legend scholars consider accounts of ghosts to be *legends.* Boy Scouts and Girl Scouts relate accounts of ghosts to each other at summer camp. Do they *believe* that these accounts are true? Many people are familiar with some account of an automobile from which the smell of death cannot be eradicated, even by the most ingenious means. Do those who relate such accounts and those who listen to them *believe* what

---

[17] This account was recorded in the summer of 1962. The principal motifs are Q552.25, "Earthquake as punishment"; and Q221.3, "Blasphemy punished."

they say and hear? Most Greek-Americans can relate to any folklorist who queries them some account of the miraculous workings
of icons or saints. But do all Greek-Americans who relate such accounts to eager folklorists *believe* them to be true? In some *individual* instances, we can be fairly certain that the answers to each
of these questions seem to be *yes;* in other *individual* instances, we
feel that the answers are probably *no;* and in the majority of instances, we would be unable to answer the questions with a simple
yes or a simple *no,* for the answers are someplace in between.[18]

What started out as a fairly typical general definition of *legend*
and what appeared to be a relatively accurate verbalization of
the general concept that underlies and is implicit in most definitions, characterizations, collections, and discussions of legend ends
up, then, as something of a *riddle:* A legend is a story or narrative
that may not be a story or narrative at all; it is set in a recent or
historical past that may be conceived to be remote or antihistorical
or not really past at all; it is believed to be true by some, false by
others, and both or neither by most. How do we solve this riddle?
The answer to this is obvious: by formulating a concept of legend
and by coining a general definition of legend that is more valid and
meaningful and sound than the concept and definition of legend
to which we subscribe, more because of past precedent than because
of conviction. And how do we do this? I think that the key to such
a concept must be sought in the nature and structure of the sets
of relationships that underlie and are implicit in what we call
legends and that constitute, on another level of abstraction, the least
common denominators of the learning process. For legends appear
to be metaphorizations of basic kinds of relationship sets in which
one or both of the parts or the nature of the relationship that is
conceived to exist between these parts is incapable of being tested
empirically to the satisfaction of every man.

This has not been an easy paper to deliver. I would *like* to be-

---

18 Littleton, "A Two-Dimensional Scheme," attempts to show how narratives
"shift categories" through space and time as attitudes concerning the "accuracy"
or "believability" of their content change. In attempting to do so, however,
Littleton clearly demonstrates that it is the *scholar* who makes the determination in all instances. He fails to realize that in a given place at a given time,
different informants might display quite different attitudes toward the "accuracy" or "believability" of the same story and hence might classify it quite
differently in terms of their own native categories. Littleton's essay—like that
by Bascom ("The Forms of Folklore") and others—clearly reveals the desire of
the investigator to order his data into universal categories, even when there
is incontrovertible evidence to indicate that such categories do not exist
except in the minds of those who insist that they must.

lieve that my thesis concerning the unsoundness of the general concept of legend that underlies and is implicit in definitions, characterizations, collections, and discussions were incorrect. But the literature on the subject supports my convictions on every count. If we as folklorists are to make significant contributions to the advancement of knowledge—and I believe that many folklorists have already done so—then we must build upon solid foundations. Much of what we now believe or accept a priori is, unfortunately, not sound. And unsound substructures in any field of inquiry cannot be depended upon to support forever the superstructures that are built upon them. I do not think that we *can* have an index of American folk legends until and unless we have a new concept of legend upon which we can build with assurance and integrity. And even if we ever *do* have such a concept, I am not convinced that legend indexes *of the kind that are currently envisioned* can be or ever should be compiled. But let us take care of first things first and begin by building a new substructure for legend scholarship.

On the Psychology of Legend

ALAN DUNDES, *University of California, Berkeley*

It is difficult to think of any area of folklore research which has continued to be as sterile and unrewarding as the study of legend. One reason for this is that the relatively few folklorists who specialize in legend have never been able to escape from the dreary concerns of endless collecting and hairsplitting classification debates. But the more important reason is that folklorists have utterly failed to convince anyone, including themselves, of the significance and relevance of legend with respect to the ultimate goal of understanding the nature of man. Collection per se does no more than provide necessary raw materials for interpretation. But without interpretation, the raw materials remain just that: raw materials. Classification attempts in which culturally relative a priori arbitrary schemes are proposed or imposed as possible universal categories have thus far proved little more than exercises in futility. Unless and until folklorists enter the area of interpretation, for example, what did and do specific legends *mean?* there is precious little hope of interesting folklore students and members of other disciplines in the masses of legend material in print and in archives.

Recent valuable surveys of legend research by Wayland Hand and Lutz Röhrich clearly indicate the major bias in contemporary legend scholarship.[1] Collecting and indexing are presented as the principal research emphases. Chapter headings in Röhrich's *Sage* are essentially subgenre distinctions (based mostly on content fea-

---
[1] Wayland D. Hand, "Status of European and American Legend Study," *Current Anthropology*, 6 (1965), 439–446; Lutz Röhrich, *Sage* (Stuttgart: J. B. Metzlersche Verlagsbuchhandlung, 1966).

tures), such as "Totensagen," "Christliche Sagen," and "Historische Sagen." In these and other surveys, there is little or no evidence that legends have even been—or could ever be—studied profitably from a psychological point of view. Nor is there much extended discussion of *any* kind of meaningful *interpretation* of legend materials, for it must be noted that the psychological approach to legend content is only one of several possible avenues to analysis. The glaring lack of mention of psychological studies raises the question as to whether legends can or cannot be usefully studied in terms of psychology. Is there perhaps something in the legend that makes it impossible to use for psychological studies? Or is it simply a matter of the professional folklorist's unwillingness to consider legends from this perspective, a possibility that if true might itself be the subject of an interesting psychological study? I suggest that folklorists once having admitted intellectually that legends contain fantasy proceed to ignore this fact, blithely ignoring the total range of academic scholarship specifically concerned with the study of human fantasy. No doubt if Hand or Röhrich had considered some of the classic psychological studies, their evaluation would have been negative. In the present context, however, I believe it to be beside the point to lift an accusing finger at folklorists who ignore psychologists. It is equally pointless to rail at psychiatrists who make analyses of legends without the benefit of any knowledge of the tools of the trade of folklore. For why should the important task of analysing the traditional forms of fantasy we label legend be left to nonfolklorists anyway? Either folklorists must begin to try to interpret legend materials as traditional products of human fantasy, or they must forfeit any claim to be anything other than antiquarian butterfly collectors and classifiers.

There are some characteristics of legend which make it a genre particularly valuable to the psychologically oriented folklorist. One of these is the temporal dimension of legends, a dimension that to my knowledge has not previously been spelled out in sufficient detail. William Bascom in his excellent survey article has delineated the standard European trichotomic division of folk or prose narrative into myth, folktale, and legend.[2] The criteria include formal features (e.g., the presence or absence of opening and closing formulas), the element of belief, and the dimension of time. Generally, Bascom's discussion accurately reflects the categories used

---

[2] William Bascom, "The Forms of Folklore: Prose Narratives," *JAF*, 78 (1965), 3–20.

by European folklorists if not the folk. In fact, one could devise field experiments to test some of the criteria. An introductory folktale formula such as "Once upon a time" could be prefixed to a story from the Old Testament, for example, in Genesis. Presumably, if members of the audience had strong religious convictions depending upon belief in the literal truth of the Old Testament, there would be some expression of outrage and indignation. "Once upon a time" means roughly that "everything that follows this fixed phrase utterance is fiction rather than truth." This is appropriate enough in the case of a fairy tale that breaks with reality in favor of a world of unreality, but it would presumably constitute an intolerable insult to members of an audience who believe the story to be true.

In Bascom's discussion of the temporal dimensions of folk narrative, he notes that myths are set in the remote past while legends are set in the recent past. This, however may be too static a description and I believe it might be more useful to describe myth and legend in terms of segments of a time continuum bounded by either definite or indefinite end points. As a heuristic device, I would suggest the metaphor or image of an hourglass *open at both ends*. The hourglass would represent a true time axis and thus folktale would not be included in it. Folktales are outside true time. In European tradition at least, they occur at no particular time or at any time. In a way "Once upon a time" means literally that the story is perched above or outside of time. In contrast, myth and legend are in true time. In terms of the hourglass image, myth would be the bottom. Here one can see the value of the open-endedness of the hourglass metaphor. There is no time before myth. Myth-time is the earliest imaginable time, and it runs roughly up until the world and man were created in their present form. The time of the creation of world and man would be the middle of the hourglass. Legend, as both a European folk and analytic category, is set in postcreation time, that is, after the creation of man. Once Adam and Eve are created (as told in a myth), their historical or pseudohistorical adventures may be in legend form. Legend is thus the upper portion of the hourglass. Just as the *beginning* of myth-time is open-ended, however, so the *end* of legend-time is open-ended. The open-endedness is again relevant because in many cases, the action or plot of a legend is not completed in the narrative itself, and in fact the action continues into the present or even into the future. The house down the road continues to be haunted;

the Flying Dutchman (motif E511) continues to roam the seas;
the Wandering Jew (motif Q502.1) [3] continues his woeful peregrina-
tion. Thus whereas the action of myth is normally completed in the
narrative (although its consequences and implications may and
indeed usually do persevere), the action of a legend may never be
completed. What this means in part is that individuals may well
feel closer to the action of legend than to the action of myth that
happened long, long ago, and closer to the action of legend than
to the action of folktale that never really happened. As a matter of
fact, in many of those legends whose actions are not yet completed,
the sense of immediacy may produce genuine fear or other emotion. This suggests that legend might be much more appropriate
than myth and folktale for psychological studies.

The greater immediacy of legend in time is paralleled by immediacy of place. First we may see the contrast between myth and
legend, on the one hand, and folktale, on the other. Whereas myth
and legend are set in this world, folktale is set in another, a fictional
world, a never-never land of make-believe. One leaves his own time
and place to enter the fantasy and dream world of the folktale. In
myth and legend, however, the fantasy is introduced into the time
and place of the real world. Here we may distinguish legend from
myth in terms of distantiation. Since myth occurred before the
world was as it is now, it tends to be somewhat removed from the
contemporary scene. Although myth does refer to the real world,
the events were of such scope and took place so long ago (although
the time period will vary with different peoples), that they may be
much less immediate than local legends. Again this immediacy of
space would seem to make legend primary source material for the
study of fantasy. One does not escape the real world into legend;
rather legend represents fantasy in the real world, an important
point psychologically speaking. It is "true" fantasy, not to be confused with the "false" or fictional fantasy of folktale.

There is yet another characteristic of legends which makes them
attractive to folklorists willing to consider a psychological approach,
and interestingly enough it is a characteristic that is the despair of
the more conservative collector-classifier folklorist. The characteristic concerns quantity and generative power. There are literally
countless legends. As Wayland Hand has phrased it, "For the

3 One indication of the difficulty in defining genres of folk narrative is provided by the fact that Stith Thompson has listed the Wandering Jew as a tale
type (AT 777) which would imply that it is a folktale rather than a legend. For
a recent study of this plot, see George K. Anderson, *The Legend of the Wandering Jew* (Providence, R. I.: Brown University Press, 1965).

systematizer, folk legends seem endless." [4] There are probably more legends than myths or folktales in most cultures. There are almost a finite number of basic myth types, for example, the creation of the world, origin of death, and so forth, but there are an infinite number of legends, especially local legends as opposed to migratory legends. Moreover, there are continual additions to the world's supply of legends. Each era contributes either new legends or at least new versions of old legends to the general corpus of texts. This does *not* seem to be the case for myths. If one uses the concept of myth in a folkloristic sense, that is, as a sacred narrative explaining how the world and man came to be in their present form, it is doubtful whether one will find many, if any, new myths created. Similarly, the majority of the folktales found in oral tradition at any one point in time are probably genetically related to older versions. Legends, in contrast, can spring anew whenever an appropriate personage, place, or event is deemed legendworthy by a folk group. This does not mean, of course, that there are not traditional patterns of legend and that apparently "new" legends do not resemble earlier legends. The point is simply that if one is interested in the origin and development of folk narrative—an area of research clearly related to the province of psychology—then one has in legend a much likelier subject than one would have with myth or folktale. New problems in society create new legends, and it will probably always be so and folklorists should capitalize on the opportunity to observe the legend formation process in progress. Thus the constant flow of new legends which bedevils the obsessive perfectionist collector-classifier who wants to obtain and/or index all known versions of all known legends represents a potentially enormous asset to the psychologically oriented folklorist.

Before attempting to illustrate the possibilities of a psychological approach to legend using specific American folk legends as examples, I should like to indicate that there is a considerable body of relevant scholarship, the bulk of which has *not* been written by folklorists. A random sampling might include Bonaparte on the legend of unfathomable waters, Isaac-Edersheim on the Wandering Jew, Róheim on the wild hunt, De Groot's extended study of the Saint Nicholas legend, and Spiro's insightful analysis of Burmese religious legends.[5] Those seriously interested in exploring the

---

4 Hand, "Legend Study," p. 439.

5 Marie Bonaparte, "The Legend of the Unfathomable Waters," *American Imago*, 4 (1946), 20–31; E. Isaac-Edersheim, "Der Ewige Jude," *Internationale Zeitschrift für Psychoanalyse*, 26 (1941), 286–315; Géza Róheim, "Die wilde Jagd," *Imago*, 12 (1926), 465–477; Adriaan D. De Groot, *Saint Nicholas: A Psycho-*

scholarship should consult Grinstein's multivolume bibliographical
aid, *The Index of Psychoanalytic Writings*, and perhaps also *Psychological Abstracts* for further references. Since it is, however,
doubtful whether many folklorists will take the trouble of giving
such psychological studies even a trial reading, I propose to present
brief psychological interpretations of several representative American folk legends. But even if none of the particular interpretative
suggestions are adjudged convincing—the question of "proving"
any one interpretation beyond a shadow of a doubt is always unlikely when working with symbolic materials—I would hope that
at least the exposure to such interpretations will demonstrate the
advantages and indeed the necessity for a psychological approach
to legend.

First, we might consider the story of George Washington and
the cherry tree. Brunvand tends to demean this classic bit of
apocrypha on the grounds that there is so little variation, and it is
true that the account inevitably ends with George confessing to his
father "I cannot tell a lie; I did it with my little hatchet." [6] I
suspect that this story comes as near to being known by virtually
everyone in the United States as any other American legend we
might name. Now what does the legend mean? Can it be usefully
explicated in psychological terms? It is probably not historical and
even if it were, its historicity could not possibly account for its
continuing widespread popularity. Clearly, it functions as an exemplum to teach a moral lesson, to wit, a child should always tell
the truth even when there is risk of anger or punishment. It is
invariably implicit if not explicit that George's father did not
punish George for the heinous crime of chopping down a favorite
cherry tree. Rather one assumes that the lack of corporal punishment constituted a reward for telling the truth. But is the legend's
role as a traditional argument-charter for telling the truth sufficient to explain its lasting appeal? I would suggest that there are
other reasons, compelling psychological reasons, which may account
for the appeal.

For one thing, the legend, brief as it is, involves a conflict between father and son. The son apparently has cut down a prize
possession of his father, namely, his father's cherry tree. Does the
act of chopping down a tree have any possible symbolic import?

---

analytic Study of his History and Myth (The Hague: Mouton, 1965); and Melford E. Spiro, *Burmese Supernaturalism* (Englewood Cliffs, N. J.: Prentice-Hall,
1967).

6 Jan Harold Brunvand, *The Study of American Folklore: An Introduction*
(New York: W. W. Norton, 1968), p. 94.

Well, if one can judge from "Jack and the Beanstalk," one might think so.[7] A son cutting down his father's tree might be indulging in a symbolic castration attempt. It is terribly tempting to make something of the fact that the tree in question is a cherry tree. Cherry in modern slang means virgin, one who has not yet experienced sexual intercourse. Thus George in cutting down his father's "cherry" tree makes the son's crime all the more impressive. Whether the cherry tree symbolized George's mother, which he cut down and thereby prevented his father from enjoying, or whether the cherry tree represented George's father's phallus, which George effectively rendered impotent, the basic nature of the crime is clear. Note that whether it is George's mother who is cherry or George's father's phallus that is cherry, the upshot is the same inasmuch as in either case, George has succeeded in preventing his father from engaging in sexual activity. If George's mother were a virgin, like the mother of Jesus and the various heroes described by Raglan in his account of the hero pattern, then this would effectively deny that George's father and mother had even had intercourse. If George's father's phallus were cherry, then similarly, its lack of sexual experience is implied. It is true that it is difficult to determine whether "cherry" had a sense of sexual innocence a century or so ago. On the basis of such evidence as the well-known riddle in Captain Wedderburn's Courtship (Child 46) in which a successful courting depends upon a man's explaining how there can be a chicken without a bone and cherry without a stone, one might think so. (Such privational contradictive riddles in which critical parts of wholes are denied can have sexual significance.) [8] In European tradition, moreover, one finds such motifs as D1375.1.1.4, Magic cherry causes horns to grow on a person, and D1376.1.1.2, Magic cherry makes nose long. In both cases, a magic cherry causes a body extremity to appear or lengthen! Such motifs would support the notion that cherry and cherries have a sexual connotation in folk tradition. In any case, the fundamental psychological import of a son's cutting down his father's tree does not really depend upon the species of the tree. It might be safer simply to say that the indisputable sexual significance of "cherry" in our own day surely could be a factor in the continued popularity of the legend.

---

[7] For considerations of the symbolism of "Jack and the Beanstalk," see Alan Dundes, ed., *The Study of Folklore* (Englewood Cliffs, N. J.: Prentice-Hall, 1965), pp. 103–113.

[8] For a discussion of the possible sexual symbolism of oppositional riddles involving privational contradictions, see Alan Dundes, "Texture, Text, and Context," *SFQ*, 28 (1964), 256–258.

There are several other comments of a psychological nature which might be made. First of all, is the legend son or father oriented? I would argue that it seems to be slightly father oriented—at least to the extent that the son does not get away with cutting down his father's tree. In this respect, the George Washington cherry tree legend differs from the Jack and the beanstalk plot. In the latter, Jack cuts down the giant's stalk (with the help of a hatchet often thoughtfully provided by Jack's mother), and this kills the giant. In George's case, he has to confess his sins. In this respect, George's situation parallels that of Jesus Christ. Jesus is supposed to be a sacrifice by, for, or to God the father. The son yields to the greater power of the father and in that sense it may not be particularly important whether one is nailed to a phallic cross or to a cherry tree. What I should like to suggest here en passant is: (1) that Raglan's hero pattern actually applies more to legend than to myth—most of the heroes' lives he analyzes were either historical or pseudo-historical; [9] (2) that the pattern's particulars have psychological significance, for example, the virgin birth is the ultimate repudiation of one's father having had intercourse with one's mother, as Otto Rank noted; [10] and (3) that to a limited extent the pattern is relevant to this legendary fragment of George Washington's life.[11]

Finally, one might remark that there is additional evidence attesting to the fact that George Washington has assumed sexual symbolic significance as an American folk image. One thinks, for instance, of the allegations or even actual signs stating that "George Washington Slept Here." Why should it matter that George Washington *slept* in a particular house? Why not George Washington ate here or visited here? That fact is that it is his presence in a *bed* of the house which the folk have singled out for emphasis. Perhaps by itself, this sleeping mania would not make much sense, but then we recall that George Washington is called the "father" of his country. Moreover, even the most adamant anti-Freudian would have to admit the possible phallic implications of the particular monument "erected" to honor the "father" of our country!

9 Lord Raglan, *The Hero: A Study in Tradition, Myth, and Drama* (New York: Vintage Books, 1956).

10 Otto Rank, *The Myth of the Birth of the Hero* (New York: Vintage Books, 1959), p. 81. For further psychoanalytic ramifications of Raglan's pattern, see Alan Dundes, "The Father, the Son, and the Holy Grail," *Literature and Psychology*, 12 (1962), 101–112.

11 There is good evidence that the folk reworkings of the biographies of historical American heroes conform to a Raglanesque pattern. See Francis Lee Utley, *Lincoln Wasn't There or Lord Raglan's Hero*, supplement to *The CEA Critic*, vol. 22, no. 9 (1965), pp. 1–33.

All these bits and pieces of the George Washington image tend to support the thesis that there may be a psychological level to the familiar legend of George chopping down his father's cherry tree. While still in a phallic frame of reference, let us turn to the modern American legend of "The Hook." This legend has been well reported by Linda Dégh, and the fact that she found forty-four versions indicates the legend's genuine popularity, at least among college age girls.[12] The essence of the plot involves a couple in a car parked in a local lover's lane. (In Los Angeles, the scene is invariably Mulholland Drive; in Berkeley it is Tilden Park; in Oakland it is Skyline Drive.) The boy hoping to make out (sexually) turns on the car radio to find some soft music to set the stage. After several minutes of "necking," the couple is startled by a news flash that interrupts the music to say that a sex maniac has just escaped from the state insane asylum. The announcement also mentions that the one distinguishing feature of this man is that he has a hook in place of one arm. The girl is upset "cause she's just sure this guy is going to come and try and get in their car." [13] Finally, after much argument, she convinces the boy to leave the area whereupon he suddenly starts the car and roars away. At the girl's home, she gets out of the car and sees "a hook hanging on the door."

What is this legend about? To say as Linda Dégh does that its function is to provide the chill of a good scare is not to say much in specific terms about its content. Dégh makes no real attempt to *interpret* the content of the legend, but rather limits herself to *surveying* the content. She remarks that some of the extended details found in the forty-four versions "emphasize the horrible looks of the hook-man, elaborating on the natural dread of the handicapped." I shall return later to the question of whether "handicapped" is really an appropriate epithet in view of the probable psychological meaning of the plot. Dégh also notes that some versions "concentrate on the fearful insistence of the girl or the disappointment of the boy, or the argument between the couple." I found most revealing her comment that "the most persistent motif is the one that renders credibility to the tearing off of the hook-arm." She also observed that "the boy's disappointment and suddenly recognized fear is an adequate explanation for the jump start of the car: the boy gunned the motor as a typical teenager while the girl rolled up the window with the hook arm caught in be-

---

12 Linda Dégh, "The Hook," *IF*, 1 (1968), 92–100.
13 *Ibid.*, p. 92.

tween." Here we have a fine example of how a professional folk-lorist, one of the very best, reports a legend. And yet the presentation is totally devoid of any real discussion of the psychological significance of the content.

One clue to the meaning of the legend is provided by the information that the narrative is normally told by girls to other girls. The majority of the informants cited by Dégh are girls. It thus appears to be a narrative from a girl's point view, a narrative that seems to summarize teen-age girls' fears about parking with their boyfriends. In the legend, we find an expression of the so-called double standard: the boy is expected to try to make out, the girl is expected to resist. According to the plot, the boy tries to set an appropriate mood for a seduction or at least necking attempt. Part of the strategy involves turning on the radio. But the stage setting backfires when the real danger in parking in lover's lane is announced by the radio, the conscience-like voice from society. "A sex maniac has escaped from the state insane asylum." From a girl's point of view, previously nice boys when parked in a car on a country road sometimes act like sex maniacs. And it is probably true that a boy feels that he has temporarily *escaped* from some of the "institutional" pressures that normally inhibit him once he is out parked in a romantic lonely lane. The radio announcement also mentions that the sex maniac's distinguishing identifying characteristic is a hook. The girl is frightened by the report of the hook that may have sexual overtones. Girls fear that boys out on dates will be "all hands," that is, that the boy's hands will be constantly engaged in exploring various parts of the girl's body. A "hook" could be a hand as in the expression "getting one's hooks into somebody," but a hook could also be a phallic symbol. The typical fear of the girl might then be that a boy's hand, signifying relatively elementary necking, might suddenly become a hook (an erect, aggressive phallus).

At any rate, in the legend, the girl insists that the boy take her home. The boy is unhappy because "you know he really had his plans for this girl" with the plans clearly being of a sexual nature. If the hook were a phallic substitute, then it would make perfect sense for the hook to be severed as a result of the girl's instigating the sudden move to return home. One informant told me the girl forced the boy to "pull out fast" referring ostensibly to driving the car away hurriedly. One way of keeping a sexually aggressive boy at bay is to castrate him! In terms of such symbolism, please note that it is entirely appropriate that the hook be ripped off just as it had made contact with the girl's "door." There is similar poetic justice in the version in which the girl winds up/closes her "window" thereby catching the penetrating hook. The attempt to enter the "body" of the car is seemingly a symbolic expression of the boy's attempt to enter the body of the girl. (The general association of cars and sexuality among teen-agers is also signaled by boys calling their cars hot rods and such automobile games as "padiddle" in which the first to observe a car at night with one light—the other presumably being extinguished—can claim a kiss.)

If I am correct in this psychological reading of the legend, then it is not the fear of an escapee from a mental institution but the fear of the sexual attack of the girl's date which provides the emotional raison d'être of the story. If this is so, then it is at least misleading and at worst wrong to claim that the story is based upon the "natural dread of the *handicapped*." The girl in the story (and for that matter the girls who are telling and listening to the story) are not afraid of what a man lacks, but of what he has. The fact that frequently actual dates end with a parking visit to a local lover's lane might account for the great popularity of this legend. It reflects a very real dating practice, one which produces anxiety for both boys and girls, but particularly for girls.

A less popular but equally interesting legend is commonly found in medical schools. A group of medical students take a cadaver's hand or arm and put a coin in its fingers. They then head for a toll bridge, for example, the Golden Gate. The toll booth attendant reaches out to take the extended coin and is startled when the entire hand or arm is left behind by the driver as the latter speeds off. In Dorson's version, the attendant drops dead of shock.[14] This legend has not been studied, but it seems to be popular on both the East and West coasts. What is the meaning of the legend?

First of all, it is one of many legends told among medical students having to do with cadavers. Clearly, one of the first hurdles that new medical students encounter is learning to face and handle human bodies, both alive and dead. As we shall see later in the "Runaway Grandmother," Americans abhor touching a dead body, and they take great pains to keep children from even observing a cadaver. I am told that after an initial period of squeamishness, medical students soon get to the point of eating their bag lunches

14 Richard M. Dorson, *American Folklore* (Chicago: University of Chicago Press, 1959), p. 259.

in the dissection room surrounded by various cadavers. The legend thus provides an outlet for the anxiety initially felt about treating a dead human body as a mere "nonhuman" object.

In the legend, the contrast between the medical students' cavalier and joking treatment of the body and the reaction of the toll booth attendant who represents the outside world is intentional. It is as if to say that the outside world finds the medical students' handling of a dead body shocking, and perhaps that a typical man on the street would be "scared to death" to cut up a corpse. This critical attitude towards medical students' handling of the human body is a long standing one, going back hundreds of years. The very fact that doctors were concerned with the body rather than with the mind was originally held against them. In essence, the idea of any-one's making his living by investigating a human body was felt to be repugnant, especially if the body was a dead one. (This attitude may still be true with respect to morticians.) This may be reflected in the legend by the toll bridge setting. The fact that future doc-tors use a cadaver arm to pay the toll suggests that they are using the limbs of others, perhaps of victims, to help pay their way in life. The connection between money (the coin) and the body part (the arm or hand) is clear. Doctors get their money in life from the sick, dying, or dead. Obviously, there are humanitarian goals at work too, but from one perspective the doctor obtains considerable wealth from the hands of his patients, even the ones who die. The doctor, after all, must charge a fee even if the operation fails and patient dies. No doubt new medical students may feel certain qualms about this. To make money from the pains of fellow human beings has its guilt-causing aspect. Thus the medical stu-dents, by offering the cadaverous arm with the coin attached to the toll-booth attendant, are reversing the normal roles. In the legend, it is not the doctor but the outside world who has to take the money from the dead man (and it is such a frightening experience that the attendant dies). It is interesting that the arm is left behind. Perhaps this shows that the doctor is willing to put such things behind him once the necessary impersonal (as the relationship between toll collector and toll payer) pecuniary activity is completed. Doctors cannot afford the luxury of becoming too involved with or attached to their patients' ailments. They must learn to be able to work with living beings and treat the bodies of these beings with the same objectivity that they learned to use with cadavers. The legend then does more than make medical students more comfortable around cadavers, since it may well provide an expression for the basic anxiety connected with taking money from sick or dying human beings.

My final example is "The Runaway Grandmother," a legend that has been carefully reported by Linda Dégh who indicates that the story is popular in many parts of Europe.[15] Her summary of the basic plot includes a pleasure trip or family vacation on which an old grandmother is taken along. Shortly after arrival at the vacation spot, the grandmother dies. The vacation ends and the pleasure trip becomes a nightmare. Various obstacles hinder the disposal of the body, obstacles such as the remoteness of the area, the unavailability of mortuary facilities, crossing a national border, and so forth. Usually, the body is strapped on the top of the car for the return home. En route, the family stops to eat at a restaurant. Upon emerging from the restaurant, the family discovers that the car parked outside has been stripped of its contents including the body. In many versions, the whole car disappears. The legend may end at this point, although often there is a brief explanation of the difficulty in probating the will or collecting the insurance of the deceased in view of the absence of the body.

Here is an excellent example of a modern bit of fantasy, and it provides another appropriate test case for the feasibility of a psychological approach to legend. First, let us see what Linda Dégh has to say about the story. After commenting on its distribution and observing its appearance in newspapers in Hungary and Denmark, she notes that the European versions make more of the problem of smuggling the grandmother across a national border. Her suggestion that the fear and danger of going through customs is much more relevant to the European experience than to the American is surely a sound one.[16] Less plausible is her suggestion that the story expresses "the fear of the return of the dead." This I suspect is a European folklorist familiar with revenant traditions misreading American versions of what may well be a cognate form of a European plot. Dégh is at least explicit: "The meaning of this legend is that the corpse has to receive a decent burial; it cannot just be left behind." She also claims "The real concern is: how to dispose of the body (at a decent place where it will rest and not haunt the survivors). The disappearance of the corpse results in the prolongation of the fear: she might return some day." I find this unconvincing and frankly I fail to see the slightest bit of evidence in any of the texts cited by Dégh (or in the versions I know from

---

15 Linda Dégh, "The Runaway Grandmother," *IF*, 1 (1968), 68–77.
16 *Ibid.*, pp. 74–75.

California) that there is any chance of the grandmother coming back
to haunt the family. If I am correct and the story is not about "the
fear of the return of the dead," what then is the legend about?

One of the principal characteristics of folklore, according to
psychoanalytic theory, is wishful thinking and wish fulfillment.
Yet the majority of folklorists choose to ignore this insight. Such
deliberate ignorance is part of the general reluctance to treat fantasy
as fantasy. Folklorists seem to prefer studying lore as if there were
no folk. If we look at "The Runaway Grandmother" as an expression of wishful thinking, we can, I think, see the content of
the legend in a new light.

The problem is basically one of a geriatric nature: What does
one do with grandmother? In a youth oriented society, a society
that worships the future and rejects the past,[17] there is no place for
the older generation. Nuclear family units resent in-laws moving in
even for a temporary visit. (Remember please that a grandmother
is a *mother-in-law*.) Rather grandfathers and grandmothers are
encouraged to settle elsewhere and more and more "old-age"
retirement communities are being built to accommodate such
exiles. In the legend, a family cannot even go on its once-a-year
annual vacation without being plagued by grandmother. Grandmother cannot or will not be left home alone and so she must be
taken along on the vacation trip. The fact that a pleasure becomes
a nightmare, as Dégh phrases it, suggests that this is the central
theme: grandmothers are *de trop* and their unwelcome presence
transforms family pleasure into nightmare. If this is an accurate
depiction of general American family attitudes toward grandmothers (though not on the part of grandchildren), then the nature
of the wish is obvious: grandmother should die! Or to put it more
metaphorically, grandmother should take a trip from which she
doesn't return.[18] This is precisely what happens in the legend. The
psychological purpose of the legend is thus to get rid of grandmother.

The wishful thinking aspect of the legend does not end with the
death of the grandmother, for there is one striking unpleasant
consequence of grandmother's death: what to do with the body?
Americans dislike discussing death in front of children. In various
versions of the legend, it is stated specifically that the parents did

---

17 Alan Dundes, "Thinking Ahead: A Folkloristic Reflection of the Future
Orientation in American Worldview," *Anthropological Quarterly*, 42 (1969),
53–72.
18 Another folk metaphor may be implied by placing the body in a sleeping
bag on top of the car (sleeping = death).

not want to alarm the children—this is one reason for strapping the body on top of the car. The children must be kept from direct contact with death at all cost, a philosophy that surely has consequences in adult attitudes towards the reality of violence and death. In any case, a secondary wish in the legend is manifest in the restaurant episode. While the family is at lunch, the body disappears. Someone else has removed the unpleasant consequence of grandmother's death from the scene. Here is a perfect reflection of American attitudes toward burials. Whereas in many societies in the world, it is the family that takes care of preparing the body for burial, in the United States, the family calls in a specialist who comes immediately to remove the body and take care of the funeral details. Normally, there may be some guilt felt by family members in calling in a perfect stranger to take care of their "beloved" grandmother. There is, I think we would agree, something unpleasant about calling in a paid professional to come take care of a corpse. Here in this legend not only is the body neatly removed but since it was *stolen* by strangers, the family need not accept responsibility for giving the body to strangers (that is, morticians). It was not the family's fault that the body was stolen. Thus the legend kills off grandmother and eliminates the body with a minimum of guilt. (There is a little guilt to the extent that someone might have stayed with the car to guard the body!)

The final element of the legend also has psychological significance. It is usually added casually as though it were not really part of the plot. It concerns the insurance and/or will probate. One of the primary reasons why Americans want grandmothers dead is related to capitalism. One way of "getting rich quick" is to inherit wealth from deceased relatives. Thus the whole wish in the legend might be expressed: (1) grandmother should die; (2) someone should steal the body so we do not have the bother, expense, and sadness of burying it; and (3) we should get all of grandmother's money. Unfortunately, wish part 2 tends to rule out or at least delay wish part 3. If there is no body, then there is no proof of death, and the family must wait until the individual in question is declared legally dead. That such a crass mercenary motive does underlie the legend is made abundantly clear in many versions. For example, in Dégh's first text, right after the body is stolen, the narrator says "Well, it wasn't very funny even though it sounds like it because they have to wait seven years now to prove that Grandma is dead before they can collect any insurance." So while I would certainly agree with Dégh that the story is a genuine folk legend, I

am not sure I accept her view that it is one "with hidden supernatural meaning stressing the unusual, the strange experience."
It is perfectly possible that the American versions do derive from a
European form in which supernaturalism and revenants play a
central part. But I would maintain that the *fear* in the American
versions is not that grandmother *will* return, but rather that she will
not. The family would like the body to turn up so that they might
enjoy their inheritance right away. In a few versions, it is stated
that the family needed the body so as to prove that murder had
not been committed.[19] The very suggestion that a family would
murder its grandmother is fantastic, but it does support the general
interpretation of wishful thinking offered here. Grandmother is a
burden whether she is alive or dead. Even after she dies, she has
to be carried by the family. The wish then is not just that she would
die, but that she would die at a convenient time (definitely *not*
during the annual two-week vacation), that somebody else will come
to remove the body, and that there will not be too much trouble or
delay in inheriting grandmother's wealth. In the legend, all the
wishes are not fulfilled. Perhaps the guilt of taking grandmother
"for a ride," to use the gangster phrase for liquidation of an enemy,
requires that the family have to wait to collect their blood money.
Still the primary wish of getting rid of grandmother is fulfilled.

In these brief speculative investigations of several popular American folk legends, I hope I have shown the rich potential that legends
have for folklorists willing to consider a psychological approach.
Even if one were to reject all the interpretations offered as being
too subjective, farfetched, and unverifiable, one could still see the
kinds of questions folklorists need to try to answer. Why is the
legend of George Washington's cutting down his father's cherry tree
as popular as it is? Are there many girls attacked by one-armed men
wearing hooks, and whether there are or not, why should such a
story appeal to hundreds of teen-age girls all over the United States?
Why should medical students tell a story in which a coin held in a
cadaver's hand is held out to a bridge toll booth attendant? Why
should a legend involving a grandmother dying unexpectedly on a
family vacation trip capture the imagination of a large segment of
the American public? I do not believe that the mere recording of
more texts or the protracted debates about genre definition and indexing can answer these questions, and I honestly think that if folklorists continue to be bogged down in the tedium of taxonomy then
questions like these will not even be asked—much less answered.

---

[19] Dégh, "Runaway Grandmother," p. 69.

The Usable Myth: The Legends of Modern Mythmakers

ALBERT B. FRIEDMAN, Claremont Graduate School

Myth is a devilishly difficult concept. People like us—academicians, intellectuals, sophisticated folk—tend to believe that we are above myth or beyond myth, thoroughly demythologized. Myths belong to an evolutionary phase in human thought which we have passed through; myths are the poignant sacred stories of primitive peoples. Paradoxically, however, from another way of looking at the matter, it is only the likes of us who have myths, that is, can entertain the concept myth; primitive people actually have no myths at all. What we regard as the myths of the primitives, according to one theoretical anthropologist, are psychological "charters of belief" for those who accept them and live by them. Belief is essential to the acceptance of "myth" and accounts for its effectiveness in a given cultural context. The very fact of belief implies that subjectively, that is, for the believer, the object of the belief is not mythological. Hence, non-belief in a given narrative, tradition, or explanation is essential for its evaluation as myth.[1] A myth, then, in this view, is not a myth if

---

Definitions: Orthodox myth is distinguished from orthodox legend in this paper very loosely. On the sacred-profane scale, legend is much further toward the profane end than myth. Myths deal with gods and near-divine heroes; legends pretend to historical validity. Though I allude, following Malinowski, to "mythic time," it would be pretentious for my purposes to distinguish the varying temporal qualities of myth, legend and folktale. The investment-of-belief discriminant between myth and legend need not be capsulated here because it is discussed in the paper, one of whose chief points is to subvert the orthodox conception of myth. Somewhere I speak of the "mythic element" in legend—a correlative subversion of orthodoxy which I shall not attempt to justify here.

[1] David Bidney, *Theoretical Anthropology* (New York: Columbia University Press, 1953), p. 294.

one believes it. Since we in this audience do not intimately believe
the sacred stories and legendary traditions of the Andaman
Islanders or the Zuni, their traditions are for us myths. Since these
peoples do believe these traditions they are not, to them, myths.

To follow this line of reasoning, we the mythless are in reality the
possessors of the richest of all mythologies, nothing less than the
assembled mythologies of all the peoples of the world—minus only
whatever myths or legends some mission-trained aborigine might
detect his civilized teachers believing in. Malinowski tells of a
conservative native's resistance to Christianity because Jesus had
left no physical traces in the Trobriand Islands:

> "Our stories about Tudava [the native insisted] are true; this is a
> *lili'u*. If you go to Laba'i you can see the cave in which Tudava was
> born; you can see the beach where he played as a boy. You can see
> his footmark in a stone at a place in the Raybwag. But where are the
> traces of Yesu Keriso? Who ever saw any signs of the tales told by the
> misinari? Indeed they are not *lili'u*." [2]

To Malinowski's Trobriand Islander, a *lili'u*, a mythic tradition,
had to be true, had to be rooted in the topography. The anthropologist I quoted above, he happens to be David Bidney, would
inform this recalcitrant native that Tudava, to the extent he left
palpable traces of his existence and was the subject of true *lili'u*,
was not really a mythic figure, whereas Yesu Keriso, alias Jesus
Christ, should be regarded from the Trobriand Islander's point-of-
view as authentically mythic precisely because he was incredible.

I doubt very much, however, that even David Bidney could convince Malinowski's informant of the mythology of the gospel truth.
But Bidney's perhaps somewhat sophistical insistence that myth
implies unself-conscious belief, that myth's quality is concealed
from the true believer, that myth is one thing from the inside and
another thing from the outside, handily establishes the terms in
which I want to pose the fundamental question of my paper, which
is this: Does contemporary American culture possess myths and
legends, that is, stories and traditions that function for us in the
way myths and legends function for members of what the English
politely term the "ruder societies"? This may well strike some
people here as a naïve question. Legends? Of course we have quasi-
historical legends of sorts, but they cannot be expected to have the
uncritical acceptance and thus the utility for us that they have for

---

2 Bronislaw Malinowski, *The Argonauts of the Pacific* (London: G. Routledge
& Sons, 1932), p. 302. This passage is reprinted in Robert A. Georges, *Studies
on Mythology* (Homewood, Ill.: Dorsey Press, 1968), p. 77.

primitives or for the folk, Myths are another matter: We do not have significant myths because we have gone beyond the mythopoeic age when mythmaking was a legitimate way of thinking and expositing ideas. Or again, one may counter that myth is impossible nowadays because myths—as do legends—depend on a vigorous oral tradition while written records inhibit the necessary imaginative play of the mythmaker.

It is true that there are poets and critics of poetry who refuse to concede that the mythopoeic mode of expression is extinct; and historiography has taught us that between the inert recorded fact and the interpretation that energizes it there is plenty of breeding and breathing space for the legendary. Yet for all that, there is no getting around the impression that the sort of myths and legends anthropologists and folklorists collect and write about do not thrive in higher civilizations. It would seem that we have restricted the areas in which myth can operate and have also developed more advanced, more civilized equivalents for myth and legend.

For example: religion. Mythology, along with dogma and ritual, is normally a vital dimension of religion. What then about the Judaeo-Christian mythology? There are, to be sure, fundamentalists who believe the whole body of mythology imbedded in the Old and New Testaments and their apocryphas, in Christian hagiography and noncanonical traditions, but the number of such literal believers is rapidly diminishing. As early as the fourth century, if not before, certain church fathers began peeling off the mythological overlay of Christianity, and in the last generation, one of the chief enterprises of theologians, Catholic and Protestant, has been to demythologize Christianity. Bultmann carried the process almost up to the point of excising the mythic Christ from Christianity, and in the last decade, he has been radically outdone by such theologians as Fritz Buri and Schubert Ogden, who have gone just about as far as it is possible to go in purging Christianity of myth and replacing a mythological divinity with an analogical one.

So much for religion. It used to be thought that the chief business of myth among primitives was to explain the why and wherefore of natural phenomena. The etiological school is now passé, but without question a good portion of any people's mythology is made up of tales about how the world and man himself originated, the origin of the traits of animals, and the rationale of natural wonders. It goes without saying that except among the folk, whoever they may be, it is the natural sciences that provide for contemporary culture the explanations and assurances that primitive people got from mythology. Similarly, the social sciences and historical sciences have taken over the work of mythology in justifying and sanctifying and tracing the origins of our social institutions, political mechanisms, codes of behavior, civic rites, and so forth.

The work of mythology thus has seemingly been preempted in our culture: it would also appear that we are uncomfortable with the logic or mental set or preconceptions that give rise to mythology. We are incorrigibly historical-minded, committed to a phasic view of process, unquestioning believers that institutions come about through successive gradations in an evolutionary continuum. The intellectual premises of Malinowski's Trobriand Islanders, which I take as representatives of the primitive mythologizing mentality, belong to quite a different order. Malinowski's informants thought of things as sudden creations. Except for occurrences in the recent past, past events for them existed on the same plane of time in one ungraded epoch. For them, cultural conditions now are not significantly different from the way they were "long ago" in mythic time.[3]

And myth, we remind ourselves, means story. Why should we, who have the ability to handle abstract thought, expound our science, theology, attitudes toward human existence in the indirectness and imprecision of narrative? Radcliffe-Brown writes that the Andamanese mythologized because they had no "power of thinking abstractly." The myth-story was their "means of expressing concretely what could otherwise only be put in an abstract statement." Even if the Andamanese, he continues, "were capable of thinking abstractly, yet, since what they need to express are not thoughts so much as feelings (not intellectual so much as affective processes) they would still need a concrete form of expression. For it is a familiar fact that the concrete has a much greater power of awakening or appealing to our feeling than has the abstract." [4] We, too, prefer our principles, theories, laws, dogmas, data, facts, what you will, to be expressed in sensuous language, to be illustrated concretely, dramatized, made to be felt on our pulses, but we like to think that the primary appeal of human discourse is to the intellect, that the affective elements are merely lubrication, merely concessions to our wavering attention.

We like to think so, but are we really less dependent than the Andaman Islanders on the affective processes? The trend of this

---

[3] Malinowski, *Argonauts*, pp. 298–305, 326–333; cf. Georges, *Studies*, pp. 72–101.
[4] A. R. Radcliffe-Brown, *The Andaman Islanders* (Cambridge: The University Press, 1933), p. 393; cf. Georges, *Studies*, p. 61.

paper thus far has been, frankly, to dramatize how much we fight
shy of the awareness that actually we live in a culture saturated in
myth. Fortunately for our peace of mind, however, we may be—
like Bidney's primitives—too much in the myth, too unself-con-
sciously credulous to recognize a myth or legend when we are
believing it. Science has without question ousted mythology from
a large area of intellectual concern, but in the moral sphere, and
in the normative aspects of life generally, myth still has power over
us. Indeed, one might go so far as to say that most Americans'
valorization of experience is keyed to a mythology. Each of us
carries around in his head a fragment of a collective national fantasy
that assures him of his society's destiny and makes him accept his
social obligations willingly. Our personal purposes, what we think
worth doing and unguilty about shirking, our notions of decency
and how to act them out, the areas of permissible pleasures we stake
out for ourselves, our whole sense of feeling comfortable in an
interpreted human universe—all depend to a large extent on
mythology. Myth certainly informs part of our political ideology.
History may not unintelligently be read—in Tolstoy's manner—as
a subtle system of mythology. And whatever our religions have lost
in mythology has been more than made up for by the mythologizing
that Jung and Freud and their epigones have woven into the
modern intellectual fabric.

Perhaps I can best underpin these assertions by citing the most
potent, pervasive, and ramified American myth—*the* American myth
in the opinion of many Americanists. I am referring to the myth of
the American Eden—America, in Bronson Alcott's words, as an
"asylum . . . the hope of man . . . there, if anywhere, is the
second Eden to be planted in which the divine seed is to bruise
the head of Evil and restore Man to his rightful communion with
God in the Paradise of the Good." [5] The myth is a strange and
wonderful conflation of the primitivistic Golden Age myth with the
futuristic millenarian myth of an earthly paradise, the goal of
human progress. In skeleton form, the myth takes its place among
Eliade's examples of the myth of the eternal return, for it combines
a belief in a lost paradise with the hope of paradise regained, that
is, combines the idea of our devolution from an age of natural
simplicity and purity with "an eschatological view of history in
which the end of time reactualizes the beginning of time." [6] From

---

[5] Quoted in Charles Sanford, *The Quest for Paradise* (Urbana: University of
Illinois Press, 1961), p. 178.

[6] Sanford, *Quest*, p. 5; Mircea Eliade, *The Myth of the Eternal Return* (New
York: Pantheon Books, 1954), pp. 141–159.

the aging Columbus to the aging Faulkner, it has been eloquently affirmed, and passages could be culled even from Kerouac, Ferlinghetti, and Ginsberg unwittingly, naïvely, proclaiming the myth. Some of the most brilliant works of American social and literary criticism have dealt with it—to name leading examples: Charles Sanford's *The Quest for Paradise*, R. W. B. Lewis's *The American Adam*, Leo Marx's *The Machine in the Garden*. It figures in Henry Nash Smith's *The Virgin Land* and in the writings of A. K. Moore, Edwin Fussell, and other critics of Turner's frontier thesis. We meet it in Sidney Mead's weighty discussion of how Americanism remolded Protestantism. No lower eminences than Karl Mannheim and Lewis Mumford have discussed its sociological implications.[7]

Thanks to this image of a once-and-future paradise, Americans are endowed with a national superiority complex that allows us to conceive of America as a land of peculiar virtue. It permits us to reconcile a self-centered isolationism with a messianic internationalism. That constant strain of antiestablishment sentiments that runs through American life styles (of which Dorson speaks elsewhere in this volume) derives much of its strength from this complex of attitudes. Most important, the myth sanctifies our activist compulsions by confounding moral and material progress. The hydrogen bomb was a temporary setback for this particular facet of the myth—onward (materially) and upward (morally) with science— but the bomb was soon buried by the computer. The bomb after all is an abstract terror; the computer and electronic data processing miraculously put airline tickets in our wallets.

But one still wonders: Are the American myths comparable to the mythologies garnered from primitive peoples by anthropologists? They function like myths, like psychological "charters of belief," for they help justify a massive ideology, a whole way of life; their form, however, poses difficulties. The American Eden myth is a confusing example of civilized myth because it is atypical in being a complication of a bona fide, anthropologically orthodox myth— the Judaeo-Christian Genesis. The more typical myth that we find in the writings of Americanists is simply, in Henry Nash Smith's formula, "an intellectual construction that fuses concept and emotion into an image."[8] Elaborate constructions are myths; simple

---

7 See Sanford, *Quest*, pp. 4–11, 40, 253–266. The Mead book is *The Lively Experiment: The Shaping of Christianity in America* (New York: Harper & Row, 1963); the Fussell book, *Frontier: American Literature and the American West* (Princeton, N. J.: Princeton University Press, 1965).

8 Henry Nash Smith, *The Virgin Land* (New York: Random House [Vintage paperback], 1957), p. v.

constructions are symbols. This is the concept of mythology he employs when he traces "the impact of the West . . . on the consciousness of Americans." [9] His myth and the myths alluded to by historians and sociologists generally are not shaped as narratives or sets of narratives in which sacred and heroic persons figure, the only sort of myth anthropologists and folklorists recognize. Here then is the difficulty: How can we reconcile these two conceptions of myth which are related on the plane of function but are otherwise so different. To resolve our problem, we are forced, I think, to hypothesize that the mythology of complex cultures is cryptotypical, that such mythologies are covert systems of assumptions, values, beliefs, personal wishes socialized and social wishes internalized, which reveal themselves only in the images and metaphors in which they get expressed, in syntactical relationships, in the articulation of incidents, in the fleshing out of archetypal personae and situations.

How this shadow world of ideality works upon reality is illustrated in a recent prize essay that traces how the myth of Eden West manifests itself in the writing of American autobiography. "In autobiography," according to the authors, "the writer explains his life by depicting himself according to culturally evaluated images of character. As he turns his private experiences into language, he assumes one of the many identities outlined in the myth and so asserts his connection with his culture. Given the millennial cast and the pervading futuristic spirit of the myth, we are not surprised to find the main character types to be the Prophets (those who interpret the complex relationship between present and future), the Heroes (those who successfully enact the prophecies), the Villains (those who throw up obstacles to fulfillment), and the Outcasts (those who fail to make a place for themselves in the great cultural program). There are, in short, a whole range of stances available to autobiographers, whether they choose to affirm the values stated in the myth or to deny the 'truth' of the myth and define themselves by the act of negation." [10]

The last sentence in this quotation strikes me as unfortunate: values are not "stated in the myth" but implied by the myth after an analysis that the myth does not invite; further, the "truth" of the myth has to be abstracted from the myth before it can be denied. That the myth be transcendent or at least covert is necessary for it to be efficacious. Myth does not bear examination by its believers.

---

[9] *Ibid.*, p. 4.
[10] W. C. Spengemann and L. R. Lundquist, "Autobiography and the American Myth," *American Quarterly*, XVII (1965), 504.

Like Cupid in the Apuleian myth of Cupid and Psyche, the mythic evaporates when light is thrown on it. It is for this reason that it is traumatic for intellectuals to glance through the *Reader's Digest,* in which articles suffused with the standard cozy mythic illusions are reduced to their sensational essence, a process that allows the vulgarity of the myth to show through with a clarity intolerable for anyone cynical enough to be critical or critical enough to be cynical.

In American legends, whether folk legends or the contrivances of popular culture, the mythic is perilously near the surface, and commentators delight in juxtaposing the historical truth with the "phony myth," as though our will to believe could be daunted by such exposures. In matters of myth, the so-called truth does not satisfy. We make an overriding truth of what satisfies us by preserving our illusions; it need only pretend to be historically verifiable. In any case, it is not the facts of the legend that are profoundly meaningful to us, but rather the ethos. Fifteen or so years ago, a couple of million boys doffed their breakfast-food space helmets for coonskin caps in tribute to Davy Crockett, king of the wild frontier, just then being deified, Disneyfied, lyricized, televised, and reinstated as a legendary hero. What does it matter that the actual Crockett was a juvenile delinquent, "indolent, shiftless," a crude boaster who deserted his wife and children and was king of nothing grander than backwoods tall-tale-tellers and bourbon samplers? What does it matter that he was "an unenthusiastic soldier," who "weaseled his way out of the Army," or that most of the humorous remarks attributed to him were concoctions of his predecessors, or that his role at the Alamo fiasco was dubiously heroic? [11] What really does matter is that in hearing and acting out the legend, his juvenile admirers were celebrating an exemplar of the national myth. And folklorists should be particularly tender toward Crockett, for some of his low-down rip-roaring antics betray the deliciously primitive traits of a trickster.

Toward Paul Bunyan folklorists are seldom tender because his legend alas is "fakelore," to use Dorson's term. But the acceptance of his legend is far from fake. Not only did the legend sell lumber—which was the intention of the adman who dreamed it up—it also abets mythic assumptions. So much so that W. H. Auden can describe Bunyan as archetypically American, a "projection of the

---

[11] The debunking remarks in this paragraph are from John Fischer, *The Stupidity Problem* (New York: Harper & Row, 1964), pp. 219–222.

collective state of mind of a people whose tasks were primarily the physical mastery of nature." [12]

With Henry Ford, the debunkers of popular legend have had a field day. As one learns from Keith Sward's book,[13] which John Greenway has wittily summarized,[14] virtually every item in the Ford legend is historically erroneous. Daimler and Benz, of course, invented the modern automobile, not Ford. Indeed, the first Ford was built by Charles B. King, but King sold out because his contraption looked so poor beside the French models. The automobiles that Ford took to exhibit in London to counter the French threat were Cadillacs built by Henry Leland, not Fords. It was Leland, also, who standardized automotive parts, having learned the technique from Colt and Whitney. Mass production was the brainchild of Olds and Walter Flanders; the assembly line was devised by Frederick Taylor and perfected for Ford by C. W. Avery. Neither the Model A, Model T, nor V8 was designed by Ford; and, capping blow, Ford had so little faith in his company that he was willing to sell out to Durant of General Motors in 1908 for three million dollars. (The company made two hundred million dollars for Ford in 1921–22.) But, as Ford is erroneously but fittingly supposed to have said, "History is bunk." Certainly one cannot detract from the force of the Henry Ford legend, which made him for decades the number 1 "symbol of American inventiveness and ingenuity," though Aldous Huxley was surely being satirical when in *Brave New World* he calls Ford "the most important person since Christ." [15]

I am aware that in speaking of American myth and legend in this setting it is easy to seem condescending, to appear to be scoffing at the optimistic cast of American mythology and its idealization of a system that too frequently does not work out as nobly or justly or efficiently as it pretends. To excuse my tone, I would conclude by pointing out that self-criticism itself is positively encouraged by *the* myth. In our history, to quote Sanford again, "orgies of self-criticism have not been less patriotic than the shouts of progress, functioning very much like the early New England institution of the jeremiad, recalling a chosen people to righteousness." [16] We demand

12 Quoted in John Greenway, *The Inevitable Americans* (New York: Random House, 1964), p. 158.
13 Keith Sward, *The Legend of Henry Ford* (New York: Rinehart, 1948).
14 *Ibid.*, pp. 159–164.
15 *Ibid.*, p. 159.
16 *Ibid.*, p. 134.

improvements because we naïvely think perfectability possible; and like the train of colonial Jeremiahs described by Perry Miller, we consider America's sins the more heinous because of our certainty of her divinely appointed mission among nations.

Definition and Variation
in Folk Legend

HERBERT HALPERT, Memorial University of Newfoundland

My title, which has unintentional ambiguities, will cover a mélange of problems and observations.[1] I propose to discuss the need for clearer definition of the kinds of folk legend and of legend terminology. My working definition of "legend" will be the conventional one: "a story told as the truth or believed to be true." As my paper will illustrate, this definition raises as many problems as it solves.

Before taking up problems of definition, however, I want to make some comments on variation, which, in turn, will lead to observations on the difficulties of using Stith Thompson's *Motif-Index of Folk-Literature* [2] for arranging legends in any practical fashion. Throughout my remarks, in fact, I will be presenting problems that must be faced in the preparation of an adequate index of American folk legends.

It is one of the clichés of folklore that there is no one "right" version for a folklore item. All variants of a folk song or a folktale have equal validity, assuming that the singer or storyteller is a competent performer in good health and memory. A folk belief may exist in a variety of forms. A custom may have variations not only from one community to another, but sometimes within the same community.

All this we know, say, and think we believe. In practice, many of us unconsciously show a literary bias, particularly when we come

---

[1] I am indebted to my colleagues George M. Story and Violetta M. Halpert for their editorial assistance without which this revised paper would have remained in the unreadable guise of an informal talk.

[2] Stith Thompson, *Motif-Index of Folk-Literature*, 6 vols., rev. and enlarged ed. (Bloomington: Indiana University Press, 1955–1958).

to the legend. We ask, if we are collectors, for *the* legend or *the* story about how a place got its name, how the haddock got its marks,[3] how the man got in the moon. Now this is all very well when you are collecting from one informant. More often than not, he has only one version of a story or song or belief, though examples of informants who know two or more distinct versions of an item are not uncommon.

Our recognition that items exist in variant forms also makes it possible for us, if we are collectors, to salve our consciences when we tell an informant that we do not know "Barbara Allen" or "The Three Little Pigs." We can say to ourselves, quite honestly, that we do not know *that* informant's version.

It is chiefly when it comes to presenting a large collection of material that we fail to do justice to legends. If we have several closely related variants, the exigencies of publication (e.g., the fact that journal editors and publishers will not allow us to publish all our treasured texts), make us select what we regard as "the best" version, occasionally adding notes on how other texts vary. I can best illustrate the so-called one legend error by briefly discussing one legend.

In the "Pines" of Southern New Jersey more than twenty-five years ago, Fiddler Sammy Buck Giberson was the central figure of several legends, of which I shall describe only one cluster. When informants referred to this, they usually asked: "Did you hear about the time Sammy Giberson met up with the Devil?" I got more than a dozen different texts introduced in much the same way.

In nearly all versions, there was agreement that the fiddler was going home late at night after a party. Sometimes he had bragged at the party that he could outdo the Devil, but this theme was not always found. At or on a bridge, he met someone, identified as the Devil, and was challenged to a contest. The contest was either in fiddling, or in step-dancing, or in both. The Devil may win the fiddling contest, or Sammy may win it, or they may declare it a draw; similarly with the separate dancing contest. When it is a double contest, we have all the possible permutations. In some versions other related themes connected with devil lore or magical music were also introduced. All these versions were in oral tradition at the same time in the same region; each was referred to as "the time (old) Sammy Giberson met up with the Devil."

My chief point is that where the legend-making process is alive

---

[3] Herbert Halpert, "Three Maine Legends," *JAF*, 70 (1957), 182 no. 1, 183n.

we get infinite variety that cannot, or rather should not, be standardized. Indeed, if in any area you find only one unchanging version of a legend told by many informants, you may begin to suspect either an extremely dominant informant, or what is more probable, the influence of print. It is well known that if a competent author weaves a pattern out of a mixture of legends from one region, and his published version becomes popular and "feeds back" to the original area, it may often replace other versions. This has been demonstrated clearly for folk songs, but I suggest that it holds equally true for other aspects of folklore, particularly for the legend.

In America there are few legend collections that present traditional material in accurate oral versions with proper documentation. "Popular" legend collections fail to meet scholarly needs in several ways: first, by their failure to identify the informants; second, by their use of sentimental or overblown prose instead of the actual words of informants; third, by their attempt to make a composite of many versions. Both authors and publishers are at fault in offering this rewritten pap, lacking in all native strength or flavor, as the legends of an area.

Let me now touch on another aspect of variation in folk legend, illustrating by examples the difficulties of using the *Motif-Index of Folk-Literature* in classifying folk legends. Here is a theme for which I have four nearly identical stories from four separate regions. Beautiful music is heard coming from a darkened room or church. When persons hearing the music go to investigate, no one is there. Three of my four texts are abbreviated from published sources; a fourth is from a student contribution to my collections. What is curious about them is that each has a different explanation of the origin of the music: (1) It was fairy music (Western Ireland); (2) It could only have been made by spirits (Isle of Skye, Scotland); (3) Perhaps the devil had "snuck" in and played (Western Kentucky, 1955, MS contribution); and, finally, (4) "No one can explain the mystery" (North Carolina).

If you attempt a motif classification of these versions of the same basic story, basing it on the informants' categories, each will land in a different section of the *Motif-Index:* the first in *F* (Fairies); the second in *E* (The Dead); the third in *G* (The Devil), and the fourth probably in *D* (Magic Music).

In the preceding examples the variation lay in the explanation given. In comparing legends we also frequently find that the stories are similar or identical but the characters vary. Barabara Allen Woods in *The Devil in Dog Form*,[4] has ably demonstrated that in supernatural legends one gets similar plots ascribed to different supernatural figures. For any international study of supernatural legends, therefore, we must recognize that Thompson's classification according to the characters makes comparative study difficult. Any legend index will have to cope with this problem.

I should like to suggest, as a hypothesis worth checking, that each geographical and cultural area tends to ascribe supernatural legends to its dominant supernatural figure. If this holds true, there are perils in the parochial approach to indexing shown in Christiansen's pioneering effort *The Migratory Legends*.[5] One of its drawbacks as a basis for an international index lies in the fact that though Christiansen does helpfully group similar legends, he lists them only under the chief Norwegian supernatural protagonist. For example, there are Norwegian versions of the legend of the Devil teaching people how to play the fiddle, which is common in the United States, but they are grouped under his Type 4090, "Music Taught by Water Sprite."

I need hardly point out that, if each national index did this, the supernatural instructor in music-playing might vary from the Devil to fairies to ghosts, and so on. I would propose for a future index that we consider a general term such as "supernatural figure" for the music instructor. We might then have a type such as "Supernatural figure teaches (or grants) skill in playing musical instrument." I suggest further that some such device may well be needed for many legend groups, that is, indexing by the action rather than by the actor.

My dissatisfaction with the *Motif-Index* for legend classification extends to another point. In at least one area, that of strong man stories, it does not have motifs for the most frequent American patterns. Let me illustrate.

There are many legends in Anglo-American tradition about men who accomplish remarkable feats of strength and/or accomplish remarkable amounts of work. When you attempt to classify such stories, you are offered two choices by the *Motif-Index: F*, marvelous characters, or *X*, tall-tale characters.

Certainly there are stories, especially in Scottish-Gaelic tradition,

---

4 Barbara Allen Woods, "The Devil in Dog Form," FS, vol. 11 (Berkeley and Los Angeles, 1959).

5 Reidar Th. Christiansen, *The Migratory Legends* (FFC 175) (Helsinki: Suomalainen Tiedeakatemia, 1958).

of strong men who are supernatural characters. There are also many tall tales about strong men told, despite their realistic anecdotal form, as humorous exaggerations. Both of these groups of stories quietly fit the *Motif-Index* arrangement. What I am interested in is an important in-between group. There unquestionably are individuals and families notable for their strength, which is described as beyond that of ordinary men. There *are* men who can lift great weights or chop large amounts of cordwood, or with a scythe mow a wheat field single-handed. But in the strong man legends, these extraordinary limits are pushed—rarely to the extremes of the supernatural strong man legend or the tall tale—but well beyond easy plausibility. What is most significant is that when these are told in oral tradition, they are regarded as true—and told with complete seriousness.

It is for such legends that I plead the need either for some new principle of classification or for a new category in a legend index. Later, I shall mention other kinds of stories that need to be examined for possible inclusion in a legend index.

Having spoken with conviction of certain aspects of legend variation and classification, I now turn to areas of definition where I confess myself baffled. Consider, for example, jests and anecdotes and parallel legends.

In the outline I give to my undergraduate students to help them classify the material they collect from their home communities, there are two sections that overlap. Under the heading *Jests and Anecdotes*, they are to include stories of fools, witty retorts, tricksters, as well as jokes about other communities, clergy, teachers, politicians, and so on. Theoretically, these are stories told as fiction and recognized as such. But for *Local Legends* (stories told as true or believed to be true), I have a nearly parallel list of story subjects.

Time and again, my students either disagree with me on the classification of a particular tale, or we are baffled about making a decision. And when it comes to tall tales, which I regard as conscious fiction that uses realism as an artistic device, many of my students flatly refuse my explanation that they should be classed as fictions, saying they are *told* as true experiences and belong under legend. In a recent conversation, Wayland Hand disturbed me by saying that he, too, would class them as humorous legends. Obviously, definition is called for.

Other of my student collectors, both in Kentucky and Newfoundland, have raised equally difficult problems of definition. They have pointed out that there are some informants who report

nearly all aspects of their past experience, whether stories of being
cured by a healer, practical jokes, hunting experiences, or trips to
Labrador, as narratives. In my fieldwork in Newfoundland, I have
been particularly impressed by the narrative patterning of stories
of shipwrecks or of narrow escapes from wrecks. Not only do informants report their own experiences in this way, but they will
also tell the experiences of their fathers and uncles or even of non-
relatives in dramatically effective narrative form.

In my comments on the first of Vance Randolph's Ozark folktale
books, I pointed out that "the repertory of storytellers includes all
yarns that interest them, not just 'folktales.' " [6] Randolph's works
have many examples of stories about customs, practical jokes, and
anecdotes of local experiences.

Several other collectors have called attention to particular groupings in oral narrative where the personal experience or *memorat*,
in Von Sydow's term,[7] often takes on distinct traditional patterns.
See Richard M. Dorson on "Sagamen," [8] Wilson M. Hudson on
"Campfire tales," [9] and Joseph S. Hall on "Bear-hunting stories." [10]
The relation of such memorats to any definition of legend will
certainly need to be considered.

May I say in passing that in considering the relationship of personal narrative to legend, scholars might well examine the work of
an important American literary group who frequently based their
sketches on oral tradition: the Southwestern Humorists, who flourished between 1830 and 1860. Franklin J. Meine in his important
anthology offers a useful classification of the topics these literary men
wrote about.[11] In his ten broad categories we find such subjects as:
sketches of local customs, hunting stories, oddities in character,
varieties of religious experience, and fights. Many of his categories
could serve equally well as a tentative outline for the many narratives still found in oral tradition, which we are just beginning to
examine.

A few of my Kentucky students contributed groups of stories told

---

6 Vance Randolph, *Who Blowed Up the Church House? and other Ozark
Folk Tales* (New York: Columbia University Press, 1952), p. 181.

7 C. W. von Sydow, *Selected Papers on Folklore* (Copenhagen: Rosenkilde &
Bagger, 1948), pp. 73–74, 87.

8 Richard M. Dorson, "Sagamen," *Bloodstoppers & Bearwalkers* (Cambridge:
Harvard University Press, 1952), pp. 249–272, and 298n.

9 Andy Adams, *Why The Chisholm Trail Forks and Other Tales of the Cattle
Country*, ed. Wilson M. Hudson (Austin: University of Texas Press, 1956), pp.
xiv–xv.

10 Joseph S. Hall, "Bear-Hunting Stories from the Great Smokies," *TFSB*, 23
(1957), 67–75.

11 Franklin J. Meine, ed. *Tall Tales of the Southwest* (New York: Alfred A.
Knopf, 1937), p. xxvi.

in their families about past generations as true stories; many, however, are clearly traditional narratives localized about some members of the family. Von Sydow recognizes such stories as family sagas (or family tales) and comments on them briefly.[12] A much fuller discussion of the traditional nature of such groups of stories is the admirable article by Mody C. Boatright, "The Family Saga."[13]

Many of these family stories are clearly legends. The first person narratives will pose more problems of definition. I suggest that Kroeber's useful term "case histories" might well be adapted for some of these narratives, and that his compact introduction to *Yurok Narratives*[14] should be kept in mind by those attempting to define the relationship between the memorat and the legend.

There are other problems: I ask for a definition on how short a "legend" can be. I assume that a single statement, for example, "There is a ghost at such-and-such a place," or "There is a man in the moon," is no more than a *dite*, to use another of Von Sydow's useful terms.[15] But how much more do we need before we have a legend?

There must be thousands of ponds and swamps in America and Europe that are called bottomless. Is such a statement a dite or a folk belief? I would say the former. If there is a local tradition (and the words "local tradition" raise another nice problem) that a man tried to plumb the depths of one of these bottomless ponds and his method is described, do we have a legend? If we are told a horse and cart or carriage were swallowed in the pond and never recovered, is this a legend? If there is the statement that the pond has an underground connection between it and a larger body of water, because some object dropped in the first later turned up in the second, have we a legend?[16] I confess that I would say yes to the

12 Von Sydow, *Selected Papers*, pp. 77–78, 87.
13 "The Family Saga as a Form of Folklore," *in* Mody C. Boatright and others, eds., *The Family Saga and Other Phases of American Folklore* (Urbana: University of Illinois Press, 1958), pp. 1–19. For further examples, see also Kim S. Garrett, "Family Stories and Sayings," in Mody C. Boatright and others, eds. *Singers and Storytellers, PTFS*, no. 30 (Dallas, Texas: Texas Folklore Society, 1961), pp. 273–281.
14 Robert Spott and A. L. Kroeber, *Yurok Narratives*, University of California Publications in American Archaeology and Ethnology, vol. 35, no. 9 (Berkeley and Los Angeles, 1942), pp. v–vi.
15 Von Sydow, *Selected Papers*, pp. 106–126.
16 See Halpert, "Place Name Stories of Kentucky Waterways and Ponds, With a Note on Bottomless Pools," *KFR*, 7 (1961), 95–96, nos. 11C and 12 and nn. 6 and 7. My colleague Gerald Thomas calls my attention to the many French versions of pools and wells with underground passages discussed in Paul Sébillot, *Le Folk-Lore de France*, 4 vols. (Paris: Librairie Orientale & Américaine, 1904–1907), II (1905), 447–449 (pools), 323–326 (wells).

last three, but would others agree? We have established no criterion.

Folklore scholars should, I think, include many etiological or explanatory stories under legend, or justify their exclusion. I should also like to see place-naming stories, absurd though many of them are, accepted as legend. Archer Taylor once wrote me asking for examples of explanatory legends about the origin of proverbs. Here is certainly another kind of legend to be included by index compilers.

Finally, let me point to an intriguing pattern that presents in an acute form the problems of definition and variation with which this paper has been concerned. We must be prepared to find in many extremely serious areas of belief, custom, and legend, such as death and burial and ghostlore, a proliferation of humorous explanatory stories and mocking anecdotes that seem to deny the seriousness of these very serious subjects. In the oral presentation of this paper, I stressed that stories of ghosts that were no ghosts only existed where there was or had been serious belief in ghostlore; and that many humorous stories of deathbed requests for burial in a certain way also reflected at least the past existence of serious concern with the way in which the dead were interred. I suggest that such juxtapositions occur particularly on topics that are emotionally charged and that the humorous tales cannot be arbitrarily separated from the serious areas, in classification, without disturbing the significance of these very complex patterns.

The "Belief Legend" in Modern Society: Form, Function, and Relationship to Other Genres

LINDA DÉGH, Indiana University

The problem of origins, spread, and verbalization of supernatural belief in modern industrial society was discussed by C. G. Jung in 1958 in a book on Unidentified Flying Objects. What the eminent psychiatrist found revealing for the manifestations of the collective psyche is also worth the attention of the folklorist. Jung pointed out the composite nature of what folklorists call the factual core of legends, be it historical event, an object, or an illusion. The process of legend formation, by which the factual core is communicated through a more or less elaborate narrative, is of major concern to scholars interested in the definition, description, and classification of the legend genre.

Indeed, the steady accumulation of data on UFO's over a lengthy period of time has not made them less mysterious. On the contrary, their continued mystery maintains an international cycle of legends. This process of legend-making calls to mind the stabilization of folk narrative plots by way of self-correctional procedures as noted by Walter Anderson.[1] In Jung's words: "Such an object (UFO) provokes, like nothing else, conscious and unconscious fantasies, the former giving rise to speculative conjectures and pure fabrica-

---

[1] Walter Anderson, *Kaiser und Abt. Die Geschichte eines Schwankes* (FFC, 42) (Helsinki: Suomalainen Tiedeakatemia, 1923), pp. 397–411. Latest evaluation of the thesis is Dieter Glade, "Zum Anderson'schen Gesetz der Selbstberichtigung," *Fabula*, 8 (1966), 224–236.

tions, and the latter supplying the mythological background insep-
arable from these provocative observations." Again he says, "one
often did not know and could not discover whether a primary perception was followed by a phantasm or whether, conversely, a primary fantasy originating in the unconscious invaded the conscious
with illusions and visions." [2] Materials known to Jung convinced
him of the possibility of both hypotheses: an objectively real, physical process might form the basis of an accompanying belief, and an
archetype might create a corresponding vision. Also, a third, noncausal relationship ("synchronicity") between independent psychic
and physic events might occur. [3]

Causal relationships, on one hand, have been usually emphasized
by folklorists working with traditional folklore materials. Arche-
types and noncausal relationships, on the other hand, have been
entirely disregarded or handled with utmost caution because they
carried folklorists away from the safe and familiar realm of archaic
and rural communities into a wider, unexplored region, not limited
to the backward social groups within complex cultures.

The definition of folklore in this broad context is a much harder
task than what folklorists have hitherto attempted. The term "folk"
has to be reformulated and our attitude radically changed toward
"oral transmission" in view of the proliferation of mass media. In
addition, folklorists have to differentiate folklore from the basic
psychological attitudes common to men. In other words, folklore
today has to be elicited from contemporary groups in all levels of
civilized industrial nations, and the folklorist should focus on lo-
cally sanctioned versions of psychological and physical stereotypes.

Folk narrative specialists recognized that primary mental needs
acted as driving forces behind the different genres when Kurt
Ranke reinterpreted André Jolles's outdated ideas on "Einfache
Formen." [4] It is by no means accidental that the interest in the
mental attitudes expressed by different genres developed in the
period that saw the fading of the classical Märchen, which for more
than a century had been the chief subject of scholarship. As industrial growth destroyed the old social forms and mass communi-

2 C. G. Jung, *Ein moderner Mythus von Dingen, die am Himmel gesehen
werden* (Zürich: Rascher, 1958). I have used quotations from the American
paperback edition, *Flying Saucers: A Modern Myth of Things Seen in the Skies*
(New York: Signet Book, New American Library, 1969), p. 17.

3 Jung, *Ein moderner Mythus*, pp. 112–113.

4 Kurt Ranke, "Einfache Formen," *Internationaler Kongress der Volkserzäh-
lungsforscher in Kiel und Kopenhagen*, Vorträge und Referate (Berlin: Walter de
Gruyter, 1961), pp. 1–11; Ranke, "Kategorienprobleme der Volksprosa," *Fabula*,
9 (1967), 4–12.

cation and population mobility devoured old values, folklorists began to study other forms of narration. They resorted first to the long neglected legend.[5] Before resolving the form and nature of this genre, they looked at related forms in order to isolate the legend from them. They also began to explore the new forms that were coming into existence.[6] Having abandoned the Märchen, they discovered a series of other genres, none of them easy to describe and isolate. The fictional distinction of narrative genres attempted by many scholars brought two important resolutions:

1. There is a continuous merging of the genres in circulation. The same story might occur in a transitional form or might easily switch over into another form.

2. The newly discovered narratives cutting across cultural borders and greatly assisted in their spread by mass media, are not really new in form, function, or meaning. Their originality is, in fact, an optical illusion; it reflects an adjustment to a modern environment and does not touch upon essentials below the surface. This elasticity is an inherent feature of folklore, and thus folklorists are justified in studying the spread of developing narrative processes.

While observing contemporary folk legends and their components, folklorists were also eager to look for them in old written sources. Wesselski's conclusions concerning the evolution of the forms of folk narration were based on the analysis of medieval literature [7] and were further substantiated by the uncovering of manuscripts and printed documents from the twelfth to the eighteenth century.[8] Parallel searches in old records as well as in modern society resulted in the recognition that present-day narratives do not differ in their form from those found in old literature. As far as the content and constituent motifs of the belief

---

[5] The most inclusive assessment of international legend research of recent years, Wayland D. Hand, "Status of European and American Legend Study," *Current Anthropology*, 6 (1965), 439–446.

[6] Hermann Bausinger, "Strukturen des alltäglichen Erzählens," *Fabula*, 1 (1958), 239–254; Bausinger, *Formen der "Volkspoesie"* (Berlin: Erich Schmidt Verlag, 1968), pp. 212–223; Siegfried Neumann, "Arbeitserinnerungen als Erzählinhalt," *Arbeit und Volksleben* ed. Gerhard Heilfurth and Ingeborg Weber-Kellermann (Göttingen: Otto Schwartz, 1967), pp. 274–284.

[7] Albert Wesselski, *Versuch einer Theorie des Märchens* (Reichenberg in B., 1931).

[8] Elfriede Moser-Rath, *Predigtmärlein der Barockzeit. Exempel, Sage, Schwank und Fabel in geistlichen Quellen des oberdeutschen Raumes* (Berlin: Walter de Gruyter, 1964); Lutz Röhrich, *Erzählungen des späten Mittelalters und ihr Weiterleben in Literatur und Volksdichtung bis zur Gegenwart* (Bern und München: Francke Verlag, vol. I, 1964; vol. II, 1967); Ina Maria Greverus, "Die Chronikerzählung," *Volksüberlieferung*, ed. Fritz Harkort, Karel C. Peeters, and Robert Wildhaber (Göttingen: Verlag Otto Schwartz, 1968), pp. 37–80.

legend is concerned, corresponding mental functions were well
known from the time of Ludwig Laistner's famed book in 1889.[9]
Fritz Harkort recently assessed facts about telepathy, precognitive
experience, vision, hallucination, and dreams as narrative nuclei
through the ages.[10]

Returning to Jung's concern with the UFO's and their relation
to the collective unconscious, there is another important fact, in my
opinion. Jung follows up the formation of the UFO-legend from
the stage of "Visionary rumor" stimulated by a psychic cause, an
"omnipresent emotional foundation" similar to the recurrent sighting of natural phenomena such as meteors, comets, rain of blood,
birth of two-headed calfs, and other heavenly signs as predictions of
major catastrophes. Flying objects, similar to UFO's have been
described and depicted since the twelfth century. Heavenly signs
were reported also during World War I. All this seems to justify
the contention that the belief in UFO's is among the products
created by "an emotional tension having its cause in a situation of
collective distress and danger, or in a vital psychic need. This con-
dition undoubtedly exists today." [11]

Jung must be right in his assumption that a regular legend has
been shaped from the different UFO rumors. He tells us that "We
have here a golden opportunity to see how a legend is formed, and
how in a difficult and dark time for humanity a miraculous tale
grows of an attempted intervention by extraterrestrial 'heavenly
powers.' " [12] The psychologist made this comment that American
folklorists seem not to have noticed. UFO's are a particularly
American phenomena, and the press has produced thousands of reports on them. Interest in them is reflected by the multitude of
paperback editions on the subject. These publications vary in their
approach as well as in their quality. Scholarly, dilettante, pseudo-
scientific, pseudoreligious, and naïve writings are lined up on the
drugstore racks, quite a few at the folklore level. Part of the material
used in the literature originated in folklore and reinforces oral
tradition. None of the books on UFO's has been written by folklorists, nor has any folklorist included UFO material in chapters
written on industrial or urban folklore. Do we expect urban studies,

9 Ludwig Laistner, Das Rätsel der Sphinx (Berlin, 1889).
10 Fritz Harkort, "Volkserzählungsforschung und Parapsychologie," Volksüberlieferung, Festschrift für Kurt Ranke zur Vollendung des 60. Lebensjahres
(Göttingen: Otto Schwartz, 1968), p. 91.
11 Jung, Ein moderner Mythus, p. 24.
12 Ibid.

popular culture, or mass communication research to do what we should do? There never has been a planned research project in which belief concepts, memorats, and legends on UFO's were collected. It is not easy to identify folklore in an enormous mass of oral and printed material. As I said before, however, modern folklorists have to expand their field of exploration far beyond the "folk" level to identify their material as it blends into mass culture.

Jung pointed out one more remarkable fact regarding the foundation of the UFO legends that might be helpful to remember in the investigation of other contemporary legends. Jung states: UFO's do not coincide only with the symptoms of our troubled age but appear at "the very time when human fantasy is seriously considering the possibility of space travel or of visiting or even invading the planets. We on our side want to fly to the moon or Mars, and, on their side, the inhabitants of other planets in our system, or even of the fixed stars, want to fly to us. We at least are conscious of our space-conquering aspirations, but that a corresponding extraterrestrial tendency exists is a purely mythological conjecture, i.e., a projection." [13]

The worldwide spread of legends about spaceships and planet men has been treated more recently by a literary folklorist in Switzerland.[14] In a systematic description, Golowin lists modern belief concepts and story contents pertaining to this theme and compares them to similar ideas on messages and messengers from the Beyond, the divine world, warnings from heaven, and the end of the world as they occur in myths, legends, and tales even before some shepherds and three kings were guided by a sign in the sky to the divine child born in Bethlehem. Golowin's nonpsychologic argumentation comes close to that of Jung in finding that the recurrence of similar stories is due to escapism in times of frustration. According to this author, enchantment with the fabulous world of the supernatural and the joy of building a fantasy-world contributes greatly to the formation of this legend complex.

The reason for dwelling for so long on the case of the UFO is to emphasize two seemingly contradictory issues:

1. Folk legend varies, but only within the narrow limits of its frame. Like all the other basic forms of narration, the legend corresponds to a basic mental attitude composed of conscious and un-

---

13 *Ibid.*, p. 27.
14 Sergius Golowin, *Götter der Atom-Zeit. Moderne Sagenbildung um Raumschiffe und Sternmenschen* (Bern u. München: Francke Verlag, 1967)

conscious functions. This attitude itself is not subject to modifications, but social and historical changes may influence the nature of the legend more than they do any other genre of folklore.

2. Conforming to basic patterns, the legend conceived in our technological age can be the vehicle of new ideas.

We are witnessing day to day changes in the social system and its norms; the disruption of the tampering mechanism of continuity in the chain of tradition. Hence, the social elements of the legend, the new climate that stimulates, evolves, carries, and maintains modern legends becomes increasingly important. The observation of functions of the process of legend formation offers us the opportunity to understand the general scope of this genre.

Since the historic statement of Jacob Grimm: [15] "the Märchen is more poetic, the legend more historic," generations of scholars have repeated it and varied it, elaborating on the contrast between the two genres. In fact, the content of the statement by Grimm was that the two genres, sharing a common stock of narrative motifs, differ in the use of these motifs as their building bricks. The Märchen incorporates them into an artistic story, whereas the legend uses them as credible facts. More recently, Max Lüthi [16] claimed that the Märchen, a polished, compositional whole ("Endform") with a consistent structure is unlike the legend, which remains a fragment, an imperfect scrap that never can reach formal perfection because the message it communicates is also fractional. Furthermore, Leopold Schmidt [17] feels the legend has no form at all, but only a message to express. In view of the efforts of legend specialists to work out an internationally acceptable system for legend classification, Schmidt's skepticism seems to be justified. Since the rather inconsistent propositions of von Sydow,[18] the activity of term fabrication found a fertile ground in the legend and exploited it to the fullest. New terms for the distinct kinds of legends, their subcategories and components, have been suggested by almost everyone concerned.[19] Catalogs known to us were set up

---

15 In the introduction of *Deutsche Sagen* (1935).

16 Max Lüthi, "Aspekte des Märchens und der Sage," *Germanisch-Romanische Monatsschrift*, 16 (1966), 337–350. In English translation, *Genre*, 2 (1969), 162–178.

17 Leopold Schmidt, "Vor einer neuen Ära der Sagenforschung," *Österreichische Zeitschrift für Volkskunde*, 19 (1965), 53–74.

18 A detailed survey, Juha Pentikäinen, "Grenzprobleme zwischen Memorat und Sage," *Temenos*, 3 (1968), 136–167.

19 Vilmos Voigt, "A mondák müfaji osztályozának kérdéséhez" (Some Questions of Cataloguing Folk Legends: What are the Motif, Type, "Stoff," Theme and Complex of Folk Legends?), *Ethnographia*, 78 (1965), 200–220; Lauri Honko,

on the principle of three kinds of content categories: the legend type, the legend motif, and the legend theme.[20] The first includes the so-called migratory legend (or Fabulate) whose relatively stable structure comes close to that of the tale and is disseminated in a wide area.[21] The motif contains the constituent elements of the first. The theme, however, was conceived as a compound of legend traditions including different plots clustering around identical actors or, conversely, identical plots forming around variable actors. The new experimental classification of the German legends on Death and the Dead,[22] submitted as a proposal for an international index-model, has not met with unanimous approval. In his significant article, Fritz Harkort [23] acknowledged old mistakes—for example, classification according to actors. The formulation of the classified units ("themes") is too brief to reveal what legend types they refer to. In their vagueness, they fit a number of legend types as well as legend particles. There is also an inconsistency in the classified material: the inclusion of types, motifs, and accounts of belief concepts in a single index is confusing, and does little to further international research.

I feel that Harkort is right in his claim that legend types and legend motifs should be classified separately, and belief concepts should be dropped, as they do not belong to the narrative genres. Nevertheless, I do not believe that any kind of sound classification can be done without a rigorous determination of what a legend really is, in regard to the belief concept or concepts it communicates, as well as the means of this communication: the narrative motif and the type. The basic belief or idea in itself is not a narrative, but it is the most stable core of a legend and is, of course, related

---

"Genre Analysis in Folkloristics and Comparative Religion," *Temenos*, 3 (1968), 48–66.

[20] Greverus, "Thema, Typus und Motiv. zur Determination in der Erzählforschung," *IV. International Congress for Folk-Narrative Research in Athens*, ed. Georgios A. Megas (Athens, 1965), pp. 130–139.

[21] Reidar Th. Christiansen, *The Migratory Legends. A Proposed List of Types with a Systematic Catalogue of the Norwegian Variants* (FFC 175, Helsinki: Suomalainen Tiedeakatenia, 1958).

[22] Gisela Burde-Schneidewind, Ina-Maria Greverus, Ingeborg Müller, Lutz Röhrich, "Deutscher Sagenkatalog. X. Der Tod und die Toten," *Deutsches Jahrbuch fur Volkskunde*, 13 (1967), 339–397; Röhrich, "Das Verhältnis der deutschen Totensagen," *Fabula*, 9 (1967), 270–284. For a general evaluation of classification attempts, Maja Boškovic-Stulli, "Beitrag zur Diskussion über die Katalogisierung der Volkssagen," *Fabula*, 8 (1966), 192–207. A provisory index of the Scottish-Gaelic legends is also in progress; Alan Bruford, "Scottish Gaelic Witch Stories. A Provisional Type-List," *Scottish Studies*, 11 (1967), 13–47.

[23] Harkort, "Volkserzählungtypen und- motive und Vorstellungsberichte," *Fabula*, 8 (1966), 208–223.

to the formal devices in the narration of the legends. The delimitation of a legend type, therefore, requires the accumulation of all constituent elements, irrespective of their narrative value. Moreover, current field experiences in both rural and urban communities convinced me that legend types cannot be isolated without a full field study of local beliefs, community attitudes, individual variations, performance, and social roles related to the narration of legends.[24] As is well known, the international folktale typology became indispensable for philological research because of the stable nature of the tale, but the legend cannot be pinned down in the same way. One often has to piece together a legend widely circulating in a given region where it lives and functions in variable forms. Some are lengthy, well-polished versions; others are independent, loosely connected stories or short accounts of facts and simple statements of knowledge of a fact or belief. The individual's talent and concern are only partly responsible for this variability in narration of legend plots. Legends are not as dependent on creativity as tales are, although people of a particular mental disposition are more likely to transmit certain legendary stories. In modern society, however, individuals usually do not accumulate a large body of legends nor do they have an audience to honor their knowledge.

Two connected traits of the legend seem to be of increasing relevance in modern society: (1) its fragmentary, incomplete form, and; (2) its tendency to be more communal than any other folklore genre in its composition and performance.

The greater the popularity of a legend within a group, the more functional it becomes, and the more and more conspicuous its incompleteness becomes. As it spreads almost like a rumor from person to person,[25] it cannot reach a consistent form but often remains incoherent. Those who pass it on do not need to tell it in detail, since the essentials are generally known. An example will enlighten this point:

One of the best known legends in Indiana, particularly in the central portions of the state, is the story of the *House of Blue Lights*. Indiana University folklore classes, as well as professional folklorists, amassed a great number of variants about a house on the north side of Indianapolis whose porch supposedly displayed a coffin lined

---

24 Iván Balassa, "Die Sagen eines Dorfes," *Acta Ethnographica*, 15 (1966), 233–242; Dagmar Klímová, "Versuch einer Klassifikation des lebendigen Sagenerzählens," *Fabula*, 9 (1967), 244–253.

25 For the formation of rumors as potential legend nuclei, see Tamotsu Shibutani, *Improvised News, A Sociological Study of Rumor* (Indianapolis-New York: Bobbs-Merrill, 1966).

with blue lights and containing the lady of the house, murdered by her husband. The story has been circulating for about twenty years, without a decline. The number of variants we possess now could be increased without any effort. There is practically no high school student, past and present, who has not heard of it. Many of the respondents also explored the premises. After the publication of an analysis in the first issue of *Indiana Folklore*,[26] readers informed me in enthusiastic letters how happy they were to read about the favorite horror site of their youth. Questioning the present owner of the house and learning about the facts behind the legend from trustworthy eyewitnesses, presenting "unassailable" though contradictory documents, I came to realize that none of the oral legend versions, including the facts, were complete in content or polished in form. I collected additional scraps, a set of separately floating motifs, personal interview materials on the background of the story, gossip and hearsay, the explanation and interpretation of its meaning. It was then possible to work out a type outline for a regional index. In view of a future American legend catalog, an analytical method of legend type determination based on depth-collection was suggested in the first number of *Indiana Folklore*. I hope our continuous efforts will improve the method of approach in the near future.

The fragmentary character of the modern legend is closely related to its collective nature.[27] Current legends seem to be generated by certain groups at specific occasions through communal cooperation. The participants of legend-sessions put together their pieces of knowledge. The opportunity of legend-telling in itself is related to situations in which the enjoyment of momentary danger, frustration, fear, and excitement is highly desirable. In this respect, without going into more details, it may be sufficient to highlight one remarkable example characteristic of the American scene. Folk legends belong to those forms of European folklore tradition that are generally carried on by mature or elderly people, whereas the village youths reject and ridicule them. As far as my own limited research experience allows conjecture, a good number of American belief legends have been developed, maintained, and used for special purposes in the life of young people between junior high school and college age. The period of coming of age, the passage

---

26 Magnús Einarsson Mullarký, "The House of Blue Lights," *IF*, I, 1 (1968), 82–91.

27 Linda Dégh, "Processes of Legend Formation," *IV. International Congress* (Athens, 1965), pp. 85–86.

from childhood to adulthood, the crisis of sexual maturation generate the tension and conflicts that convert supernatural and horror stories into suitable outlets. I believe this profound motive behind the legendry of young Americans, divided in many cases according to sexes, is greatly supported by three facts:

1. Human habitations are not too dense in this country. Settlements are often surrounded by forests, mountain ranges, desert land, or marshland, catering to the visionary imagination of young people craving for a scary adventure in their rather uneventful affluent world.

2. Cars are important factors in the process of growing up, and learning how to drive. The resulting mobility awakens a new sense of freedom in the enjoyment of a brand new operator's license as a key to the adult world.

3. The period of coming of age coincides with the time of leaving home and facing the unknown world alone. The faraway boarding school or college campus functions in many respects as a training camp—an initiation seclusion, as it were—bridging the sheltered family life with the responsible life of the adults.

These facts are well attested in all kinds of American folk legends used by young people although not with equal emphasis. A few examples selected at random will show the role of folk legends in the life of young people.

There is a legend used by teen-agers for keeping away their smaller brothers and sisters from a hidden clearing in a wood, used as a ball-playing ground near the small town of Dover in north-central New Jersey.[28] Here is the essence of the variable story:

Dewhy Deevers murdered his wife in Upstate New York and escaped. When finally caught, he was tied by his wrists to one car (or wagon), and by his ankles to another car, and pulled apart until he was twelve feet long, after which he escaped and ran away to haunt the woods of Dover. He eats kids if you bother him in the woods.

One ten-year-old informant's addition to the story shows how it is passed on: "You should see the little kids run when we tell them that. They tried to scare me once, my brother and his friends, but it didn't work—that's because I heard them talking about him one day and laughing and stuff—but my little brother is afraid of him, and it's funny. We sure scared him, all right." This legend is handled as a group secret, and the uninitiated are warded off.

There are a good many other functions the ghost legends per-

---

28 *The Story of Dewhy Deevers*, collected by Cecelia Wickes, Indiana University student, April 9, 1969.

form. Indiana and most other states are populated with them. Whole cycles cluster around particular cemeteries, as well as abandoned houses, bridges, and objects that have unusual features.[29] Would-be adults ready for adventure pass on and multiply the fragments they have heard from others and then prepare for a visit in whole gangs to see for themselves the dangerous spot. It is a kind of initiation ritual performed by challenging danger. This act is very similar to the tests of courage and ability which village youths have to pass in order to gain admission to the adult men's group in folk society in many parts of the world. It also reminds one of the "dare" presented in the Grimm fairy tale, "The Youth Who Wanted to Learn What Fear Is" (Aa-Th. 326). In the Indiana legend versions, the boys climb fences at the ghostly hour around midnight on a moonless, rainy, foggy night when the place is even more "spooky looking" than usual. There is a unanimous emphasis on the eeriness of the place. Some of the informants tell that the time of the visit to be paid to the local haunted place—and there seems to be one in each location—should be Halloween night when the story itself has to be recited while standing on a particular spot. Others claim that one should stand silently on a designated place, looking at the object from a certain angle and wait in silence till the expected ghostly sound would come. It is very likely that under the impact of the resulting group psychosis, the young explorers of the supernatural world will see and hear what they expect. There is also an obligation to perform certain acts such as lifting the arms above the head, turning the head in the right direction, touching the object, climbing in or under it (the middle chamber of bridges are of major concern), jumping around it, spitting three times while spelling out a particular text, or sometimes saying an obscene word. In other cases a tabu against speaking or looking in a given direction is observed. The ritual usually concludes with recording the evidence of the act, as one can infer from the initials, class symbols, obscene graffiti common to haunted buildings.

Besides the all-male adventure-seeking exploit, a smaller number of informants related visits to the haunted places to dating customs of the young people. That the scene of narratives such as *The Hook* or *The Boyfriend's Death* is sometimes localized at haunted places,[30] is an obvious error due to the similarities of the gettogethers when haunt and horror stories are told. The narratives

29 Dégh, "The Haunted Bridges near Avon and Danville and their Role in Legend Formation," *IF*, 2, no. 1 (1969), 54–89.
30 *Ibid.*, I, 1 (1968), 92–106.

telling about "lovers' lane" horrors belong rather to the female type of legendry that has strong sexual overtones and reflects the function of dating, only to a lesser extent. In this case, parked in a "lovers' lane," boys tell their girl friends a scary story or persuade them to come to a haunted place. There the boy recites the legend while the couple stands on the right spot looking into the designated direction in order to obtain the desired effect: the girl would be scared out of her wits and would draw closer, seeking protection from the "fearless" male.

Similar to the lovers' lane narratives, stories forming a cycle of predominantly feminine legends told by girls to other girls at girl pastimes concern the hatchet man. This sex maniac, a threat to the virginity and the life of helpless girls, hides in parking lots, in the back seat of cars, on windy roads asking for a hike, in college dormitories under the cover of the night.[31] Fear of unknown danger is the camouflaged theme of this legend-complex: fear of assuming adult responsibilities and fear of attaining sexual maturation.

The facts pertaining to a ramified and intertwined group of current belief legends are by no means equivalent in their value. They seeem to belong only partly to a main legend text. They seem rather to feature the circumstances, the background, the aims of the legend; they give account of related ritual acts, attitudes, mental disposition of the involved people and of the telling situation. Literary folklorists, not familiar with this kind of data, might classify them according to different categories—belief concept, memorate, fabulate, experience story, ritual, custom, and personal information of the respondents. All these, however, are important constituents of the legend text itself and contribute to the inconsistency of the legend, in contrast with the consistency of the message. As a matter of fact, the formal elaboration depends on what the legend wants to tell.

Legend experts continually commit one mistake. Misunderstanding the role of the belief factor in the legend, they are eager to find out whether the informant believes in the veracity of his story or not. They sometimes ask him, directly, whether the story is true or not and build theories on the usually irrelevant, garbled, haphazard statement forced out by the insistent collector. Telling a belief legend might have many personal and cultural reasons besides believing in it.[32] Nevertheless, most people never raise the question of

---

31 *Ibid.*, "The Roommate's Death and Related Dormitory Stories in Formation," *IF*, 2, no. 2 (1969), 55–74.

32 Brynjulf Alver, "Category and Function," *Fabula*, 9 (1967), 65–66, deals with the same problem.

truth concerning their stories—their rational mind might be un-
aware of a strong unconscious belief. A carefully directed interview
might reveal the hidden reasons why someone is telling a legend.
And, yet, a legend teller does not have to believe his story. The
variable individual attitudes do not change the essential quality of
the genre. In other words, the legend is a realistic genre because of
its setting and its style rather than because of the feelings of individual bearers. As a genre of folk literature, the legend focuses
on its aim: the communication of an open or hidden message. All
its roughness, seemingly poor composition, the mixing of story
motifs and everyday facts, furthers the acceptance of this message.[33]

All the same, the legend as a genre might lose its credence and
might merge with other genres. It also might undergo a process of
desacralization in our time.[34] It also might be converted into a
humorous story, an anecdote. As it has been recognized, the legend
and the anecdote built against a realistic background have a close
affinity. Sometimes it is not too difficult to change the tragic outlook
of the legend into a comical antipode. Kurt Ranke[35] views this
phenomenon as a corruption process as does Károly Gaál,[36] who
reports from field experience instances of converting legends into
anecdotes by way of discrediting them. Not only a process of corruption or of ethnic modification of stories passing through ethnic
borders, however, might lead to the shift of genres[37] but also to our
inquiry it is far more significant that the anecdote denied, with a
hearty guffaw, the belief concepts of the legend.[38] This twist of the
tragic face of the legend can be observed in many cases, when it
really conceals a belief and fear of its reality by rendering it harm-
less through an abrupt, humorous conclusion.

An example of a very popular current story will show what I am
trying to say:

Many subvariants are known about a haunted house in which the
intruder is pursued by a floating coffin.[39] At the climax, when the

[33] For a detailed discussion see Dégh, Folktales and Society (Bloomington:
Indiana University Press, 1969), pp. 130–134.

[34] Mircea Eliade, The Sacred and the Profane (New York: Harper and Row,
1961), pp. 151–155.

[35] Ranke, "Schwank und Witz als Schwundstufe," Festschrift für Will-Erich
Peuckert (München, 1955), pp. 41–59.

[36] Károly Gaál, Angaben zu den Erzählungen aus dem südlichen Burgenland,
Wissenschaftliche Arbeiten aus dem Burgenland, 33 (Eisenstadt, 1965), 26.

[37] Ranke, "Grenzsituationen des volkstümlichen Erzählgutes," Europa et
Hungaria. Congressus ethnographicus in Hungaria (Budapest: Akadémiai
Kiadó, 1965), pp. 297–300.

[38] Will-Erich Peuckert, Deutsches Volkstum in Märchen und Sage, Schwank
und Rätsel (Berlin: Walter de Gruyter, 1938), p. 168.

[39] William L. Clements, "The Walking Coffin." IF, 2, no. 2 (1969), 3–10.

victim is almost run over by the coffin, he produces a box of Smith Brothers cough medicine and stops the coffin (coughing). Erroneously, the Baughman-Index lists this type with the Catch Tales—along with a related type in which a man, who murdered his wife is haunted by eerie sounds: "It floats, it floats." Almost crazy with fear and guilt feeling, he blurts out: "What floats?" "Ivory soap, stupid!" answers the spook. Bausinger lists German parallels of this type.[40]

Informants might often display indifferent or hostile attitudes toward the belief legend or might even be likely to scoff at the believer. Nevertheless, it is obvious that our world of modern miracles of technology does not destroy supernatural belief and its narrative formulation. We still have plenty of work to do.

---

[40] Bausinger, "Strukturen," p. 252.

How Shall We Rewrite
Charles M. Skinner Today?

RICHARD M. DORSON, Indiana University

SKINNER'S LEGEND BOOKS

Consideration of American folk legends should begin with the clever volumes that Charles M. Skinner, once a correspondent on the *Brooklyn Eagle,* published at the turn of the present century. Folklorists have paid him no heed, perhaps because we have done so little with the legend and, too, because he was so frankly the popularizer. Still we must admire the scope of his enterprise that led him to set forth 266 narratives in regional clusters in the two volumes of *Myths and Legends of Our Own Land* in 1896 and to follow these with 171 more, traversing the same terrain in the two volumes of *American Myths and Legends* in 1903. Between these he sandwiched in an 1899 swatch of 78 Caribbean and Pacific traditions, hard upon the imperialistic gains accruing from the Spanish-American War, in *Myths and Legends of Our New Possessions & Protectorate.* We can admire also his limpid Hawthornesque prose, evoking tinted landscapes and dark deeds in little masterpieces of mood painting. Meanwhile, we are vastly irritated by the suppression of all sources and almost all clues to sources. Yet Skinner knew his public and gave them what they wanted: pretty tales cloaking the American hills, coasts, rivers, and prairies with romantic associations culled from a past skimpy by European standards but approaching a respectable three centuries in his day.

Operating by instinct, Skinner did grasp part of the concept of American legend. He understood what we might call "Legends on the Land," in paraphrase of George R. Stewart's much later book, *Names on the Land*. The course of American history, from its colonizing footholds through its westward march to the Pacific, had left in its wake local events remembered in tradition. Regional cultures and the moving frontier thus are acknowledged as regulating elements in legend-making. Not of course that Skinner indulged in any overt theory. But he provided brief prefaces indicating that he had a fair idea what he was up to and felt, if not misgivings, some sense of responsibility. "The bibliography of American legends is slight," he wrote in 1896, "and these tales have been gathered from sources the most diverse: records, histories, newspapers, magazines, oral narrative—in every case reconstructed." [1] He adds that he has devoted so much time to the pursuit of these materials that he believes they are reasonably complete. But seven years later he retracts this claim in the preface to a second series, and alludes to "many stories, poems, and essays that have for their subjects these transmitted but unverified histories." [2]

From whence these legends? One indication of provenance is geographical; they are linked to places. The first of the four volumes, and the first section of the second volume deal with the Middle Atlantic and New England states, leaving less than half the total contents for the South, the Central States and Great Lakes, and the Rocky Mountain and Pacific states and territories. The balance shifts in the second series (which is not divided by regional headings, although the tales are presented in the same geographical arrangement), with the Southeast wedging into the first volume, and the second commencing with Mississippi. As he moved West where the pickings were leaner, Skinner had to rely increasingly on Indian tales, and the vignettes cease to represent the coagulating lore of white settlements. Yet even with his overdone Indian narrations he sought out those rooted in the soil. "Many are the legends that account for the presence of Indians on this continent," he noted, "but few of these traditions have any interest of locality." [3]

It is this feeling for locality, for the terrain of the vast, varied American continent, that gives much of the power to Skinner's editions. He sensed, what folklorists have often commented on, the connection between topography and legendry, and his prize speci-

---

[1] Charles M. Skinner, *Myths and Legends of Our Own Land*, 2 vols. (Philadelphia and London: J. B. Lippincott, 1896), I, 5. (Hereinafter cited: *Own Land*.)

[2] Skinner, *American Myths and Legends*, 2 vols. (Philadelphia and London: J. B. Lippincott [1903]), I, 5.

[3] *Ibid.*, II, 146.

mens illustrate the close linkage. Thus he introduces "The Walled Herd of Colorado" with one of his deft word pictures.

> In a lonely part of Colorado, seventy-five miles northwest of Meeker, famed as the scene of the deadly revenge of the Utes for the faithlessness of our government, is a valley five miles long by three in width, completely environed by rocks about six hundred feet in height that actually overhang in places. . . . The Yampa (or Bear) River rushes past the lower end under arching crags, so that there is an abundant water supply. In no way could one reach the valley alive unless he were lowered by a rope or could descend in a balloon or a parachute.[4]

Here is an arresting natural formation, symbolic of the rugged West, and set in the historical frontier with an allusion to an Indian uprising. The legend then tells of a fleeing Mormon group who with their stolen cattle were stampeded over the cliffs into this sequestered valley, where only the last to fall survived, thanks to the cushion of dead beasts beneath them. A thousand head of cattle supposedly now roam this valley, "Lower Earth" as the Utes called it, secure from bears or mountain lions, and harmed only by an occasional hunter who fires on them wantonly from the cliffs.

In his attachment to place, Skinner necessarily foreswore those kinds of legends not strongly affixed to the soil, particularly those of celebrated persons who did not stay put. So strong was his urge to localize that, coming across "A Travelled Narrative," as he properly called it, he set it in a crossroads grocery store in Rutland, Vermont, simply to give it a specific home among numerous claimants.[5] This story stands out as a unique example in Skinner's repertoire of the antebellum Yankee trickster yarn so popular in the periodical press of the 1830's, 1840's, and 1850's; there is a text in my *Jonathan Draws the Long Bow* from the *Spirit of the Times* of January 23, 1841, credited to the New Orleans *Picayune*,[6] with the same plot of a Vermont storekeeper who spies a hanger-on filch a pound of butter and pop it under his hat and exacts revenge by seating the fellow close to the stove and detaining him until the butter oozed over his face and clothes. Skinner speaks of the prank as "formerly common in school-readers, in collections of moral tales for youth, and in the miscellany columns of newspapers." He had, of course, access to hundreds of such jocularities, but the wonder is that he included even one, for Yankee and frontier humor were not his style

---

4 *Ibid.*, II, 122–123.
5 *Ibid.*, I, 54.
6 Richard M. Dorson, *Jonathan Draws the Long Bow* (Cambridge, Mass.: Harvard University Press, 1946), pp. 89–91, "A Melting Story."

and furthermore, as he recognized, these new strains of American comedy did not anchor in special localities so much as in regions. In another Vermont legend, from Cavendish, roguishly titled "Yet They Call It Lover's Leap," [7] Skinner does make the connection between local landmark and Yankee understatement. In typical fashion, he describes a sheer, rugged precipice over which fated lovers might well have jumped, but for once it was an unromantic farmer who lost his footing while quarrying rock and was saved from a jellied end by landing on a projecting table of stone directly beneath; all he called up to his companion was, "Waal, I ain't hurt much, but I'll be durned if I haven't lost my jack-knife." "Ask any good villager thereabout to relate the legend of the place and he will tell you this," recommends Skinner in a rare reference to oral sources. These examples need stressing because they are so uncharacteristic of the wild, somber, mournful mood that Skinner delights in; all his other Lovers' Leaps are dead serious.

Accompanying the firm sense of place is an equally definite sense of time. The legends occurred in the receding past, beyond the memory of living man, "for the past is ever more picturesque than the present." [8] Colonial and Revolutionary times best suit Skinner. He clearly relishes the Puritan era and the Dutch days of New Netherlands. The Indians always loom large in his pages, both in relation to the white man in the early days of settlement, and in their own historical and mythological traditions. Most of the nineteenth century he eliminates; legends originate in the American Revolution but not, for his readers, in the Civil War. Tales of the Gold Rush and the forty-niners are suppressed in favor of creation myths of the western Indians and an occasional miracle reported by a Catholic priest in New Spain. When he does allude in one or two instances to the Civil War, the scenes are far from the main fields of battle. A longish involved legend, "Spell Tree of the Muskingum," [9] tied to Tick Hill in Federal Bottom on the Muskingum River in Ohio, concerns a spectral scare put into the local farmers by a Confederate guerrilla named Jim Crow. "The gallant defense of the Bottom is still recounted at the cross-roads grocery, but it is not included in the official records of the war." [10] Every once in a while Skinner will bring traditions up to his own time. "The Barge of Defeat" [11] deals with a spectral vessel loaded with

---

7 Skinner, *Own Land*, I, 225–226.
8 *Ibid.*, I, 257.
9 Skinner, *American Myths and Legends*, II, 49–54.
10 *Ibid.*, II, 54.
11 Skinner, *Own Land*, II, 71.

gigantic dancing Negroes seen on the Rappahannock River in Virginia shortly after the Civil War, prior to a Democratic party meeting at Rappahannock. Next day the Democrats were defeated at the polls, chiefly by the Negro vote, and again in 1880 and 1886 the sight of the ominous vessel preceded a Republican victory. In addition Skinner mentions the appearance of the Virgin in 1889 in Johnstown, Pennsylvania, on the occasion of the celebrated Johnstown flood, for the purpose of protecting her image in the local Catholic church (*Myths and Legends of Our Own Land,* II, 210). He speaks of a cursed treasure in Columbia City, Oregon, dating from a mutiny in 1841 on a Spanish ship that came to harbor, and continuing through a spiritualist seance to uncover the loot forty years later, until the search was abandoned in March, 1890, when one of the diggers went mad (pp. 292–293). Spirits in the air, said by the red men of Tishimongo, Indian Territory, to presage disasters, were seen in May, 1892, by John Willis, a United States marshal hunting horse thieves (pp. 237–238). These are rare excursions into the near-present for Skinner, who by and large holds to his self-denying ordinance that traditions must have weathered a century or more, and acquired an aura of the remote and impalpable.

Even with elements of space and time thus defined, Skinner still possessed some range of choice, but he imposed other limiting factors in determining the subject matter of his legends. They should involve the tragically romantic, the supernaturalistic, and the moralistic, preferably in conjunction. Romantic is here meant literally, as the blighted romance of star-crossed lovers. An endless array of ill-fated swains march across Skinner's pages: the couples may be Indian, or Spanish, or Indian and white, or Tory and patriot, or English and American, or French and American, or highborn and lowborn. Much of the time a jealous third party seeks to wreak vengeance on his rival. Skinner appears happiest when one lover dies, through foul play or mischance, and the other goes witless and pines to an early death. Where he dug up all his enamored pairs will probably remain an unfathomed mystery. The net effect is to make the path of true love in America appear unbearably tortuous and leading only to a memorial cliff, or cave, or pond where one or both of the tormented duo met their untimely end. He himself comments in one such affair, "As so often happened in Indian history, the return of these lovers was seen by a disappointed rival." [12] Not that he was unduly sentimental; deriding the excessive sentimentalities of Susannah Rowson's *Charlotte Temple*

---

[12] Skinner, *American Myths and Legends,* I, 86.

and Chateaubriand's *Atala*, he shows no qualms in relating the sadistic punishments inflicted on an adulterer by a grieving husband. In "A Trapper's Ghastly Revenge," a hunter and trapper of Coxsackie on the Hudson, Nick Wolsey, returns to his cabin one day to find his babe beheaded and his Indian wife witless. She dies within two days. The trapper requests from the tribe the jealous Indian who has committed the deed, and forces him back to the cabin.

> Tying his prisoner to a tree, the trapper cut a quantity of young willows, from which he fashioned a large cradle-like receptacle; in this he placed the culprit, face upward, and tied so stoutly that he could not repress a groan of horror as the awful burden sank on his breast. Wolsey bound together the living and the dead, and with a swing of his powerful arms he flung them on his horse's back, securing them there with so many turns of rope that nothing could displace them. Now he began to lash his horse until the poor beast trembled with anger and pain, when, flinging off the halter, he gave it a final lash, and the animal plunged, foaming and snorting, into the wilderness.[13]

Nick Wolsey left his cabin never to return, but passersby were said to hear the steed crashing through the woods along the Hudson and the Mohawk to the accompaniment of curses and maniacal laughter. This requital seems harsh enough, but Skinner presents a still more ghoulish variation on the theme—and in reading his legends one has a continual sense of *déjà vu*, or perhaps more accurately *déjà lu*, as the same episodes recur with different nomenclature. In "Riders of the Desert," a Spanish trader betrays the trust of Ta-in-ga-ro (First Falling Thunder) who has been living happily with his wife Zecana (The Bird) in the Colorado foothills. Zecana, bereft of reason, plunges a knife into her bosom. When Ta-in-ga-ro catches up with the Spaniard, he strips him, ties him naked with wooden thongs astride a wooden saddle on a half-trained horse, and then binds Zecana's corpse to him face to face. Ta-in-ga-ro follows him on his own mount, watching the Spaniard alternately sweat from the sun and bleed from the cords, shiver from cold at night and moan from hunger at day, until he was forced to eat the flesh of The Bird. When the Spaniard at length went mad, Ta-in-ga-ro lashed the horse into the plains, where the ghost riders yet wander.[14] This revolting torture should be counted on the credit side of Skinner's ledger, showing that he was not wedded simply to the picturesque, the pathetic, the scenic, but could stomach, and perhaps even savor, a brutal legend.

---

13 Skinner, *Own Land*, I, 45.
14 *Ibid.*, II, 197–200.

Crowding the unlucky lovers in the legend books are gibbering ghosts. Skinner's ghosts usually gibber—one of his favorite words—at the scene of a murder or suicide, and they fail to assume the personal and nonmalevolent roles we find in modern collections of ghost stories. It is not the ghost story as such that interests Skinner, but the haunted spot that serves as reminder of a gruesome or macabre happening. Throughout the legends he strives to create an atmosphere of the unearthly, whether he deals with the Great Spirit of the Indian tribes, Indian wizards, colonial witches, or recluse alchemists who make magic, or the fevered visions of ordinary mortals who behold apparitions and hear uncanny sounds. Thunderous reports from the heavens, exploding blue lights, midnight revels of spectral hordes, and shimmering mists that take on human forms continually adorn the legends and engender some suspicion as to how much is tradition and how much is atmosphere. When Skinner has definite supernatural materials to work with, as in his exposition of "Salem and other Witchcraft," [15] he is particularly effective in conveying the sense of foreboding and awe that clung to hags scattered throughout New England. One surmises that Skinner yearned for the lower mythology and demonology so available in Europe, and he made a few gestures toward vampires, werewolves, and Indian fairies and mermaids, but for the most part he relied on the prevalent if less exotic English ghost, witch, and devil to carry the burden of his supernatural needs. One of his most striking legends recounts the sighting of a phantom train at Marshall Pass, Colorado, twelve thousand feet above the sea, barreling down upon a real enough train.[16] But this is a lone departure from his antique ghosts.

A strong moralistic tone pervades the legends and raises them above the level of the merely picturesque. Pride is humbled, courage rewarded, faith upheld, faithlessness punished. They are in good part cautionary tales whose message is writ clear. The patriot farmer's son who joins the British redcoats and kills his father unwittingly atones for the acts of parricide and treason by trampling his uniform in the dust and spurring his horse off a cliff ("Parricide of the Wissahickon," *Myths and Legends of Our Own Land,* I, 162–164). A fisherman's son on Cape Cod braves the rolling surf to rescue a storm-tossed British ship on Thanksgiving eve of 1778 and leads the hated foe to shore; the captain sups at the father's table next day in amity ("The Revenge of Josiah Breeze," *Myths and*

---

15 *Ibid.,* I, 226–238.
16 *Ibid.,* II, 192–195.

Legends of Our Own Land, I, 269–272). Fairplay, Colorado, enjoys
its name in memory of an incident when Bob Lee, a miner's son,
pointed a gun to shoot his partner, Luke Purdy, who had gotten
Bob's sister in the family way; Bob asked for fair play and a gun of
his own, and went on to say that he had struck it rich and meant to
do right by Rosie. Now Luke asks for fair play, and all three lived
happily ever after in Fairplay ("Fairplay," *American Myths and
Legends,* II, 116–120). While Skinner gives nothing as hackneyed as
the cherry tree legend about Washington, he does offer several
pieces portraying the commander-in-chief of the Continental Army
in a manly and gentlemanly light. As a young officer with Brad-
dock's troops, George chased a rascally half-breed from the cabin
of the damsel Marion, and tarried under her roof while she nursed
away his fever. He promised to return, and did, only to find her
cabin in ashes, but he kept until his own death a brown tress folded
in a paper marked "Marion, July 11, 1755" ("Marion," *Myths and
Legends of Our Own Land,* I, 180–181). Another maiden, a Tory's
daughter betrothed to an American soldier at Valley Forge, saves
Washington's life when he tarries at their dwelling for the night.
The Tory stabs his guest as he sleeps, only to discover next morning
that it is his daughter, who has deliberately switched bedrooms with
the general, whom he has killed. We recall Type 1119, "The Ogre
Kills His Own Children," wherein the bogeyman murders his own
offspring with whom the hero has changed beds ("A Blow in the
Dark," *Myths and Legends of Our Own Land,* I, 153–155). Even
Indian polytheism is condemned. Because the red men honored
lesser gods instead of the one Master of Life, signs of heavenly anger
ruffled the waters of Lake Initou, Massachusetts, and the game and
fish fled. A spirit told Chief Wakima in a vision to pray to the Great
Spirit instead of permitting his medicine men to indulge in their
follies. As a sign of his goodwill, the Great Spirit sent a giant swan
to the lake whose wings covered all the tribe assembled there in
boats; when the swan left, an island arose in the lake, since called
the Swan ("The Swan of Light," *American Myths and Legends,* I,
83–85).

These examples could be almost indefinitely expanded, but the
point is clear enough that Skinner selected his legends with a view
to reinforcing Christian morality and Yankee patriotism.

Sooner or later we must come to the question of Skinner's sources.
If he is to be taken with any degree of seriousness, we need assurance that he has dredged up and not dreamed up these legends,
and dealt with them fairly. On this score we can to some extent be
set at ease. A number of well-established American folk traditions

appear in his pages in versions that, allowing for Skinner's deft style, convey their story justly. Here are "The New Haven Storm Ship," sighted in the air by a throng of Puritans in 1648 and reported by John Winthrop and Cotton Mather; "The Windham Frogs," that notorious business of thirsty frogs who startled the Connecticut villagers from their beds thinking Indians were attacking; "Micah Rood Apples," whose red centers betray the murder of a peddler in the orchard of farmer Rood in Franklin, Connecticut, in 1693; "General Moulton and the Devil," commemorating the pact that Jonathan Moulton made with Satan in Hampton, New Hampshire, to sell his soul for all the gold his Sable Majesty could pour down the chimney into Moulton's boots—whereon the wily Yankee cut off the soles of his boots; "The Leeds Devil," the monster that rampaged the New Jersey piney woods until it was exorcised by a minister in 1740 for a hundred years, reappearing duly in 1840 and seen as late as 1899. These and other hardy traditions had taken firm root in the American soil, and we can judge pretty well where Skinner plucked them. In my own researches for *Jonathan Draws the Long Bow* I came across a number of early printings of these and other legendary narratives available to him. For instance, behind his telling of "Passaconaway's Ride to Heaven" (*Myths and Legends of Our Own Land*, I, 212–213), the wizard chief of the Merrimacs, sometimes identified with the missionary Saint Aspenquid, and credited with many marvels, lies a long lineage of sources. As early as 1635, the transient colonist William Wood reported in *New England's Prospect* the Indian's belief in "one Passacannawa that he can make the water burn, the rocks move, the trees dance, metamorphize himself into a flaming man," with other like wonders.[17] Two years later Thomas Morton echoes the report in his *New-English Canaan*. The town histories of Barnstead, Concord, Manchester, and Warren, New Hampshire, and Kennebunk Port, Maine, published between 1837 and 1872, referred to the shaman. Whittier wove Passaconaway into his extended poem "The Bridal of Penacook." For the strange phenomenon of "The Gloucester Leaguers" (*Myths and Legends of Our Own Land*, I, 238–241), the spectral force of French and Indians that plagued Cape Ann throughout the 1690's, Skinner could have had recourse to Cotton Mather's *Magnalia Christi Americana* of 1702, Niles's "History of the Indian and French Wars," and the 1860 town history of Gloucester. Among the possible accounts of Moll Pitcher that Skinner could have tapped were stories about the fortune-telling witch

---

17 Dorson, ed., *America Begins* (New York: Fawcett World Library, 1966), p. 285.

in the *American Comic Almanac* for 1837, in the *Granite Monthly*
for 1879, in the *Life, Letters and Wayside Gleanings for the Folks at
Home* that Mrs. Bathsheba H. Crane published in 1880, and in the
town history of Brookline, New Hampshire. Certain prominent
landmarks, like the White Mountains of New Hampshire, have
continually attracted montane biographers of lore and legends, before and since Skinner's day, and he would have had no trouble
securing his choice sheaf of traditions associated with "The White
Mountains" (*Myths and Legends of Our Own Land*, I, 215–220),
from such a work as John H. Spaulding's *Historical Relics of the
White Mountains,* published in 1855.

One obvious source to which Skinner sometimes points, and
which even he could not readily conceal, is literature. Some literary
treatments of what might or might not have been bona fide traditions did undeniably give an impetus to subsequent tradition. He
levies upon Hawthorne for colonial legends of the Province House
in Boston, the Maypole of Merrymount, and the Gray Champion;
upon Longfellow for Evangeline and the courtship of Myles
Standish; upon Irving for Rip Van Winkle, the Devil and Tom
Walker, and the legend of Sleepy Hollow (titled "The Galloping
Hessian"); upon Whittier for the ghost-vessels of the "Palatine" and
the Dead Ship of Harpswell, and Skipper Ireson's Ride; upon
Susannah Rowson for Charlotte Temple. Skinner recognizes the
potency of literature and the arts in establishing legends in the
popular imagination. He begins his series by stating forthrightly,
"The story of Rip Van Winkle, told by Irving, dramatized by
Boucicault, acted by Jefferson, pictured by Darley, set to music by
Bristow, is the best known of American legends." As to the tradition
behind Irving, he does not speculate. In utilizing Hawthorne's *The
Scarlet Letter,* he does refer to the "alleged foundation" behind the
romance in charges of adultery with two of his parishioners leveled
against the Reverend Hanserd Knollys of Dover, New Hampshire;
and similarly he presents a legend of cursed pirate's gold supposed
to have suggested "The Gold Bug" to Poe.[18] One wonders why
Skinner did not follow the trail of local-color writers in the South
and West leading to local traditions. An incident in the Miami
valley, Ohio, when a soldier fleeing Indians in 1791 hid in a deep
hollow oak, there to perish until a cyclone tipped over the tree and
revealed the skeleton inside, along with a pitiful diary of eleven
days, leads Skinner to remark how the novelist James Payn had
used such an episode in *Lost Sir Massingberd.* Hearing of the skel-

---

18 Skinner, *American Myths and Legends*, I, 49–52, "The Confession of Hanserd
Knollys; cf. II, 292–294.

eton in the tree, Payn complained against "Nature's acts of plagiarism." [19]

Reconstructing Skinner's sources is probably a hopeless and unprofitable venture, but one comes away with a grudging respect for his legend-books as a source in themselves. Tucked away in a passing reference within his extended account of "Lost Mines" is the name of Packer, the prospector of San Juan County in Colorado supposed to have eaten his comrades during a hard winter, a name revived this past year on the national news media when the students of the University of Colorado changed the name of their cafeteria in his honor, or dishonor.[20] Mary Richardson in Calvin, Michigan, told me how her father in slavery times belled a buzzard, which then flew in distress from North Carolina to South Carolina; Vance Randolph knows the tradition in the Ozarks, and Ira Ford in *Traditional Music of America* (1940) speaks of a hoodoo buzzard with a tinkling bell heralding an epidemic of typhoid fever, and he supplies a fiddle tune that simulates the sound of the bell. But Skinner antedates these reports with his own of "The Belled Buzzard" that settled in Roxbury Mills, Maryland, shortly after the Civil War and, spoiled by the feasts from that carnage, would thereafter eat only human flesh; its bell foretold some disaster that would enable the bird to gratify its appetite.[21] The pseudo-Indian Nebraska legend of the salt pillar, so suggestive of the biblical story of Lot and so cleverly unraveled by Louise Pound, has a version, which apparently she missed, in *Myths and Legends of Our Own Land*.[22] For the murdered peddler cycle, Skinner offers, besides the Micah Rood apple, the gruesome tale of "the crab-clawed Zoarites" of upstate New York, who bore the deformities on their hands and feet which their forebears had caused to a hapless peddler; the ghost of a Hebrew peddler dispatched in 1853 near Lebanon, Missouri, which, seven years later, shocked his murderer into suicide; and the haunting of Orleans Cross-roads, Maryland, until the ghost of the peddler slain there was laid by branches thrown on his grave.[23] In short, Skinner's compilations are not to be overlooked when one traces histories of American folk legends.

Still we recognize at the same time how much must have been

[19] *Ibid.*, II, 248.

[20] *Ibid.*, II, 318–319.

[21] *Ibid.*, I, 274–275; Dorson, *Negro Folktales in Michigan* (Cambridge, Mass.: Harvard University Press, 1956), pp. 46, 207.

[22] Skinner, *Own Land*, II, 186–188, "The Salt Witch."

[23] *Ibid.*, I, 63–65, "The Deformed of Zoar"; *ibid.*, II, 182–183, "How the Crime Was Revealed"; and Skinner, *American Myths and Legends*, I, 275–278, "Stick Pile Hill."

omitted. He is wanting particularly in the field of the post-Revolutionary historical folk legend. One example that he does include suggests the possibilities. This is "The Escaped Nun," dealing with the notorious burning of the Ursuline convent in Somerville, Massachusetts, in 1834 by outraged neighbors filled with buried rumors of disobedient nuns walled alive, Protestant girls seduced by priests, and critics sealed in dark dungeons. When Sister Mary John fled the convent and spread these stories, a mob broke in and set fire to the building. This ugly chapter in what historian Ray Billington has called *The Protestant Crusade* usually receives passing mention in general American histories, and it belongs squarely in the middle ground between historical fact and fictional folklore where traditional prejudices, bogies, slanders, and horror tales flourish. Skinner recognized the genre, saying "this story of the convent has already become a tradition rather than a history." [24] We would vastly prefer that Skinner had substituted more of these mainstream American legends for his interminable Indian romances and myths.

At the end of both of his two-volume editions, Skinner departs from his strictly geographical scheme to pursue topical themes, still related to the land but crossing state lines. In these, perhaps his most interesting and forward-looking sections, he glances at Buried Treasure, Lost Mines, Snakes and Sea-Serpents, Storied Cliffs and Waters and Trees and Mountains, with special attention to Captain Kidd and the Wandering Jew. "Every Western State has its lost mine," he observes, "as every Atlantic State has a part of Kidd's or Blackbeard's treasure." [25] Commenting on "How Some Places Were Named," he remarks, in appropriate folkloric vein, that the classical names affixed by scholars to towns and cities have far less appeal than the "Doodletowns that are indigenous to the soil." [26] And he allows himself some humorous etymologies of New Jersey towns. "We are entitled to have doubts when we are told that Beatyestown is Irish; that Boilsville was named in commemoration of Sufferin' Job Hitchins, who stood it as long as he could and then died there; that six of the most ancient settlers named Feebletown for themselves, just before they shuffled off the coil." [27] This rather unexpected light touch is best displayed in the one entry that departs from places, on "Deadheads," "Crackers," "Hoodlums," and "Panhandlers," although here too he ties their origins to Michigan,

---

24 Skinner, *American Myths and Legends*, I, 59.
25 *Ibid.*, II, 301.
26 *Ibid.*, II, 228.
27 *Ibid.*, II, 223.

Georgia and Florida, and San Francisco. "Hoodlum" is supposed to have originated with rowdies, drifting to California after the Gold Rush, who gained their name from the misspelling of the name of their leader, the bully Muldoon, by a San Francisco newspaper editor, who spelled the name backward, but slipped in an *h* for an *n*.[28] In Mitford Mathews's *A Dictionary of American English on Historical Principles,* entries for 1871 and 1881 associate "hoodlums" with San Francisco, although not with Muldoon. Mathews lacks the anecdotal origin Skinner gives for deadhead.

In the first half of the nineteenth century a new toll-road was built out of Detroit, replacing a rough plank-road leading to Elmwood Cemetery. As the burial-ground had been laid out before the toll-road was created, and a hardship was involved in refusing access to it, the owners of the road agreed to let all funeral processions pass free. A physician of the town, Dr. Pierce, stopping to pay his toll one day, remarked to the gate-keeper, "Considering the benevolent character of my profession, I ought to be allowed to travel on this road without charge."

"No, no, doctor," answered the toll-man; "we can't afford that. You send too many deadheads through, as it is."

The incident was repeated, caught up all over the country, and "deadhead" is now colloquial, if not elegant English.[29]

This kind of anecdotal legend, so characteristic of the American scene, is, regrettably, quite out of character for Skinner, but here too, as in other matters, he surprises us with an occasional deviation.

We have one last series of questions to consider about Skinner's legend-books: the extent to which he consciously recognized folkloric patterns. More specifically, how aware was he of the migratory legend, or of the folktale that assumes the guise of a unique local event, or of variant versions? As his terminal essays show, he certainly perceived some of the recurrent themes in American landscape legendry. Sometimes he also indicates a sensitivity to traditional narratives, and alludes to likenesses of Endymion and Diana among the Ojibways, and to the "Helen of a New-World Troy" among the Zuñis and the Wintus; a New York Dutch tradition makes him think of the Hat Rogue of the Devil's Bridge in Switzerland; he rejects a relationship between the lost tribes of Israel and the northern Indians on the basis of flood legends, but sees other analogies, for instance between biblical patriarchs and the medicine

28 *Ibid.,* II, 215.
29 *Ibid.,* II, 212–213.

men.[30] Once he remarks drily on "Folk-lorists who take their work
very seriously" interpreting Helen as a moon myth because her
name means "shining," as if the siege of Troy never took place.[31]
This solitary acknowledgment of the swirling controversies in folklore theory places Skinner on the side of the euhemerists, as we
might expect from a dealer in physically based legends. The question of variation did not seem to disturb him, and every once in a
while instead of synthesizing a narrative he sets down the options.
Under the caption "Various Grindstone Hill," he relates distinctive
Indian, Yankee, Irish, and French-Canadian explanations for the
odd-shaped hill on Maine's Penobscot River.[32] (To the Indian, it
was a moon peopled with imps that Melgasoway shot down from
the sky; to the Yankee, a wizard's conjuration to enable mowers to
sharpen their scythes; to the Irish, the wheel of a barrow on which a
"stout fellow" was pushing a monument up to the North Pole; to
the *habitant*, the devil's response to a lusty oath of a captain of
French troops marching to reinforce Montcalm in Quebec, who
swore that he wished it would rain grindstones and harrowteeth.)
He gives two forms of the celebrated legend of the tribal suicide of
the Biloxi. In one, the remnants of the Biloxi, besieged by the
Choctaws, march into the Pascagoula River in Mississippi. In the
other, a postcontact version, the Biloxi who have willy-nilly accepted Catholicism, hear a mermaid singing atop a mound of the
Pascagoula waters; they encircle the mound, entranced, and the
waters recede and drown them. A dying priest, taking the blame on
himself for this pagan lapse, declared that if a fellow clergyman
would row to the spot in the bay where music was heard in the
deeps, and drop a crucifix at midnight on Christmas, he could save
the souls below, at the cost of his own life.[33] While not pausing to
speculate on these discrepancies, Skinner did recognize that some
geographically separated legends showed closer community than
variants in the same locale, and he treats "Besieged by Starvation"
under one head, although he discovered places in three different
states where Indian forces made their last stand on rock formations
since associated with their lost cause.[34] By and large, origins did not
concern the adroit legend-spinner, yet he does cite as "an example

---

30 Skinner, *Own Land,* II, 119; *ibid.,* II, 219; Skinner, *American Myths and
Legends,* II, 195; Skinner, *Own Land,* I, 38; Skinner, *American Myths and
Legends,* I, 194.
31 Skinner, *American Myths and Legends,* II, 195.
32 *Ibid.,* I, 15–19.
33 Skinner, *Own Land,* II, 90–92, "Last Stand of the Biloxi."
34 *Ibid.,* II, 203–204.

of the way in which legends sometimes grow" the case of No-Head Pond, about which Thomas Nelson Page wrote his story "No Haid Pawn." Fed by underground springs, the pond seemed to have no source, and the blacks on Page's plantation attributed its existence to a headless ghost.[35] As for the reverse process, where the itinerant tale finds a congenial roost, Skinner sometimes perceived its workings. In the account of farmer Lovel, for whom Lovel Mountain in New Hampshire is named, capturing six Indians with the old trick of knocking out a wedge in a cleft log they were holding (Type 38), he observes that Lovel must have read ancient history to be so prepared.[36] On the other hand, while he uses the title "The Singing Bones" for a graphic rendition of Type 720, *My Father Slew Me, My Mother Ate Me,* and ends it with the terse statement, "A Louisiana negro legend," he gives no indication of its folktale nature.[37] The way in which Skinner introduces dialogue—of a literary turn of phrase particularly ill suited to his characters—and his development of personality conflict between the hard-pressed husband and evasive wife, confers a plausibility on his legend while reducing its folktale quality. In one apocryphal legend, Skinner invents a place called Lonetown, New Jersey, as the setting of what he concedes is a "quip of long endurance" that might indeed have originated in the courts of Egypt or the caves of the Stone Age. It is the plaint of the stranger in town—the towns vary—who was sentenced to death by hanging or six months in Lonetown. After a spell in Lonetown, he publicly admits the error of his choice.[38] This kind of prank on the reader, revealed in the final paragraph, reveals Skinner in a lighter moment that he could not indulge in more than once or twice without destroying his reader's faith, but it does show his alertness to migrating legends, and even his willingness to give them a little push. His open-mindedness on origins appears in his observation on Lovers' Leaps, that "while in some cases the legend has been made to fit the place, there is no doubt that in many instances the story antedates the arrival of the white man." [39] Occasionally, he lets drop provocative generalizations on the matter of American legendry, such as the view that American witches for all their magic live in poverty compared to their European counterparts, or the perception of an odd recurrence of assaults on people and their homes by "imps of darkness"—this latter comment as a

---

35 Skinner, *American Myths and Legends,* II, 266.
36 Skinner, *Own Land,* I, 207–208, "A Chestnut Log."
37 Skinner, *American Myths and Legends,* II, 33–36.
38 *Ibid.,* I, 238–240, "The Lonetown Mystery."
39 Skinner, *Own Land,* II, 318.

preface to the poltergeist legend of the George Walton house in
Portsmouth, New Hampshire.[40] We must however score him down
for alleging that "ghosts cannot abide factories, locomotives, brew-
eries and trolley-cars." [41]

On the mechanism of legend transmission, Skinner again has
little to say, but here too he suddenly surprises us by declaring that
the school and college around Bryn Mawr and Harverford have
kept alive the traditions and superstitions of early Pennsylvania
settlers. Somehow Skinner does not seem the man to appreciate the
vitality of collegiate lore. He then proceeds to tell the undergraduate legend of "The Man With the Skates," anticipating such current dormitory horror legends as "The Pickled Hand" and "The
Hook." In this earlier prototype, one student accidentally throttles
another, and in panic clothes the corpse with overcoat and hat, ties
skates to its feet, and drops it through a hole he breaks in a frozen
pond. The coroner returns a verdict of accidental death by drowning, but each night thereafter the killer hears a dragging, shuffling
sound, and sees his victim climb over the transom. On the third
night he was found dead, with finger marks on his throat.[42]

Further to his credit, Skinner did recognize and give space to
what we might call the impostor legend. One longish narrative
concerns a scamp named Ransford Rogers who came to Morris-
town, New Jersey, in 1788 and organized the local citizenry to seek
for Kidd's treasure on Schooler's Mountain, selling them shares in
the enterprise in return for his guarantee to lay the guardian ghost,
which turned out to be Rogers himself.[43] The whimsical and even
irreverent manner in which Skinner relates this and some other
traditional escapes—such as Captain Kidd's unintentional bequest
of a magic gold tooth to a Dutch goodwife ("The Golden Tooth,"
American Myths and Legends, I, 176–186)—provides a welcome
change of pace to the romantic tragedies, even if they seem too
lighthearted for genuine legends. In his boyhood in New England,
Skinner tells us, in an unexpected confidence, he had once played
the poltergeist himself, until rudely apprehended by the "unpopular
gentleman" whose house he was plaguing.[44]

What progress have we made since Skinner? The answer would
seem to be, surprisingly little. Field collections of American folk

40 Skinner, *American Myths and Legends*, I, 270; Skinner, *Own Land*, II, 305.
41 Skinner, *American Myths and Legends*, I, 226.
42 *Ibid.*, I, 260–264.
43 *Ibid.*, I, 224–234, "The Spooks of Schooley's Mountain."
44 Skinner, *Own Land*, II, 310.

narratives have pleasantly multiplied since the 1920's, but the legend remains still pretty much an orphan, ill defined, poorly collected, unheralded—I was about to say unsung. One looks hopefully through the major field books—Frank C. Brown, Vance Randolph, Emelyn Gardner, Leonard Roberts—and finds small pickings. The *Legends of Texas* in the Publications of the Texas Folklore Society offer mostly retold texts on trite themes. An example of what appears to me a representative American place legend is the account of Everlasting Water at High Knob, Kentucky, in Leonard Roberts's *South from Hell-fer-Sartin*. There is a literal, and dramatic, text told by Felix Turner, 60, of Burning Springs, Clay County, Kentucky, of how an old Baptist preacher, denied the use of a well by his brother-in-law, prayed on a dry bank by his home for God to send him everlasting water. After three tries the section of a hollow black gum tree he had cut down overflowed with water.

> And it's never failed since. And they's been sawmills, cattle watered out of it, and they've never been able to sink that one foot down in that gum. And that happened at High Knob, Kentucky. That's a true fact now. And I can find you twenty different old men and old women that will swear to the facts of that.[45]

Here are combined the ingredients of the oral folk legend, as opposed to the well-publicized mass media legend: a remarkable local happening, accepted as fact, with an identifiable motif at its core (D1766.1, "Magic fountain produced by prayer"), a specific locale, and a general knowledge by the community of the episode. What we would like, however, are the statements of the score of persons to whom Felix Turner refers. A local legend, to my thinking, can never be accepted in one text, for the proof is on the legend collector to demonstate that it pervades the social group. We are not dealing here with folktale variants, but with awareness of the tradition, perhaps in something like entirety, more frequently in fragments. Consequently, there arises a publishing problem: how are these fuzzy bits and pieces to be presented? My answer is, just as they are told, without any attempt at reconstructing a synthetic —truly a synthetic—narrative. The publishing outlet will have to be, and should be, a scholarly monograph. Vance Randolph once told me that he had collected many tales of so local and disjointed a nature that he never attempted to print them. Charles Neely did set down eighteen narratives he called "Local Legends" in *Tales*

---

45 Leonard Roberts, *South from Hell-fer-Sartin* (Lexington: University of Kentucky Press, 1955), p. 173.

and Songs of Southern Illinois, and they ring true because they are formless, filled with local references, personal and anecdotal, and not particularly interesting as story stuff. But they are rich in the stuff of human experience in a back country setting, with their accounts of wolf and panther scares; the self-strangling of a hog thief; the escape of a Confederate sympathizer who kissed a pretty girl on his way out the window; the execution during the Civil War of a government informer by a group of deserters, at lonely Dug Hill, thereafter said to be haunted; the recovery of a stolen horse with the aid of a herb doctor. Neely was on the right track.

On the basis of my earlier paper, "Defining the American Folk Legend," and the present review of Skinner's two series, I would like to throw open for consideration the following general propositions.
1. *American folk legends belong in large part to a different universe from the Sagen of the Old World.* The fairies, trolls, nissen, and sea-spirits of Christiansen's *The Migratory Legends,* or the *kappa, tengu, oni,* and fox-demons of my *Folk Legends of Japan,* have no counterparts in the United States. Skinner sought to cover the American land with legendary associations like those in Germany and Japan, chiefly on the basis of Indian spirit-beings, but this scheme simply does not work in America. Indian mythology, or legendry, does not carry over into American life. American legends begin with colonization.
2. *Many American folk legends can be divided into three large divisions:* those connected with the land and with communities, according to Skinner's premise; those attached to legendary individuals, whether strong heroes, badmen, healers, saints, characters, or celebrities; and those involving experiences alleged to have occurred to a given individual, but which are attached to many persons in different places. These three classes of traditions, while all falling under the head of believed narratives, are so dissimilar that perhaps they deserve distinguishing labels. Category one covers events of local history that have struck the imagination of the townspeople; from my fieldwork in upper Michigan, I think of the Lynching of the MacDonald Boys in Menominee, How Crystal Falls Stole the Courthouse from Iron River, and Pat Sheridan's Speech at Escanaba. Category two covers cycles of legendary anecdotes, such as those about the Three Nephites, or John Darling, or Barney Beal, or the Healer of Los Olmos. Ballad heroes like John Henry may actually not be heroes of prose legends. Political figures in the United States have never attained the legendary status say of Mexican leaders like Emiliano Zapata and Pancho Villa. A

character may sometimes be local, or he may belong to an occupation or profession, like the late Stephen Visscher, professor of geography at Indiana University, and the subject of jovial anecdotes among his colleagues in Bloomington and in the national fraternity of geographers concerning his niggardly habits, such as retrieving the Sunday *New York Times* from his neighbor's garbage can, or attempting to cart his mother-in-law's corpse across the state line from Indiana to Kentucky to save a burial fee. Category three covers floating single-episode legends, like the Vanishing Hitchhiker, the Stolen Grandmother, the Dead Cat in the Package, the Hook, the Killer in the Back Seat, the Graveyard Wager, and the Death Car. These are usually told as second-hand memorats, and this genre is represented in four of the eighteen "Folk Legends of Indiana" in the first issue of *Indiana Folklore* (1968). The same tradition may of course take a "free floating" or "bound place" form, in the words of de Caro and Lunt commenting on the unusual legend in that issue of "The Face on the Tombstone," but a decision can be rendered as to its basic emphasis; in that case, involving the theme of the ineradicable likeness on the stone, the element of place predominates.

3. *Other categories of American legends are required to deal with urban, ethnic and Negro traditions.* Immigrants, slaves, and city dwellers bear a different relation to the land from the direct possession and cultivation of farmer-settlers; they are often, as John Higham has titled his history of immigration, *Strangers in the Land.* We are only beginning to investigate the folklore of cities, but one omnipresent city legend, sinister and foreboding, and defying any existing classification, is already visible, that of the Mafia or the Syndicate. Ethnic societies frequently cherish legends and heroes of their homelands, which they renew and reinforce by visits and artifacts. Negro narratives of slavery and postslavery atrocities and terrorism, such as the bogey of the night riders uncovered by Gladys Fry, also transcend the simple categories of place and person.

4. *Regionally limited depth collecting is needed to excavate historical or community place legends.* Our model here can be the *Folklore of Adams County, Illinois,* by Harry M. Hyatt, who turned up eleven thousand beliefs and memorats within an area of ten square miles around Quincy. The current enterprise of one folklorist, to write his brethren for the most popular legend in their respective states, will simply perpetuate mass-culture pseudolegendry. Besides we need more than legend texts; we need their ethnographic, historical, and psychological settings.

5. *American folk legends should be published with a maximum*

*of variant texts and annotation, and with no attempt to appeal to
the general reader.* Social scientists have gently warned us about
succumbing to the intrinsic appeal of our materials at the cost of
scientific detachment. The legend issue of *Indiana Folklore* moves in
this direction.

6. *In speaking about American folk legends, we will have to
differentiate between the forty-eight contiguous states and other
territory flying the American flag.* Here too Skinner has anticipated
us. The cultural history of Hawaii, Alaska, Puerto Rico, Guam,
American Samoa, and other odd islets deviates so widely from the
story of colonization and the westward movement that we will have
to look at their legends with different binoculars.

7. *The vitality of American folk legends is directly related to the
epochs of American history.* Times have changed since Skinner's
day; the population has doubled, and its ways are profoundly
altered by the automobile, airplane, radio, television. But times had
changed before Skinner's day. Legends that he revived had already
lost their force, and legends that he excluded were in full vigor. In
a society as dynamic as that of the United States, legends continually grow and wither, to be embalmed in tourist books and bro-
chures. Any presentation of American folk legends should take into
account these temporal periods.

AMERICAN LIFE STYLES AND LEGENDS

American history may be viewed as falling into three periods
dominated by particular life styles, to use a term currently in vogue,
with the 1960's marking a convulsive transition into a fourth. Each
life style reflects the dominant goals and aspirations of the period,
and it is reflected in turn in the prevalent social philosophy, in the
educational institutions, in the culture heroes and popular heroes,
and in legends and folklore. Characteristically, the American life
style has sought to express a freedom of action and belief against
an enemy of freedom, against the Establishment of its day.

The first life style was that of the Religious Man, and his oppres-
sor was the Established Church of England. This style dominated
the seventeeth century and prevailed perhaps halfway through the
eighteenth, when revivalism, on one side, and arminian rationalism,
on the other, choked off the Puritan thrust. Religious Man, in his
Protestant reforming guise of Puritan, Quaker, or Mennonite, con-
centrated on the salvation of his soul. He came to America to place
himself in a stronger position to attain this priceless end, free from

the medieval shackles of a hidebound Anglican church, still close to Rome, which mixed saints and sinners. The theology of Calvinistic Puritanism controlled the public and private lives of New Englanders, with its formidable dialectic of covenants, election, predestination, congregationalism, perseverance of the saints, justification by faith, and preparation to receive God's predetermined grace. In the Bay Commonwealth, all magistrates must be saints, for sinners could never govern God's elect. Harvard College, first of American universities, was founded in 1636, the precursor of other denominational colleges intended to train ministers who could exegete Scripture and to graduate a laity capable of understanding such exegesis. The leaders of the first settlements—William Bradford, John Winthrop, Francis Daniel Pastorius—bent their energies to safeguarding their new autonomous religious societies. Cotton Mather is the greatest of the culture heroes—splenetic, unquenchable, oracular, preaching on every event and issue within reach, from Salem witchcraft to smallpox inoculation, and finding God's providence behind every act. His crowning work, the *Magnalia Christi Americana* (1702), celebrated the achievements of Christ in the American wilderness, according to his general providential design and his specific providential judgments. In their somber dress, austere meetinghouses, and strict code of biblical conduct, the Puritans molded their daily life style on their theology. Jonathan Edwards in the 1730's and 1740's is the last of the religious culture heroes, fighting with all his genius of intellect and fervor of spirit to recapture the glory of God in an Enlightened Age when man exalted his own reason. Parrington called Edwards an anachronism and Perry Miller called Parrington misguided for not perceiving that Edwards reasoned with the concepts of the eighteenth century. But Edwards *was* anachronistic in trying to preserve the religious life style that had become outmoded.

The folklore of the colonial period echoes the life style. It is first and foremost a religious folklore, strewn with remarkable providences, devilment, and witchcraft. One of the most hair-raising books in American folklore is Increase Mather's *An Essay for the Recording of Illustrious Providences* (1684), contrived by the New England clergy to preserve, and thence to study, God's marvelous actions in the New World through which He communicated His satisfaction or His wrath to His saints. So Increase and his fellow divines gathered in the unfathomable accounts of remarkable escapes from storms at sea and from savages on land; of preternatural phenomena, such as demon-possessed houses and bloody apparitions; of blasphemers struck down by lightning, thunder, tempests, and earthquakes. In effect, they collected local legends. The wars of the Lord, whether against the Indians of the forests or Satan's witches within the gates, bred legends of red sorcerers and goodwives versed in the black arts. Balanced against these hellfiends are the popular heroes and heroines delivered by God's grace from Indian captivities and yawning whirlpools. Cotton Mather enlarged his father's work into one of the six books of the *Magnalia*, where it has remained a quarry for legend revivers to the present day.

The Religious Man was succeeded along about the 1760's by the Political Man, when agitation of the colonists against the Coercive Acts of King and Parliament mounted to the point of revolution. Now the foe is the State, based on an irrational theory of divine right monarchy that permits a tyrant to injure and destroy his subjects. The patriots espouse the philosophy of natural rights, with its corollaries of government based on a social compact among sovereign individuals, each inalienably entitled to life, liberty, and the pursuit of happiness. Democracy replaces salvation as the good to be achieved. It promises secular salvation. With democracy comes political freedom to reinforce the religious freedom already won.

The culture heroes are political men, even Presidents: Jefferson, architect of the Declaration of Independence; Jackson, promoter of the common man; Lincoln, savior of the republic. Dress, speech, behavior, attitude reflect the life style of practical democracy. The patrician Jefferson, friend of the people, but still a Virginia aristocrat with his shiny pumps, velvet breeches, white waistcoat, and powdered wig, gives way to the commoner Jackson, himself a wealthy Louisiana slave owner but ushering in the reign of King Mob, it was feared, and attracting to himself much popular symbolism—Old Hickory they called him. At the end of this line came the true man of the people, Honest Abe, log-cabin born in Kentucky, ungainly and ugly like the butt of frontier tales, full of salty sayings and apt stories, the most legendary of our Presidents. With the emergence of the republic comes a new concept of education, encouraged by Jefferson, free public schools to educate a citizenry for the tasks of democratic responsibilty.

In this second period, his life and legends spanning it neatly from the close of the Revolution to the signals of Civil War, arises David Crockett, frontiersman, congressman, folk hero in a new style that shocked and excited the nation. The historical Crockett is not much of a figure, a Jacksonian turncoat exploited by the Whigs, but he is above all a political personality, electioneering from the stump in democratic fashion, arguing the issues of the national bank and paper currency with frontier saws, lending his name and personality to political writings. Crockett, like Lincoln, is the backwoods humorist, and his tall tales catch the spirit and soaring rhetoric of Manifest Destiny. Other legendary heroes who emerge in these buoyant years of early American nationalism share Crockett's homespun manners, rough-hewn speech, and daredevil outlook: Mike Fink, Mose, Sam Patch, Yankee Jonathan, and in the subliterature of the frontier, Simon Suggs, Sut Lovingood, and Jim Doggett—all shaggy heroes of a democratic folk, mocking the genteel dandies of the drawing room.

A new mood and a changed set of historical conditions usher in the period of Economic Man in the hundred years from the close of the Civil War to our own time. The latter decades of the nineteenth century witnessed the spectacular growth of American industry, and the shift of wealth and power from farm to factory, from country to city. Now the ordinary American faces a new foe, the Corporation that throttles the small businessman, gouges the consumer, and buys the legislature. The right to vote counts for little in the jungle of competitive warfare, and reformers like Henry George sought formulas to distribute more equably the goods of the land. Well-being, or material success, is the target and the dream of American youths and oldsters. Happiness lies not in a state of grace, nor in free suffrage, but in property and income. Freedom to vote is meaningless if one is chained by poverty and want. Yet wealth itself was never questioned, nor productivity, but only distribution. Wealth was the great desideratum. The philosophy of social Darwinism buttresses the status of the millionaires, who represent the bloom of civilization. Fair competition, the survival of the fittest, and the laissez-faire role of government, whose only obligation is to protect property, are the rules for economic man laid down by the Creator of an evolutionary world.

The underlying myth of this era is the rags-to-riches ladder scalable by every assiduous, thrifty, hard-working, patriotic American boy. Horatio Alger's badly written and immensely popular novels related the rise of Ragged Dick the Bootblack to chairmanship of the board. In the realm of fact Andrew Carnegie exemplifies the dream, as the poor immigrant lad from Scotland who became the king of the United States steelmakers. Carnegie particularly qualifies as a culture hero because he set forth the doctrines of social Darwinism in a context of Presbyterian Calvinism; the wealthy industrialist deserved his means, but he had a responsibility to his fellow man, as a steward of God's wealth, to supervise its disbursal during his lifetime to ensure maximum benefits to society.

Conspicuous consumption and keeping up with the Joneses now characterize the life style, as Thorstein Veblen mordantly explained in *The Theory of the Leisure Class.* Democratic simplicity of manners yields to honorific display of acquisitions and useless learning. In the 1880's and 1890's the graduate school enters the educational scene, and begins to change the college into the modern university with its emphases on doctoral degrees, specialized research, and scholarly productivity. The university comes to mirror the corporation, as a departmentalized organization of productive experts.

Ambivalence toward the corporation characterizes this third life style. Populists, progressives, and Socialists challenge the social Darwinists, but to regulate not destroy the giant trusts. Jack London vacillated between individualism and socialism, Nietzsche, and Marx; he himself is the virile, handsome culture hero who loves, hates, defeats, and is defeated by competitive capitalism. Were the Robber Barons despoilers or empire-builders? Allan Nevins changed his mind and in his later years wrote eulogistic biographies of John D. Rockefeller and Henry Ford.

The folklore of the period too is ambivalent. It is a pseudofolklore, offering in the 1920's and 1930's a series of contrived jolly giants, at first taken seriously. In an age of gigantic productivity, why should not these demigods illustrating American size and might be manufactured for a ready market? The Red River Lumber Company adopted Paul Bunyan as a trademark, and United States Steel accepted Joe Magarac as their representative supersteelworker. Folklore was packaged and peddled like bright plastics, and Paul Bunyan became a household name. When cavils were raised that these heroes lacked proper folk credentials, heated rejoinders came forth: why impugn a national symbol? The illustrator for the *Life Treasury of American Folklore,* James Lewicki, observed, "If the American people think Paul Bunyan is their folk hero, then he is." The *Daily Worker* as well as the Red River Lumber Company extolled Old Paul, who does indeed reflect the dilemma of the period.

We appear to be struggling today toward a new life style. While it is too early to be sure of the terms, I think this present era of revolt may introduce the age of the Humane Man. The incubus he seeks to discard is not so clearly defined as Church, or State, or Corporation, although it is clearly enough the Establishment, and capitalized words for the Establishment are beginning to appear: the System, the Structure. To blacks in Watts "The Structure, the omnipresent, accursed, obstinate, filthy rich, miserly, racist Structure is the common enemy." [46] A law school senior speaking at the Harvard Commencement on June 12 [1969] said, "Almost every one of us receiving a degree today has faced the inflexibility and insensibility of our system. To those who would argue that the system has been responsive, there is a one-word answer: Vietnam." [47] The under-thirties, with sympathy from some over-thirties, feel a mortal threat to their freedom of spirit, heart, and mind from the acquisitive values and military-industrial bureaucracy of the System. To them the multiversity is a mirror of and training ground for the Structure, and they demand a Free University, free from authoritarian grades, curricular requirements, impersonal lectures, parietal restrictions. Their highly visible life style of beards, beads, flowers, kooky get-ups, pot, LSD, and street-living rejects the norms of wealth, health, status, and daily routine in the Structure.

The clash of life styles was dramatized in the recent episode of May 16 [1969] of the so-called "People's Park" near the Berkeley campus. University authorities attempting to deal with the hippies and street-people quartered on the university's vacant lot "repeatedly expressed irritation with the failure of the Park people to 'organize' a 'responsible committee' or to select 'representatives' who might 'negotiate.' " The authors of this report in the *New York Review* on "The Battle of Berkeley," Sheldon Wolin and John Schaar, continue:

> The life-styles and values of the Park people were forever escaping the categories and procedures of those who administer the academic plant . . . the organized system must strive to extend its control and reduce the space in which spontaneous and unpredictable actions are possible. The subjects, on the other hand, come to identify spontaneity and unpredictability with all that is human and alive.[48]

---

[46] William Buckley, Jr., "Coming Up From Watts," *Herald-Telephone,* (Bloomington, Ind.), June 12, 1969, p. 10, col. 5.

[47] *Courier-Journal* (Louisville, Ky.), June 13, 1969, p. A24, col. 3, quoting Meldon E. Levine. Levine's address, "A Conflict of Conscience: Our Practice of Your Principles," is given in the *Harvard Alumni Bulletin,* vol. 71, no. 14 (July 7, 1969), pp. 47–48.

[48] Sheldon Wolin and John Schaar, *New York Review of Books,* vol. XII, no. 12 (June 19, 1969), pp. 29–30.

Defenders of the System, and older liberals sympathetic to the dissenters, express puzzlement at their objectives, while conceding that there may be something missing in the quality of American life. One void in the United States, as compared with her sister Latin American republics, that has struck me, and other folklorists such as Américo Paredes, is the fiesta, with all its gaiety, color, exhilaration, movement, and sense of community. A remarkable statement from the editor of the Harvard *Crimson*, Nicholas Gagarin '70, who took part in the assault of Harvard's administration building on April 9 [1969], expresses this fiesta spirit:

> There were two kinds of emotions in University Hall. The first were dreamlike and euphoric. They came from the weird realization that now at the University, Mr. Big, Harvard U., we finally had a building. They came from the carnival, open, free-wheeling life-style inside. . . . What was most euphoric, however, was us and what we were to each other. For those few hours we *were* brothers and sisters. We did reach out and hold onto each other. . . . The second emotion, of course, was fear.

Gagarin goes on to describe the miscellaneous nature of the group in University Hall, one of whom was a drunk in a tuxedo, some commuters, some club boys, some who did not even know what the six demands were. He reaches this conclusion:

> What is really at stake—and what I think that small apolitical group of us was sitting in at University Hall for—is not a political revolution, but a human one. And if we could bring that about, if we could bring ourselves into the beautiful human togetherness that existed inside the Hall, if we could end the inhumanity, competitiveness, and alienation that the University teaches us so that we may fit neatly into an inhuman, competitive, alienated society—then such things as the war, ROTC, and slumlandlording would be inconceivable.

And he anticipates a new, open university, with courses being whatever the "students and faculty present at any given time wanted to talk about, sing about, or dance about." [49]

How does folklore reflect this emerging life style? In a discussion of the free university movement, *Time* magazine mentions a New College course at Harvard on Claude Lévi-Strauss taught by a senior majoring in folklore and mythology. A teaching fellow in history called the sessions "the best intellectual discussions I've ever participated in." [50] Lévi-Strauss, however, hardly represents the correlation. On the level of national culture heroes, Jack and Bobby Kennedy contributed youth, buoyancy, and a sense of mission to the style of the free humane man. Malcolm X and Eldridge Cleaver

---

[49] Nicholas Gagarin, *Harvard Alumni Bulletin*, vol. 71, no. 11 (April 28, 1969), p. 39.
[50] *Time*, vol. 93, no. 23 (June 6, 1969), p. 56.

from another direction have shown the power of the eloquent, passionate man of words. The Beatles and Bob Dylan from still another angle have redirected styles of song, dress, and entertainment. In common these culture heroes open doors to free expression closed by the Structure. The hero challenges the Establishment; he is an antihero hero.

This point was brought forcibly home to me with an exciting series of folklore collections turned in to me by alert students on the Berkeley campus in the spring of 1968. A number of these students simply crossed Sproul Plaza to interview the street-people on Telegraph Avenue. One entire collection and parts of others were devoted to the antihero of the LSD pill-peddlers, Augustus Stanley Owsley III, and his outwitting the "narks" (narcotic agents) and "fuzz" (police). Another collector accumulated stories of Vietnam draft-dodging antiheroes who employed ingenious schemes to deceive the military. Still other collections presented the rituals, anecdotes, argot, and symbolism of Hell's Angels, homosexuals, pot parties, Synanon (the organization of ex-drug addicts), and similar groups developing a life style opposed to that of the System. The initiation rite for Hell's Angels, for instance, called for the neophyte to soak a fresh T-shirt and pair of jeans in human urine and feces, and wear them until they rotted. Meanwhile in the San Francisco *Chronicle* a series of news stories featured antiheroes attracting attention: a hippy who walked nude for fourteen blocks downtown before being taken into custody; police officer Sergeant Sunshine smoking a marijuana cigarette on the courthouse steps a moment prior to his arrest; a society of homosexuals parading before city hall with placards "Hire a Homosexual"; a wild-looking young man who knocked down several electric generating towers with a bulldozer—literally attacking the power structure. This is the lunatic fringe gradually moving toward the center. As in earlier periods, the culture heroes and the folk legends mirror the dominant forces of society. When we rewrite Skinner, we should take into account these temporal as well as his spatial divisions.

Note: Many more references could be added from contemporary writings in support of the Humane life style theory, but I would like only to cite Arthur M. Schlesinger, Jr., *The Crisis of Confidence* (Boston, 1969). His section on "Joe College, R.I.P." (pp. 194–237) contains a number of statements from college students attacking the System and the Structure and the acquisitive life style, and eulogizing the new style SDS and young people's heroes (Bob Dylan, the Beatles).

Mexican Legendry and the Rise of the Mestizo: A Survey

AMÉRICO PAREDES, University of Texas at Austin

Folklorists have many ways of defining "legend," and Latin Americans are no exception. They may speak of *caso, relato,* and *tradición,* as well as of *leyenda*. For the purposes of this paper, however, I accept "legend" as defined by Bronislaw Malinowski in "Myth in Primitive Psychology" and more lately by William Bascom in "The Forms of Folklore: Prose Narratives." [1] That is, I refer to narratives with historical or pseudohistorical basis, told as supposedly true events. I am quite aware that this classification has been under attack recently by structuralists and students of folklore as process, while scholars of the historic-geographic school long ago expressed their doubts about it. Structuralists object that the term "legend" tells us nothing about the internal structure of the texts; those interested in folklore as process say it tells us nothing about folk narrative as an aspect of human behavior. But these are objections that are neither proved nor disproved. No one to my knowledge has conducted any really thorough study to show whether or not the term "legend" identifies a particular kind of folk narrative from the viewpoint of structure or narrative performance. And there is at least some evidence it may.

Most Mexican legendary narratives about buried treasure, for example, follow a definite pattern that suggests an identifiable structure. The much-maligned Malinowski long ago pointed out

---

[1] Bronislaw Malinowski, *"Magic, Science and Religion" and Other Essays* (Garden City, N.Y.: Doubleday, 1954), pp. 102–117; William Bascom, "The Forms of Folklore: Prose Narratives," *JAF*, 78 (1965), 3–20.

that legends in the Trobriand Islands were performed under conditions different from those in which fictional tales were told. As a
participant in folk narrative sessions who much later became an
observer, I myself have noted much the same thing in Border
Mexican legendry. There was a marked difference between the way
wonder tales and legends were told: in the composition of the
groups participating, in the events immediately preceding and following narration, in the style and pattern of the narratives, in the
emotional tone surrounding the whole performance. The objection
made by scholars of the Finnish school is that the "same" story—
that is to say, the same "type" or "plot"—may be told as myth or
legend in one place and as wonder tale in another. But to my mind,
legendry is not to be distinguished primarily by plot content but
by the conditions of telling and the attitudes of the narrator and
his audience.

For my purposes, then, legends are ego-supporting devices. They
may appeal to the group or to individuals by affording them pride,
dignity, and self-esteem: local or national heroes to identify with,
for example, or place-name legends giving an aura of importance
to some familiar and undistinguished feature of the local landscape. Whether in doing so they validate or challenge the social
structure, ease tensions or exacerbate them, is beside the point. One
may feed his ego just as well with frustration and defeat as with
victory and conformity. Legends, however, are important in providing symbols that embody the social aspirations of the group,
whether these be embodied in an ideal status quo or in dreams of
revolution. For this reason, I would say, we are justified in isolat-
ing legends as a category.

I would base this survey, then, on the premise that the general
category "legend" may be distinguished in the history of Mexican
folklore, that it serves to express or project certain sets of Mexican
attitudes, and that the preference for certain kinds of legendry at
certain periods in Mexican history reflects changes in the historical
process resulting in the emergence of modern Mexico. To say
modern Mexico is to say the mestizo—the distinctive blend of Spaniard and Indian, with contributions by the Negro and other ethnic
groups, that has produced the Mexican national type. It is my
thesis that the rise of the mestizo as representative of the Mexican
nationality may be illuminated by the study of Mexican legendry.

Mexican legendry, as I would define it, begins with the arrival
in Mexico of Hernán Cortés. Indians and Spaniards had their own

traditions, of course, but it is the contact between the two that interests us. This contact is reported mostly from the Spanish side. We know little of the way Indian traditions were affected by the Spanish during the conquest or even in colonial times. The early accounts of Indian myths, legends, and miracles either are reported by Spaniards, as in the case of Father José de Acosta's *Historia natural y moral de las Indias,*[2] or by Hispanicized Indians like Fernando de Alva Ixtlilxóchitl.[3] Written in Spanish for Spaniards, they give us a European point of view, but modified by the New World experience and by contact with Indian cultures. That is to say, they give us a mestizo point of view, if we are willing to accept "mestizo" in a cultural rather than a racial sense. And for Alva Ixtlilxóchitl even the racial definition applies, since he was born of a Spanish father and an Indian mother.

In recent times folklorists and anthropologists have collected many legends from the Indian villages, where Indian culture—already profoundly affected by sixteenth-century Spanish influences—took refuge and held on down to the present. These legends—in which werewolves, witches, ghosts, and other supernaturals abound—are extremely worthy of study in their own right. From our point of view, however, their most important aspect is their illustration of the conservative attitude of the Indian villages, their ability to transmute borrowings from sixteenth-century Spain into something very much their own. Thus, in the religious conflicts after the Revolution of 1910, one usually finds the mestizo fighting on the anticlerical side and the Indian fiercely defending the religion of the Spanish conquistadors. Had the Indian villages been the dominant force in Mexico, Mexican history might have been much like that of China up to the time of the Boxer rebellion. But the future belonged to the Indianized creole, the Hispanicized Indian, the Negro slave, and their issue—the mestizo. And it is in those legends identified with the mestizo that we can trace the development of Mexican nationality.

From the conquest to the beginning of the nineteenth century, the most prominent themes in this type of Mexican legendry were those dealing with marvels and miracles. Exploration and conquest of new, hitherto undreamed-of lands excited the sense of the marvelous, this being true not only of Spanish and Portuguese Amer-

---

2 José de Acosta, *Historia natural y moral de las Indias* (Seville, 1590).
3 Fernando de Alva Ixtlilxóchitl, *Obras históricas,* ed. Alfredo Chavero, 2 vols. (Mexico: Editora Nacional, 1952).

ica but of North America as well.[4] But the legends about Amazons, mermaids, and griffins, which were brought back by explorers, had as their ultimate source Old World literature, religion, and folklore, projected on an environment so new that anything might happen there. We must look upon them as purely European, for they reflect no interaction of Spaniard and Indian, being merely the effect of the American environment on the imagination of Europeans.

The earliest legends one could consider as Mexican are the accounts of supposed events in Indian history, either before or after the arrival of the Spaniards, retold by Spanish writers or by Hispanicized Indians. One of these first truly Mexican legends is Bernal Díaz del Castillo's account of Doña Marina's meeting with the relatives who had sold her into slavery. The story, as Díaz himself recognizes, is a retelling of the tale of Joseph and his brothers, transferred to an American setting and imbedded into the context of Indian history.[5] This may have been the earliest attempt by a Spaniard to interpret the Indian's experience in terms of his own. The Indianized Christian myths to be collected by ethnologists in the late nineteenth and the twentieth century would be the other side of the coin.

With Father José de Acosta we go one step farther. In the Mexican part of his natural and moral history, he recounts the portents and omens that preceded Moctezuma's fall in terms reminiscent of the mythical accounts about early rulers of Greece and Rome. Fernando de Alva, on the other hand, attempts to reconcile the resentment of the conquest and the loss of his mother's civilization with acceptance of the Christian religion brought by men like his father. His accounts of preconquest Aztec history also have echoes of Old World classical literature. Writings such as those of Díaz, Acosta, and Alva may be said to mark the beginning of the literary kind of legends that would come into full flower after Mexican independence. But they also are interesting as examples of the first attempts to come to terms with the Indian-Spanish synthesis that would dominate Mexican national life.

It is interesting that the Spaniards who conquered Mexico had

---

4 See for example Richard M. Dorson, *American Folklore* (Chicago: University of Chicago Press, 1959), and Agustín Zapata Gollán, *Mito y superstición en la conquista de América* (Buenos Aires: Editorial Universitaria de Buenos Aires, 1963).

5 Bernal Díaz del Castillo, *Historia verdadera de la conquista de la Nueva España* (Madrid: Espasa-Calpe, 1928), I, 114–116.

as their narrative folk song the *romance,* a free and highly flexible form. Likewise, the mestizos who fought their own war of conquest (or reconquest) in the Mexican Revolution of 1910 sang the *corrido,* a form descended from the romance and also a vigorous and adaptable form. But the intervening generations seem to have preferred for their folk song forms the highly structured, rigid *décima,* borrowed from literary and aristocratic circles, or the neat packaging of a single thought afforded by the four-line *copla.* As the ebullience of the conquest passed and the colonial mold settled and hardened, there were changes in Mexican legendry, too. The sense of the marvelous was considerably diminished by the narrowing of colonial horizons. Legends of wonders persisted, and in the later colonial period they were often cast into décima form and printed by the broadside press. But these were very much like the wonders bruited about in medieval Europe: accounts of places where it rained blood, of disobedient children eaten up by fiery serpents, of animals born with human faces—all exhibiting a strong didactic character.

More typical of the colonial period, and important because of their political and social effects, were the legends about miracles. Chief of these is the account of the appearance of the Virgin of Guadalupe at Tepeyac in 1531. Miracle legends had important functions from the viewpoint of the rulers of the land: Christianizing the Indians and redirecting some of their frustrations as a conquered people. But the Virgin of Guadalupe had another effect—unexpected by the crown—that of welding the many elements that formed the population of Mexico into something like a common consciousness. She was the one symbol to which creole, mestizo, Negro, and Indian eventually would relate. During the period between the achievement of independence and the attainment of a true feeling of national identity, "the mother of the Mexicans" was the most important factor holding the Mexican people together. In modern Mexico the Virgin of Guadalupe is not the all-embracing symbol she once was, but historically her legend has been so decisive as to raise the question—among sociologists and literary historians at least—whether her story should not be classified as myth rather than legend. She has influenced the behavior of generations of Mexicans, from the Indians and mestizos who followed Hidalgo into battle to the cry of "Long live the Virgin of Guadalupe and death to the Spaniards!" down to the contemporary lover who, despite his fascination with blonde movie queens from Hollywood, still can sing:

Yo a las morenas quiero	I love dark-skinned women
desde que supe	Ever since I've known
que morena es la Virgen	That dark is the skin
de Guadalupe.	Of the Virgin of Guadalupe.

Legends of miracles have been devoutly believed in Mexico, but since the rise of liberalism and anticlericalism, the clergy has been accused of deliberately concocting such stories. Accounts of the miracle of the Lord of Chalma, coming so close on that of the Guadalupe, do sound like efforts by the Augustinians to do at least as well as the Franciscans had done with the Virgin of Guadalupe. But one must take into account the spontaneous generation of saints' legends, given the right conditions. Under the pressure of battle and threat of defeat, Santiago (Saint James) more than once appeared to Spanish conquistadors in Mexico and what is now the southwestern United States. Under different kinds of pressures, the Virgin has appeared to Mexican-American believers in south Texas as recently as ten years ago. In south Texas too, a *curandero* or folk healer, Don Pedrito Jaramillo, is considered a saint by many people, who pray to him and tell stories about his miracles, though he is not recognized by the church. Curanderos such as Don Pedrito give rise to another kind of legend, in which the healer effects miraculous cures that confound medical science. In general pattern these narratives resemble medieval legends about saints who performed miracles and confounded unbelievers. In function they are attempts to maintain a status quo in the face of culture change.

With independence there was great attention given in Mexico to the romantic legend of literary origin. Mexicans, on the verge of becoming a nation, looked back with some nostalgia toward a colonial past already tinged with romance. The closest North American analogue to the "legends and traditions" writings in Mexico is in the folk-inspired sketches of Washington Irving. Like Irving, Mexican spinners of literary legends tended to borrow from their readings in European literature and folklore.[6] Their works are strongly Gothic, reflecting European literary tastes of the time. These are stories about old churches, half-ruined houses and historic bridges, headstrong young blades and kindly priests, and corpses risen from the grave to punish overweening pride, as well as stories about thwarted young lovers who find a way out. Most of

---

[6] José Joaquín Fernández de Lizardi (1776–1827) was probably the first Mexican writer to make use of his country's folklore. An early book of legends was Pablo J. Villaseñor's *Leyendas históricas y tradicionales* (Guadalajara, 1853).

this material was disseminated only by means of print. But some literary legends, because they were rooted in Mexican tradition, were taken back by the people and have remained vigorously alive up to the present time.

Of these none has been more widespread than that of the Weeping Woman (La Llorona). Even a cursory discussion of La Llorona would take up more time and space than I have at my disposal. Suffice it to say that it is basically a European narrative, as Bacil F. Kirtley has pointed out, emphasizing a Europeanized milieu and European values.[7] The story may be based on medieval legends, as Kirtley argues. It also owes something to a love-them-and-leave-them theme common in Old World literature from classical to modern times, from Euripides' *Medea* to Puccini's *Madama Butterfly*. But the literary legend of La Llorona struck deep roots in Mexican tradition because it was grafted on an Indian legend cycle about the supernatural woman who seduces men when they are out alone on the roads or working in the fields. At times she destroys her lovers after giving herself to them, but often she is helpful as well as passionate and may make a man's fortune or help him raise a fine crop of corn. She is *matlacihua* or Woman of the Nets among Náhuatl speakers,[8] and other language groups such as the Mixes and the Popolucas know her by other names.[9] As *la segua*, she has been reported as far north as Texas,[10] and she also is known as far south as Panamá.[11] How adaptable the legend of La Llorona can be is shown by Bess Lomax Hawes in her sensitive study of the Weeping Woman among a group of young girls in a correctional institution.[12] So La Llorona appears in many shapes, now Malinche, now Medea, now matlacihua, now Madame Butterfly, she still haunts the night—no better example of the Spanish-Indian synthesis in vigorous life today.

While romanticists were rewriting the legends of Mexico's colo-

---

[7] Bacil F. Kirtley, "'La Llorona' and Related Themes," *WF*, 19 (1960), 155–168.

[8] See Manuel Pérez Serrano, "El duende y la matlacihua," *Anuario de la Sociedad Folklórica de México*, 5 (1945), 35–40.

[9] Walter S. Miller, *Cuentos mixes* (Mexico: Instituto Nacional Indigenista, vol. 2, 1965), tales nos. 14 and 15 and pp. 234–240; George M. Foster, "Sierra Popoluca Folklore and Beliefs," *University of California Publications in American Archaeology and Ethnology*, vol. 42 (1945), tale no. 11 and pp. 180–181.

[10] Miriam W. Hiester, "Tales of the Paisanos," *Texas Folklore Publications*, 30 (1961), 229.

[11] Robert L. Plasker, "Folk Beliefs and Rituals Connected with the Sacrament of Baptism," unpublished manuscript.

[12] Bess Lomax Hawes, "La Llorona in Juvenile Hall," *WF*, 27 (1968), 153–170.

nial past, another kind of legendary hero was being created by the
people out of the protagonists in the struggles for independence,
the civil wars, and foreign invasions—local figures who expressed
national aspirations in one form or another. And as the feeling of
national identity intensifies, the Mexican legend seems to move
away from belief in the miraculous toward realism and historical
events. This realistic and historical emphasis—often noted of the
Spanish *romancero*—appears not only in the Mexican counterpart
of the romance, the corrido, but in the legend as well. The legend,
in fact, often becomes associated with the corrido. One may profitably compare a hero like Agustín Lorenzo, whose exploits date
from the 1860's and about whom no corridos are known, with
corrido heroes of the 1880's and later. Musket balls cannot enter
Lorenzo's body, and his horse can fly through the air. When
trapped by federal troops, he disappears in a burst of flame. It is
interesting that Agustín Lorenzo's legends are related to ritual
festivities that are part of the carnival at Huejotzingo, Puebla.[13]
Heraclio Bernal, conversely, is one of the early heroes of the corrido tradition that reaches its height in the Revolution of 1910.
An outlaw early in the Porfirio Díaz regime, Bernal fights for social
justice and against Spaniards, North Americans, and other foreign
exploiters of the Mexican poor. A stanza common to many variants
of his corrido tells us how formidable he was.

Dicen que cargaba el diablo	They say he carried the devil
en una caja de bronce;	Shut up in a box made of bronze;
pero el diablo lo cargaba	But the devil that he carried
en su carabina de once.	Was in his eleven-bore rifle.

Obviously, people were telling stories about Heraclio Bernal that
were much like those told about Agustín Lorenzo; Bernal could
call on the devil to help him out of tight spots in his battles
against the rural police. But the corrido maker simply does not
buy that; he is too realistic in his point of view. Bernal had no
devils to help him, says the corridista; his only allies were his
courage and manhood, and his trusty rifle. Thus we have traveled
a considerable distance on the road from miracles to *machismo*,
the much-discussed Mexican "cult" of maleness. As Mexican nationalism begins to develop in the years before the revolution, the
more dynamic mestizos are turning to their own resources to solve
their problems, rather than hoping they will be solved by miracu-

---

13 Frances Toor, *A Treasury of Mexican Folkways* (New York: Crown Publishers, 1947), pp. 194–196, 509–512; Luis Leal, "The Legend of Agustín
Lorenzo," *WF*, 24 (1965), 177–183.

lous means. It is strange that so many North Americans still persist in defining Mexican machismo in terms of miscegenation and oedipal conflicts, coming as they do from a country where rationalism and self-reliance have been a sort of fetish—at least until very recently.

Certainly most of the legends accompanying the corridos of the revolution and of border conflict are of this realistic type. Their heroes accomplish extraordinary feats and kill hordes of their enemies, but all this is done by exaggeration of ordinary, everyday events rather than by appeals to the supernatural. There are some exceptions, such as the miraculous legends reported about Zapata and Villa. I cannot be a judge of their authenticity, but all such examples I know of I have found in printed sources. The Villa legends I have heard from oral sources are all realistic: Villa captures American airplanes by disguising his soldiers as Americans and setting up a fake airstrip; Villa enters General Pershing's camp in disguise; Villa confounds his enemies by making tremendous forced marches and falling on them unawares.

Perhaps realistic legends about corrido heroes are not easily told to outsiders because they involve partisan feelings and hostility toward strangers, especially North Americans. Social protest, nationalism, and resentment of foreign powers play a large part in them, especially resentment toward the United States. Legends about conflict with the United States were not very common in central Mexico before the turn of the century, though they were well known in the northern provinces and among Mexican-Americans since the 1850's. By the end of the nineteenth century, as North American capital entered Mexico while *braceros* came in greater numbers into the United States, there was a change that can be noticed in popular reaction to news and rumor. In 1905 repairs to the cathedral in Mexico City gave rise to reports that the cathedral had been bought by United States interests, who were going to turn it into a factory or a Protestant church. Among the premature manifestations of the revolution were the riots in Mexico City, Guadalajara, and other major cities on November 9, 1910, following news reports that a Mexican had been lynched in Texas. The outbreak of the revolution and intervention by the United States intensified Mexican feelings.

From such situations we have legendary narratives such as "The Burning of Antonio Rodríguez," in which a young Mexican is lynched because of the false accusations of a North American woman who falls in love with him—a New World version of the story of Potiphar's wife. In a version collected in the 1960's the narrator compares the lynching of young Rodríguez to the atomic bombing of Hiroshima. In narratives such as "The Two Virginias," the American woman is declared to be immoral, and her immorality is explained as a historical trait. Mexican legendary heroes are betrayed by American guile, so that the narrator of a legendary version of the betrayal and death of the Cerda brothers ends by saying, "I am scared of an American with a pencil more than if he had a .30/30 or an automatic. Because I can shoot back at the man with the gun. But as for the man with the pencil, watch out for him."

I have attempted a survey of the history of legendry in Mexico, in the words of the message that brought us here, an attempt "to chart directions in which systematic legend study might be profitably carried on." Even where data were at hand, time and space limitations and the broad scope of this survey made it necessary for me to state generalizations without elaborating on them. My hope is that these hypotheses may point in directions that further research will find fruitful. But to fill the interstices in the framework I have outlined, much work needs to be done in specific matters concerning Mexican legendry—both in the library and in the field. This is true even of legends such as La Llorona, about which so much has been written. Most studies on La Llorona, however, make sweeping historical generalizations for all Mexico on the basis of one or two variants. In spite of all that has been written about this legend, we know relatively little about its history and distribution, much less about the conditions under which it is told. In other words, if an index of legends is desirable for the United States, the same may be said of Mexico.

Systematic legend studies, it is my belief, may tell us much about the mestizo. Too often the mestizo has been simplistically explained in Freudian terms, or in the language of North American race consciousness, that cannot suppress a thrill of horror at the idea of miscegenation and thus sees all kinds of morbid behavior (such as machismo) as a consequence.

Mestizaje in Mexico has been fundamentally a social phenomenon, though we should not be surprised that a class of many ethnic origins and no racial snobbery should become thoroughly mixed. There are in Mexico, however, many "village Indians" with mixed European ancestry, while many "mestizos" are village Indians recently escaped into town. From the very beginning, the mestizo included disinherited creoles and unsuccessful Spanish immigrants among his numbers, not to mention the petty merchant, the small rancher, and the village priest. If the mestizo was the disinherited and classless element, he also was the restless, dissatisfied, and dynamic element in a stratified, static social structure. To be in such a predicament is to suffer from incredible tensions.

In the end, it was the mestizo who needed the Virgin of Guadalupe the most. The Spaniard had his European religion; the Negro, his African gods. To the Indian, Guadalupe could also be Tonantzín; Santo Tomás could be confused with Quetzalcóatl; Christ could merge into Tezcatlipoca. But the mestizo needed a powerful symbol like the Guadalupe as an anchor for his identity in a world that offered him no place he could call his own. And it was the mestizo rather than the quietistic village Indian who formed the core of the rabble that followed Hidalgo to defeat. After independence, his history was one continuous struggle for self-determination until today, in a less believing age, he has found his identity in the nation rather than in his saints. His legends, I submit, have mirrored this change.

Hispanic Legend Material: Contrasts Between European and American Attitudes

STANLEY L. ROBE, University of California, Los Angeles

The Spanish-speaking countries constitute one of the major culture areas of the modern world. A significant effort of contemporary scholarship is focused on problems of the language and popular traditions of this extensive segment of the earth's surface, which holds within its confines something over thirty-one million people in the Iberian peninsula and another one hundred fifty million, in conservative figures, principally in America, but with lesser groups elsewhere.

Comparative studies have been concerned with the transmission of folk materials from the mother country, Spain, to her outlying colonies during the period of Hispanic expansion, beginning in the last decade of the fifteenth century and holding on, one might say, through the nineteenth. Dialectologists have prepared careful studies relating American Spanish to various types of regional peninsular speech. Much of the basic work has been done in determining routes of transmission of the folktale between Spain and America. Brighter still is the situation in regard to the riddle, the proverb, and the ballad, fields that have been explored carefully on both sides of the Atlantic. Political and geographical factors, however, have determined to a large degree the direction of research, which has set up a dichotomy of the mother country, on the one hand, and the Hispanic areas of America, on the other. Even within these two geographic polarizations, the traditional attitude of fragmentation of government, cultural jurisdictions, and even scholarship has prevailed, first in Spain and then in the Spanish American countries.

This attitude has affected legend scholarship to a considerable degree. The strongest motivating force behind this activity has been love for the *patria chica,* the regional rather than the extended national homeland that has won the native's devotion, definitely in cultural and social matters and often in questions political as well. Thus the legend in Spain and Spanish America is viewed within narrow physical boundaries. Available data refer to the *patria chica* rather than to the *patria grande,* and the general survey of a reasonably extensive geographical area is definitely the exception rather than the rule. Thus differences rather than unifying features are much more apparent, and a broad, sweeping vision of the legend in Hispanic culture awaits the compilation and collation of material contained in a multitude of publications that have but a regional scope. Later, I shall have occasion to refer both to these unifying features, or similarities, if you wish, and differentiating factors in citing specific kinds of legends as they occur in the Old World and the New.

The absence of a broad perspective has created a variety of problems in legend research. Certainly the principal one is the frequent inaccessibility of published materials or even texts, which often appear in journals, pamphlets, and books of extremely limited distribution and circulation. Scholars in Spain and Spanish America, where funds for research are often severely restricted or unavailable, operate under a handicap far greater than those ordinarily encountered in the United States. But in Spanish America, the limitation of horizons in regard to the legend and the folk narrative may have other consequences and I should like to cite one of these. Much of my own research relates to Mexico and the forms of its popular narratives. In preparing the notes for a collection of texts that I had recorded from informants, I had occasion to refer to a short article published by the late Robert Barlow in which he sought to point out to beginning fieldworkers certain narratives that gave promise of being of authentic indigenous origin, present in Mexico before the arrival of Europeans and with the implication that they were not to be found elsewhere.[1] Of the sixteen then suggested by Barlow, approximately half give evidence of deriving from a native source. The remainder, in varying degree, show affiliation with similar themes present in the legend tradition of Europe or elsewhere. I shall cite examples of these.

A youth sees his betrothed at the edge of the village. He follows

---

[1] Robert Barlow, "Los *kwawxochipixkeh* y otros temas del cuento indígena," *Anuario de la Sociedad Folklórica de México,* VI (1950), 433–438.

her, calling, but she leads him toward a cliff. She turns around and he sees then that she has no face [F511.1.0.1]. He rushes back to the village and finds that his betrothed has never left her house. He has seen a phantom [G264]. This narrative, with numerous variants, occurs in extensive areas of America and has been reported from points as far away as Argentina.

A woman and her lover, who is a sorcerer, remove their heads when they go hunting at night. One time they stay out late and in their haste to return home they inadvertently exchange their heads when they replace them.

The patron saint of the village, while fleeing from his enemies, leaves the impression of his hands or feet in rock. Occasionally in Mexico these prints are attributed to Quetzalcoatl, who figures prominently in the preconquest pantheon [A972.2.1].

A woman gives her husband tacos made of blood. Other peasants become suspicious and tell him to watch his wife. At night he sees her remove her own legs and replace them with those of a turkey. She then flies to a nearby village where she sucks children's blood [G61, G216, G262.1].

One further résumé will suffice. In fulfillment of a vow, a man is provided with adequate food and drink, then buried in a spacious tomb beside his deceased wife. One day a mouse carrying a flower in its mouth enters the tomb. The man takes the flower and with it resuscitates his wife. They leave their respective tombs, return to the earth's surface, and engage in various and sundry adventures. This narrative, which enjoys wide circulation in Mexico, is none other than Aarne-Thompson type 612, *The Three Snake-Leaves*.

Barlow's enthusiasm and his devotion to Mexican indigenous culture have unfortunately played a trick upon him. No clear line of demarcation can yet be drawn between native contributions to Mexican legendry and those that have come from European and African immigrants. The problem is not markedly different in other Spanish American countries. Legend themes that appear in peninsular Spanish tradition can be identified and documented more readily than those that derive from native groups, especially in those areas where the two have been in contact since the first half of the sixteenth century.

Without attempting to tread on the treacherous ground of European versus American origins, I feel that a number of valid observations can be made on the characteristics of the legend in peninsular Spain as compared with Spanish American oral tradition and offer some tentative conclusions. The latter must be based in large part upon published collections from these areas. Scholarship, particularly in Spain, has largely been historically oriented, and straightforward texts, except in a few areas, are rare. The tendency has been to fall back upon literary works that have utilized legend material and to cull pertinent information wherever possible from reliable historical documents. I have been able to supplement these with texts gathered personally in Mexico and other Spanish American countries and during a briefer period of fieldwork in Spain.[2]

Certain points of similarity are immediately apparent in the religious legends of Spain and Spanish America, in those involving religious shrines, the appearance of the various manifestations of the Virgin Mary, and the images of saints. Legends explain the origin of two of the most important shrines of Extremadura, both of which have had repercussions in the popular belief of Spanish America. Tradition reports that the Virgin appeared to a shepherdess near Garrovillas, in the western portion of the province of Cáceres. The girl went home and told her parents, to whom the Virgin also appeared. At her instructions, they lifted a large rock and found beneath it an image of the Virgin of Alta-Gracia, who is still venerated on that spot.[3] Similarly, the Virgin appeared to the cowherd Gil Cordero in one of the more remote sections of the Sierra of Guadalupe around the middle of the thirteenth century. Here was erected the Spanish sanctuary of Our Lady of Guadalupe.[4] These legends, which are typical of those that circulated in Spain in the medieval period, have set the pattern for numerous congeners in America, of which perhaps the most notable deals with the vision of the Indian Juan Diego, to whom the Virgin reportedly appeared in 1531 on the hill of Tepeyac on the northern outskirts of Mexico City.

America also has its quota of images that were found to have grown miraculously in the form of Christ as part of a tree trunk, others that sweat, shed tears, or have muddy shoes from having left their niches to travel across the countryside.[5] Some refuse to be moved from their shrines [6] and a physical defect in the image may

---

2 The Del Amo Foundation generously provided financial support for narrative recording in Extremadura in the spring of 1968.

3 José Perianes Rodríguez, Breve historia y novena en honor de la Santísima Virgen de Alta-Gracia, Patrona de Garrovillas (Cáceres), (Plasencia: Spain: Imprenta Sanguino, Sucesora, 1953), p. 10.

4 Carlos Callejo Serrano, Guadalupe y la hispanidad (Madrid: Blass, S.A., Tipográfica, 1965), p. 6.

5 Elaine K. Miller, "Mexican Folk Narrative from the Los Angeles Area" (Ph.D. diss., University of California, Los Angeles, 1967), no. IX.

6 Ignacio de J. Valdés, Jr., Cuentos panameños de la ciudad y del campo (Panama: Editorial Gráfico, 1928), pp. 33-36.

be explained by a legend that indicates that damage occurred when the image was transported to its destined shrine. Clearly, the missionary labors of the Spanish priests in the sixteenth century were supplemented by an ample supply of legends that were current in Spain in the late medieval period.

The sixteenth century in Spain was a period of intense concern with witchcraft, and the surviving records of the trials and investigations of that time have provided abundant documentation of the nature and extent of belief in witches and the legend material that surrounded them.[8] In this connection, Spanish scholars have preferred to work with documentary sources rather than with texts taken from contemporary oral tradition, although Aurelio M. Espinosa in his *Cuentos populares españoles* includes narratives that give a clear indication of an awareness of witchcraft in the twentieth century.[9] My experience with peninsular informants indicates that they are somewhat more reluctant to discuss witchcraft than are their Spanish American counterparts. In Spanish America it is relatively easy to elicit from an informant a narrative that relates the customary activities of a witch (male or female) in his community, with precise details concerning the salve with which the witches anoint themselves, the holy incantation in reverse "Without God and Saint Mary!," the flight of the witch to a feast with her kindred spirits, the pursuit by her husband who imitates her acts and incantations, and finally the breaking of the spell by the use of salt at the banquet or uttering the name of Christ or the Deity.[10] It is not uncommon for the informant to assert that the seat of witchcraft is in Spain, even in areas where one would expect the predominance of indigenous tradition. Julio Vicuña Cifuentes notes that Chilean witches refer to their meeting place as "Salamanca" or the "Cave of Salamanca," [11] in reference to the reputed academy of Spanish witchcraft and sorcery located there. Generally, Spanish American legends of witchcraft resemble quite closely those

---

7 A specific legend of this type is attributed to the image of the Virgin venerated in the church of Santa Cruz de las Flores, Jalisco, as recorded for me by María del Refugio Leal Moya of San Agustín, Jalisco, Mexico, in July, 1960.

8 Julio Caro Baroja, *The World of the Witches* (London: Weidenfeld and Nicolson, 1964). There are several Spanish versions, the most recent of which is Caro Baroja, *Las brujas y su mundo* (Madrid: Alianza Editorial, 1968). Subsequent references are to this edition.

9 Aurelio M. Espinosa, *Cuentos populares españoles* (2d ed.; Madrid: Consejo Superior de Investigaciones Científicas, 1946–1947), I, 403–404.

10 Sebastián Morales of Jalapa, Veracruz, recorded for me on July 22, 1965, a narrative that includes these incidents. The text will appear in a volume of Mexican tales and legends from Veracruz, presently in preparation.

11 Julio Vicuña Cifuentes, *Mitos y supersticiones* (3d ed.; Santiago: Editorial Nascimento, 1947), p. 15.

from northern Spain, in particular the Basque provinces and Navarra, as reported by Julio Caro Baroja [12] and José María Iribarren, [13] yet these legends exist in many areas alongside a parallel native tradition.

The widespread legends in Spanish America that deal with the mischievous spirits who disrupt a household by keeping its members awake at night, throwing dishes about the kitchen, rearranging the furniture, or causing stones to rain down upon the house have been transmitted through the Iberian peninsula. Informants in Spanish America readily converse about these *duendes*—kobolds would be the nearest equivalent in English—and legend texts can be obtained with little difficulty. Thus the sources for study of the duendes in Spanish America are largely contemporary. In Spain they date from the sixteenth through the nineteenth century and current reports are uncommon,[14] yet the duende is a familiar concept to the Spaniard. The traveling legend assigned number 7020 by Reidar Christiansen [15] has been reported at least three times from Spain,[16] and it is to my knowledge the only such legend among those listed by Christiansen which has appeared with any regularity in Spanish America. I have noted to date seven versions from Mexico [17] and one each from New Mexico,[18] Costa Rica,[19]

---

[12] Caro Baroja, *Las brujas y su mundo,* pp. 202–218.

[13] José María Iribarren, *Retablo de curiosidades* (3d ed.; Pamplona: Editorial Gomez, 1954), pp. 46–57, 166–173.

[14] Pablo Hurtado, *Supersticiones extremeñas* (Cáceres: Tip., Enc. y Lib. de Jiménez, 1902), pp. 105–107, and Eugenio de Olavarría y Huarte, "El Folklore de Madrid," in *Folk-lore español: Biblioteca de las tradiciones populares* (Madrid, 1884), II, 66.

[15] Reidar Christiansen, *The Migratory Legends* (Helsinki: Suomalainen Tiedeakatemia, 1958).

[16] Olavarría y Huarte, "El Folklore de Madrid," II, 66; Hurtado *Supersticiones,* p. 105; and Espinosa, *Cuentos populares de Castilla* (Buenos Aires-Mexico: Espasa-Calpe Argentina, 1946), tale no. 54.

[17] The references to these seven are as follows: Mary Blake, "The Elves of Old Mexico," *JAF,* XXVIII (1914), 237–239; Paul Radin, "El duende Fihurití," in *El folklore de Oaxaca* (New York, 1917), no. 165; Vicente T. Mendoza and Virginia R. R. de Mendoza, "La familia que tuvo que cambiar de casa," in *Folklore de San Pedro Piedra Gorda* (Mexico: Secretaría de Educación Pública, 1952), p. 387; Miller, "Mexican Folk Narrative," nos. LIV and LV (both attributed to Jalisco, Mexico); Stanley L. Robe, *Mexican Tales and Legends from Los Altos* (Berkeley and Los Angeles: University of California Press, 1970), no. 193; and "La familia que mortificaban los duendes," recorded for me in Coatepec, Veracruz, by Consuelo Olmos de Martín. The last narrative will appear in my forthcoming volume of tales and legends from Veracruz.

[18] Espinosa, "New-Mexican Spanish Folk-Lore," *JAF,* XXIII (1910), 400.

[19] Víctor Lizano H., *Leyendas de Costa Rica* (San José: Editorial "Soley y Valverde," 1941), pp. 133–134.

Colombia,[20] and Chile.[21] The legend is related to the oral tradition of Western Europe and has been given careful treatment by Archer Taylor in "The Pertinacious Cobold." [22]

The hope of finding buried treasure seemingly springs eternal in the human breast, and certainly in the Spanish-speaking countries. Among small-town Spanish informants, the mention of treasure is a sure-fire spark to set off a series of legend narrations. A specific instance from my own field experience will serve to illustrate the vigor of the tradition in the village of Garrovillas, in Extremadura. At an informal gathering of twenty or thirty men in the town's plaza, a field laborer mentioned that his brother-in-law had dreamed that a treasure was buried inside a tower constructed in medieval times and located on the banks of the Río Tajo some five or six miles away. Popular legend associates this tower with the Moorish princess Floripes, who figures prominently in the legend cycle of Charlemagne and the Twelve Peers of France. The informant accompanied his brother-in-law and several other men to the tower where, armed with picks and shovels, they began to remove earth. This went on for several days after which time the informant reported that they began to approach the treasure. Through some process of magic, however, the treasure was denied to them and instead was transported to a point beneath a fountain several miles distant from the tower. The villagers were anxious to continue the search at the treasure's new location but were dissuaded from doing so by their wives, who were tired of cooking for them at the site of the treasure and complained that their husbands had abandoned their work and were without income during the days of digging. The narrator kept his audience spellbound not so much because of his ability as a storyteller but because of the content and suspense inherent in the legend itself and the points that were familiar to all. Despite the presence of recording equipment, old shepherds, farm workers, and hangers-on engaged the treasure hunter in a lively discussion concerning this and other treasures.

Dreams enter prominently into locating treasures in Spain, as does the use of a certain type of book or guide that carries instructions, frequently enigmatic, for finding wealth. Informants were

---

[20] Arturo Escobar Uribe, *Mitos de Antioquia* (Bogotá: Editorial Minerva, 1950), pp. 196–200.

[21] Vicuña Cifuentes, *Mitos y Supersticiones*, p. 71.

[22] Archer Taylor, "The Pertinacious Cobold," *Journal of English and Germanic Philology*, XXXI (1932), 1–9.

not able to provide precise information concerning the provenance of such books.

The seven-hundred-year occupation of Spain by the Moors and the reported secreting of wealth by Christians during this period have fortified belief in these stories. In more recent times the invasion of Spain by Napoleonic troops during the early nineteenth century and reports of the hiding of movable property have spurred further the search for treasure. In America, frequently unstable political and economic conditions, plus a reluctance to entrust one's savings to banking institutions, have kept interest high. In these circumstances, the treasure is often pointed out by an unlaid ghost who must wander until a living person pays a debt that the soul has neglected to pay during his life on earth. The Spanish American seeker is often frustrated and unable to possess the treasure when it is nearly within his grasp, as happened to the *extremeño* from Garrovillas, but the cause of his frustration is most likely to be a perverse ghost or the devil who intervenes in animal or other form to distract the treasure seeker. When he can again devote attention to the treasure, it has disappeared.

Within the general boundaries of Hispanic legend tradition there are, nevertheless, certain features that contrast expression on one side of the Atlantic with that on the other. For example, the devil appears frequently in Spanish American narratives in a variety of roles. In didactic legends, still called *ejemplos* "exempla" in many areas, Satan punishes the wayward or disobedient, but in other narratives he still enters into pacts with humans and fulfills his part of the bargain by providing them with wealth or protecting them from adversaries. There are still popular heroes, like José Bailón of Pinoltepeque in lowland Veracruz, who could never be contained in a jail because Satan aided him to escape immediately each time that Bailón's enemies had him imprisoned.[23] Spanish works on the legend infrequently refer to the devil. His absence there may be an oversight of Spanish folklorists but neither did small-town informants in Spain seem eager to speak of him.

Legends concerning ghosts and souls of the dead seem to be more prevalent in America than in Spain, although they are known in the latter area. Spaniards look upon such legends as belonging to the realm of the bizarre and the fantastic, an attitude that perhaps explains a general reluctance to grant them entry into text col-

---

[23] Recorded by Sebastián Morales of Jalapa, Veracruz, August 9, 1965. This legend will be included in my forthcoming volume of narratives from the state of Veracruz.

lections and narrative studies. In wide areas of Spanish America they abound in great variety and in the Los Angeles area even include divergent versions of the legend of the vanishing hitchhiker that was in vogue following World War II.[24]

Some comment must be made concerning the vigor and the nature of the historical legend in the two areas. Among Spanish informants there is a strong awareness of history, a collective memory not necessarily of the present century or the one that preceded it but those of the Renaissance or the medieval period. The time span of history is extremely deep when compared to that of even the richest country of Spanish America in matters of tradition. In both legend and ballad, for example, residents of the city of Cáceres in Extremadura recall the stratagem used by the Christians in retaking the city from the Moors in 1229, when a Spanish knight, taking advantage of the infatuation for him of the Moorish commander's daughter, was able to lead a band of soldiers through an underground passage into the stronghold and decide the day in favor of the Christians. In punishment, the father imprisoned his daughter in the subterranean passage to wait there until the Moors should recapture the city, so the legend runs, but the entrance to the passage became invisible to ordinary mortals and the Moors were never able to recapture Cáceres.[25] Such legends are far from unusual in Spain. The nearest broad parallels in Mexico involve the activities of the last monarchs of the Aztec empire, Moctezuma and Cuauhtémoc, and Malinche, the Indian woman who served as interpreter and mistress to Hernán Cortés. At more than one preconquest archaeological site I have been assured by local natives that the crown of the last Indian monarch rests beneath the soil of one of the mounds. The birthplace of Malinche, like the bones of Columbus, is sought after by various communities, who seek identification with her through legend.

The types of legends that I have cited thus far are common in varying degree to both Spain and America. Some of the thorniest problems of legend research lie in the area of widespread themes that show up in American tradition but seem to be unknown in Europe. In such circumstances one would normally seek parallels in local indigenous tradition. For example, reports of transformations of humans into animal form are fairly frequent in both Spain and Mexico. In Spain the transformation of a woman into a cat or a pig is ordinarily related to legends involving witchcraft, but

---

24 Miller, "Mexican Folk Narrative," nos. XXVIII–XXXI.
25 Hurtado, *Supersticiones extremeñas*, pp. 63–67.

in Mexico an entirely different tradition is involved, that of the
nahual, a set of beliefs, practices, and legends clearly inherited from
preconquest Mexican culture.[26] A similar source seems likely for
legends involving *chaneques,* invisible wood spirits of lowland trop-
ical Mexico who cause travelers to become lost in the woods, who
annoy travelers by whistling, and cause them to hear the blows of
a phantom woodcutter in lowland thickets.

The legend of the *llorona,* the weeping, wailing woman who
frequents creeks and rivers looking for her murdered children is
one of Spanish America's most widely disseminated narratives
and at the same time the one that is the most puzzling. Probably
it is a complex of legends, sometimes involving infanticide by the
mother and the curse that God places upon her, condemning her
to seek her children eternally; other times dealing with a phantom
who first appears as a beautiful woman to lonely male travelers
at night and then frightens or kills them, revealing herself as having the hideous face of a mule or a skull in its place. In America
it appears as far north as the Hispanic Southwest of the United
States and extends through Mexico and Central America into
Colombia and Venezuela, with isolated examples from southern
South America. Ordinarily, such a wide geographic distribution
would argue strongly for a Hispanic source of the legend, on the
assumption that the native groups present in the llorona's modern
habitat display a variety of cultures and traditions and that the
uniformity present in the legend derives from the other element
that has contributed to these mestizo cultures, namely Hispanic
tradition.

Published studies on peninsular Spanish folklore say absolutely
nothing about the llorona, either by this name or any other. Again
it is possible that folklorists have neglected to report the legend,
although it is hardly likely that a theme so frequently noted in
America would have left no traces in Spain, assuming that its
route of transmission led through that country. I have questioned
informants in Spain concerning the presence of such a legend but
the results have been equally negative. Contemporary Spanish folklorists have been able to provide little information concerning a
possible peninsular llorona but the only parallel (and this is a
remote one) involves a Moorish princess punished by her father
(as was the Moorish lass at Cáceres) who can still be heard at night
wailing at the walls of a castle set atop an eminence above the Río

---

[26] An excellent survey of this belief is George M. Foster, "Nagualism in
Mexico and Guatemala," *Acta americana,* II (1944), 85–103.

Tajo. The similarities are slight and unconvincing. The time is ripe for a careful study of available texts by one who is not previously committed to any particular position concerning the origin or transmission of the legend.

At present there is nothing available that approaches an accurate register of legends for either Spain or its former American territories. Thus it is difficult to determine with any degree of precision the nature of the stock of legends that came to America with Spanish colonists or to trace the development of a body of creole or mestizo narratives in the New World. It would seem that in a number of cases legends that arrived with Spanish settlers reenforced narratives and beliefs already held by native groups.

Using the imperfect tools and materials at our disposal, one can perceive, however, both similarities and differences. I should like to state explicitly the two major differences that are implied in the discussions that have gone before. First, there appears to be a definite time lag as far as certain Spanish American legends are concerned. One notes a high frequency of legends that relate to witchcraft, kobolds, apparitions, and ghosts, which in Spain, for the lack of more precise information, seem to be on the wane. It is precisely this realm that Spaniards qualify as bizarre and fantastic, yet they underwent an intense preoccupation with such activities in the sixteenth and seventeenth centuries.

The second contrasting feature is closely related to the one just mentioned. In America there is an extremely close affinity between the oral narrative and the local or regional system of belief. The legend plays a key role in any examination of the body of belief and superstition of a community, not through simple affirmation of such a superstition or even its practice but through exemplification in the form of a well-defined narrative.

I should have liked to afford the informants a greater role in my discussion, with perhaps a consideration of personality traits and personal reactions to individual legends. That will have to await a detailed discussion on an appropriate occasion. I should like, however, in closing to give the informant his brief say and I shall do so by quoting another Mexican informant from Veracruz, who sensed something of the difference between denizens of the Old World and the New, as he knew them.

As they travel in Mexico, a Spaniard asks an Indian the names of various animals that he sees. The Spaniard inquires: "What animal is that?"

"Sir, that is a cow," the Indian replies.

"That can't be a cow. In my country cows are the size of that church you see over there," retorts the Spaniard. "There are no cows in my country of this size."

Next they see a horse, which the Indian identifies correctly, but the Spaniard is incensed: "Horses in my country are really big! That one is just a rat."

And so it goes. As they travel onward they meet other animals and in each case those known to the Spaniard are of giant stature when compared with those known to the poor Indian. But soon they reach a river that they must ford. The Indian dismounts from his horse, undresses, then kneels on the river bank and begins to pray.

The curious Spaniard asks: "Indian, why are you doing that, praying and crossing yourself?"

"Sir," he answers humbly, "this is called the River of Truths. Anyone who tells a lie will be swept away by its waters."

The Spaniard meditates briefly, then replies: "Then nothing that I have just told you is true. Everything here is the same as in my country."

I presume that the two then crossed the river without further incident.

The Making of the Popular Legendary Hero

HORACE P. BECK, *Middlebury College*

As I have listened to the various speakers during this conference, I am even more impressed by an idea that I have held for some time—the immediacy of folklore in this country. A story after twenty-odd years is a legend. Further, I am impressed with the ephemeracy of folk belief in America. For these reasons I am going to digress and speak for a moment on European legends.

During the past three summers my wife and I have been collecting material on the islands and in the outports of England, Scotland, and Ireland. It is good, I think, for us as folklorists to refresh our interest now and then by working abroad where folklore is often more viable than it is in the United States. In our three summers we have seldom heard a legend told with the apology formula of "people say" or "I have heard." Rather, the tale begins—"There is a cursing stone on this island that kills people." Further, the age of the stories is often amazing. Let me give one illustration. A fisherman came aboard at Kilcummin Roads, Ireland, and told us about a box that had washed ashore. After a cow licked it for three days a woman opened it. Inside was a baby that grew to become a saint. Today if clay is taken from the saint's grave by a direct female descendant of this woman, it will protect the possessor from drowning. The saint lived in the sixth century. Our informant's sister was the woman who could get the clay today and she and her brother lived on the same spot—if not in the same house—as their ancestors fourteen hundred years ago. With this story to keep me humble, I would like to approach my topic.

A good deal of ink has been used in discussions of the hero. Currently Lord Raglan holds the field with the view that history has little to do with the hero figure, which really is a stereotype—highborn, dying on a hill without issue, and so forth. But Raglan, like most of the other writers, is talking about mythological, epic, or culture heroes. I am interested in legendary heroes—popular, national legendary heroes and what makes them tick. These heroes are to Christ, Beowulf, and Arthur as a rat is to a beaver. Were we to study legendary folk heroes the analogy might be reduced from rat to beaver to mouse to rat.

For the purposes of this study three historical entities have been chosen for examination. Of the three, one figure has reached the stature of popular legendary hero, known to both folk and sophisticate—thanks in part to Walt Disney and Richard Dorson. One hero has nearly made it, having regional fame and peasant acclaim in his native area. The third is the control—a man who had everything but who never made it past the graveyard. The three are Davy Crockett, Ethan Allen, and Joshua Barney.

As children we used to think of heroes as men who were in all respects "gooder" than others. They were brave, strong, kind, courteous, and God-fearing. They protected the innocent, sheltered the weak, and set their hand against evil. Sometimes they died for what they believed in. Briefly, they stood for outstanding national and cultural virtues. But children dream and adults have nightmares. In order to bring things into some perspective the first step in the problem is to give a brief biography of the three men. Since of the three Crockett is the best known, he will be handled first and briefly.

David Crockett,[1] the sixth of seven boys, was born of Irish parents in 1786, in Tennessee. The father was both poor and dubiously honest. From time to time he bound the boy out to pay his debts. Fear of his father's just wrath for not attending school made young David flee home, and for a while he wandered about the country picking up odd jobs and being cheated out of his hard-earned money. Like the prodigal son, he returned at the age of fifteen only to depart for North Carolina to work off a debt incurred by his father. One job led to another and finally, at the age of seventeen, he managed to obtain some schooling. During a wolf hunt he became lost, succored a young girl, and married her. After a few years farming, he struck out for the territory ahead

---

[1] For a more detailed analytical account, see Richard M. Dorson, *American Folklore* (Chicago: University of Chicago Press, 1959), pp. 199–214.

and settled his family in Lincoln County, Tennessee, in 1809. He then served in the Creek War as a volunteer and endured a good deal of hard marching and privation as a scout. His principal military activity seems to have been foraging for food for his company —a chore at which he appears to have been relatively successful, for he kept them supplied with venison, turkey, squirrel, and an occasional cow. As to his Indian fighting ability, he participated in several slaughters, but if he killed any Indians personally he makes light of it, simply referring to the tactics used, the numbers killed and burned by the militia of which he was a part.

Following the war, he moved farther westward with his family and spent a considerable amount of time hunting bears. He tells us he killed only for meat, but in one year nearly three hundred of the animals fell before his gun—eleven in one day! About this time he became a justice of the peace and from such a small beginning rose in fame, partly by his magistrate's work and partly by his reputation as a bear hunter, until he was elected to the state legislature. Flushed with success, he then ran for Congress and won twice. A third attempt failed and Crockett immediately— either out of disgust or in an attempt to regain lost ground—set out for Texas where he joined Colonel Travis and perished with him in the Alamo.

His chief claims to fame appear to have been as a bear hunter, a crack shot, a woodsman, and a man who could wade through swamps in chilly weather. Strangely enough this ability seems to have been of a local nature, for when he went West to join with Travis, he first totally missed the target in a shooting match, then missed a buffalo, got himself lost, then lost his horse, was clawed by a cougar and captured by the Comanche—in short, he acted very much as any Eastern greenhorn in similar circumstances. These things, of course, were forgiven him by his final act, which was to vanish with the defenders of the Alamo.

Ethan Allen, also the son of a poor man with a large family, was born in Vermont in 1739, at a time when that area was still wilderness and a refuge for scoundrels. Early in his career he became a real estate agent and leader of the Green Mountain Boys, a group recruited to contest New York's claim to Vermont. At this time he achieved considerable fame as a hunter and community strongman. In 1775 under the command of Benedict Arnold, he surprised and took Fort Ticonderoga with the Green Mountain Boys. Although the battle was nearly bloodless, his finest hour came when he supposedly shouted, "Surrender in the name of the

Great Jehovah and the Continental Congress." Flushed with victory, he planned an attack upon Montreal inspired somewhat by Wolfe's actions at Quebec. The attack was poorly planned, uncoordinated, and undisciplined. Allen's forces were speedily put to rout, and he was captured with many of his men. He was carried abroad and spent much of the war in prison. By the time he was exchanged, all the prisoners taken at the same time he was had either escaped or died. Following the war, he and his brother made a fortune in questionable land transactions. He subsequently died in bed.

During his career he was accused of trying to betray Vermont into British hands—a charge that was never proved, thanks to perjured witnesses and the fact that the court was convinced he could not have been both in Bennington and in New York in so short a length of time. What the court did not know was that Allen had established a pony express for himself between Bennington and New York which enabled him to kill a horse every five miles and make phenomenal time.

From the time he was captured until he was exchanged, Allen not only stoutly refused to escape but thwarted the plans of others in this line. At one point he prevented a privateer captain from seizing an ill-manned British frigate and sailing her into an American port. Meanwhile, he demonstrated his rage against the British by biting on nails and challenging his captors to duels—knowing full well prisoners were not allowed weapons.

A couple of his escapades during less troublesome times might be mentioned to fill out his career. In taverns one of his particular delights was to make the customers swallow live troutlings thereby giving venerability to the goldfish swallowing craze of several decades ago. He bet his brother, Ira (a short man), that he could outdistance him in a footrace. The terrain was familiar to Ethan but strange to Ira, and when the two set off Ira soon found himself hopelessly bogged down in a quagmire while Ethan romped home the victor. According to what law there was in Vermont, no land could be sold for taxes without being duly advertized in the paper. Ethan posted a notice of a land sale for six o'clock. When the prospective buyers arrived at 6:00 P.M. they discovered that Ethan and his little brother had bid it in for pennies the acre at six in the morning.

Like Crockett, Allen achieved considerable acclaim as a hunter able to kill game and endure hardship. On one occasion he is said to have gone after deer in the wintertime for he was low on provisions. Hunting was good but the weather cold. Every time he killed a deer, he left a bit of his clothing with it to identify his kill. A hundred deer later, he was running through the forest in subzero temperatures clad only in snowshoes, bullet pouch, and powder horn, with his trusty fowling piece in his hand. He can be forgiven not shooting bears, since there never was a plethora of these creatures in Vermont as there was in the West.

Although he demanded that Ticonderoga be surrendered "in the name of the Great Jehovah," he later caused to be published an atheistic tract entitled *Reason, the Only Oracle of Man* which he stole from one Thomas Young. This was a limited edition for the printinghouse was struck by lightning as the books were coming off the press and the printer refused to run off any more.

When he died his tombstone bore the inscription "A Man who tried God's Spirit to the Utmost." He now shares whatever affection Vermonters are capable of along with the Morgan horse, a breed sired by a nag who eked out his days drawing a peddler's cart.

At this point it is interesting to note that Ira Allen had a much greater effect upon history than his more flamboyant brother. He lacked the stature, the bluster, and the abilities "to take a social horn," but he was endowed with a good deal of financial ability. It was Ira, not Ethan, who was responsible for founding and endowing the University of Vermont, but outside those halls his name is largely unknown in the state.

Joshua Barney was born in 1759, one of fourteen children of a successful farmer-businessman near Baltimore. At ten he terminated his schooling, knowing "as much as the school master" and after trying two business ventures went to sea, aged eleven. By the time he was fourteen he was a second mate. At fifteen, he became master mariner of a sinking ship, when his uncle-skipper died in mid-ocean in the dead of winter. He brought the wreck safely into Gibraltar, repaired her, and discharged his cargo at a $30,000 profit.

In 1775 Barney was the first man to display the American flag while recruiting for a privateer in Baltimore. By June of 1776 he had been commissioned lieutenant in the Continental navy and helped to capture the armed brig, *Betsy*. Within a month he brought in his first prize. In the *Andrea Doria* in November, he received the first salute given an American man-o'-war at St. Christopher in the West Indies, and only days later took H.M. Brig *Racehorse* in a heavy engagement. A few days after that another prize was taken and Barney took command of her. She went ashore in a snowstorm off Virginia but by superior seamanship was got off. The prisoners rebelled. Barney shot one. Finally, she was captured just off the Delaware capes and Barney was paroled. Seven months later an English officer was exchanged for him and Joshua went to sea again. Almost immediately he was engaged in a battle, which he won. Later he was captured and then nearly retook the ship.

The year 1779 found him bound for Bordeaux. He was overtaken by a superior vessel, the *Rosebud,* which discovered that Barney's vessel had no stern ports. Accordingly, the *Rosebud* hung astern and pounded the American at leisure. During the night Barney cut ports in the stern, trundled a six-pounder into the great cabin and loaded it with crowbars. At daylight the unsuspecting Englishman closed in to continue his bombardment. Joshua knocked down the false covering and let fly. Forty men were killed and the *Rosebud* put totally out of action.

Captured a fourth time in 1780, Barney was incarcerated in Mill Prison, Plymouth, England. He promptly escaped, masquerading as a British officer, and tried to sail a fishing smack to France. Captured again, he again escaped and made his way to France disguised as a dandy, in company of a mysterious young lady. Here he was befriended by Benjamin Franklin.

In 1782 he was home again and took command of the *Hyder Alley.* In this vessel he engaged the much larger *General Monk.* The battle was hot. In order to see the action Barney was in the habit of standing on the binnacle to get above the smoke. Here he stood sword in hand on this occasion. His hat was shot away, his uniform riddled by bullets, but in twenty minutes the *General Monk* was his. Of all the battles of the Revolution, this one has been considered the most outstanding by naval tacticians.

The war over, Barney tried going back to merchantmen but on his first voyage he was captured by three British privateers. They took his vessel, whereupon he immediately retook it (blowing the arm off the prize captain in the process) and brought the gang into Baltimore. On his next trip he was captured and tried for piracy, but he was exonerated.

Like Paul Jones, Barney was overlooked by the navy and, disgusted with the merchant service, he accepted a commission as commodore in the French navy, a post he held until shortly before hostilities broke out with France, when he resigned his commission.

In the War of 1812, Barney continued the wild career he had begun in the Revolution. At one point he put into Newport,

Rhode Island, where he received a rousing salute. Not to be thought impolite, Barney fired one in return. Unfortunately, he had forgotten his guns were shotted and he blew the leg off a Negro woman standing on the pier.

His greatest day came, however, when the British decided to take Washington. Jefferson had thought the best way to take British frigates with sides thirty feet high, bristling with hundred-pound guns, was with a flotilla of rowboats—not with other frigates. The British showed the folly of this idea in one easy lesson.

In control of Chesapeake Bay, the English under General Ross, decided to attack Washington. The assault was begun on August 24, and was carried out almost without a hitch. The American troops were easily dispersed and the British marched out of Blanderburg for the capital. A mile outside of town on a little rise overlooking the road waited Barney astride a horse, since no binnacle was handy. Before him squatted five naval guns. For nearly six hours those five guns stopped the progress of history until, badly wounded, Barney fell from his horse, and the battery surrendered.

Here the story all but ends. The commodore never fully recovered from his wound. He had been given fifty thousand acres in Kentucky to which he repaired for a while and then returned to the East. On his second trip out, his old wound acted up and Joshua Barney died and was buried in Pittsburgh, Pennsylvania.

In the Naval Academy at Annapolis there is a bust of Barney. A dirty alley in Newport, Rhode Island, is called Barney Street, and an inhospitable shoreline in Buzzard's Bay is still called Barney's Joy. That is the memory of Commodore Joshua Barney, the tall, golden haired, blue-eyed hero of two wars and nearly twenty pitched battles.

These, then, are the capsule lives of three men, one of whom might be called a buffoon, another a scoundrel, and only the third, a hero. What can we find that makes them "go"—aside from the fact that all three died in their fifties? [2]

In the first place we are faced with a problem of background. Crockett and Allen both have similar origins in that they came of poor, prolific families. All three were farm boys. Only Barney could

---

[2] Dorson feels that the Crockett popularity comes from the Heroic Age when people were interested in the violent life, but since this age seems to span several millennia and a variety of heroes, I feel we can determine the reasons for Crockett's rise, along with others of his kind, more closely in America. See Richard M. Dorson, "Davy Crockett and the Heroic Age," *SFQ*, VI (1942), 95–102.

lay claim to an education and only Barney was in a sense "to the manor born." This may well serve as a demerit for Barney because it would seem that most American heroes from Franklin to Fink were poor and uneducated in the formal sense.

Both Crockett and Allen came from the frontier. Crockett from the West, Allen from the North. Although the lives of the two men actually overlapped, Allen was of the eighteenth, Crockett of the nineteenth century. The Louisiana Purchase, the exploration of Lewis and Clark, and the Embargo Act had tended to heighten interest in the Western Man. It was further enhanced by Jackson's election to the Presidency, and even though Crockett was his implacable enemy, he benefited from Jackson's term in office. This can be easily seen from the reception Crockett received during his tour of northern states where people came to lavish upon him the same interest they were later to give Jumbo the elephant.

Allen, on the other hand, flourished in a day when the frontier was too close to civilization to be a curiosity. Later, local interest focused on seafaring and the industrial revolution, and Vermont remained a kind of backwater quite overshadowed by both the wilder frontier in the distant West and the glitter of the industrial revolution at home.

Both Allen and Crockett were dishonest—at least to a degree. Crockett admits to winning votes through the use of liquor, to swindling a tavern owner, and to padding his expense account. He even suggests chicanery in vote counting. Allen's backsliding has already been discussed. Both of these men, however, were dishonest in a peculiar way. They cheated the cheatable—government where people still say "one must expect dishonesty in Washington." They cheated the landlord and the absentee landowner; they outsharped the sharpie. The rather substantial results of these dealings accrued to them but always a few scraps were thrown to the poor. The result was that they achieved a largess of nature not really in keeping with their small ways.

Allen and Crockett had a remarkable way of telling a story, spinning a yarn, and taking a "social horn." They had a degree of personal charm to display at public meetings. Crockett lost an election, Allen a battle, but there was about them a glib ability to affix the blame to other quarters. There is little evidence that Barney ever had this ability. Rather, he stood out in times of stress— handling a ship in a gale, standing on the binnacle wreathed in smoke, driving his men. There is good evidence that he had a quick mind, but little in the way of evidence that he was either an opportunist, a storyteller, or a man who was more than reserved on public occasions.

We now move into what I take to be one of the most important areas of the three men. Ethan Allen and David Crockett were both writers. Although he could scarcely read or write when elected justice of the peace, Crockett wrote, later, an autobiography that was a success partly because of its content but largely because of its style. Crockett, like Allen, was a supreme egotist and just as his election to Congress whetted his appetite for the Presidency, so did the success of the autobiography lead him to compare himself favorably with Shakespeare.

So successful was Colonel Crockett's *Autobiography* that numerous other volumes followed—mostly ghostwritten, judging from the style. Among them was a life of Van Buren, *Colonel Crockett's Tour,* and *Colonel Crockett's Texas Exploits.* Davy Crockett had become good copy and publicity agents in the guise of money-grubbing literary hacks decided to capitalize on him. Davy Crockett plays, and especially the Crockett Almanacs had a great deal to do with making him a hero of the first water.

That popular acclaim may best be achieved through the use of a trained intercessionary has been known since before Davy Crockett. We know the part Parson Weems played in creating the figure of Washington. (He even borrowed the story about King Phillip who was said to be in league with the Devil because he could throw a rock across Narragansett Bay and applied it to the General who threw a dollar across the Potomac to show his strength.) Those who have studied Irish folklore are aware that the would-be hero was more afraid of antagonizing the filé (bard) than he was of an armed host. Should "the maker of songs" choose, he could compose a satire that would destroy his enemy.[3]

Colonel Allen's *Narrative,* concerned mostly with the first person singular and treating the period of his life from the time he took Ticonderoga until he returned to Vermont an exchanged prisoner, did a tremendous amount to further his career, especially since it came out at a crucial point in the war and inspired men of courage to strive harder. Although the book went through nine editions in twenty-six years it was expanded upon only by Jared Sparks and Herman Melville who included Allen in a little-read novel, *Israel Potter.* The popular hack writers of the day paid little attention to him, and although Allen had written and was to write

---

[3] T. W. Rolleston, *Myths and Legends of the Celtic Race* (New York: T. Y. Crowell, 1911), p. 108.

other tracts, they were mostly political and narrowly aimed, such as
*A Concise Refutation of the Claims of New Hampshire and Mas-
sachusetts Bay to the Territory of Vermont,* and so forth. The fact
he felt compelled to publish *Reason, the Only Oracle of Man* in
1784 did him no good, for it branded him "Atheist." Crockett can
inveigh against Old Hickory and it becomes him like David facing
Goliath without a sling, but to be a "real" hero there are two
sacred areas wherein no man dare tread—theology and national
supremacy. Allen trespassed in both areas, and although he escaped
the charge of treason, the other charge stood.

Joshua Barney, first of all, was not born of "poor but honest"
parents and he had "book larnin'." His feats of courage were
performed far from the grog shop, and his advice and time does not
appear to have been spent upon the mob. Both his calling and his
background did not admit it. Further, he did not write a book or
advertise himself in any way. Indeed, of his contemporaries, only
Philip Freneau was moved to write two poems in his behalf. While
Crockett and Allen were usually around to defend themselves from
detractors, Barney was half-a-world away. Another point to be
made returns us to the times. The Westering movement that so
favored Crockett's star served only to dim Barney's. The country
was not inclined toward a navy at that time, and Barney's image
was one that, like John Paul Jones, would be kept under wraps.

From all this material then, we can, I think, draw some conclusions. First, it is not necessary—indeed it may well be detri-
mental—to be endowed with the manly moral virtues to achieve
heroic stature. Were it otherwise Joshua Barney would have
loomed very large. Second, it is imperative that the times be
fortuitous to make the special flair a man has shine out. The times
for Crockett were ideal. Third, personal flamboyance and the
ability to talk a good game far overshadows the ability to "cut
the mustard." A drinking bout with Crockett or Allen did more
for their reputation than being victor of two pitched battles against
heavy odds could ever do for Barney. Fourth, and perhaps most
important, is the power of the written word and the publicity
agent. Taken together they form a team that is hard to beat.

So far I have talked about three men, two of whom became
popular, national legendary heroes. Both Crockett and Allen, like
many other scoundrels, are also known to the folk, but it would
seem that the ideas about them retained by this group are neither
of nor from the folk but have been introduced from outside their
society. To demonstrate this point it might be well to glance at

some typical legendary heroes whose only appearance in literature has been in textual recordings.

In Maine we have two such men, Barney Beal and Fred Carver. Near Doylestown, Pennsylvania, resided the Doan Brothers and in the Chesapeake Bay area we meet the Reverend Joshua Thomas and Lickin' Billy Bradshaw. The number could be extended by moving West but these are sufficient. All these men seem to bear a striking similarity. First, they all are narrowly known—Barney Beal around Jonesport, Fred Carver in Penobscot Bay, the Doans in the vicinity of Cross Keyes, Pennsylvania, Joshua Thomas—a miracle worker—only in Chesapeake Bay, and Lickin' Billy is best known to the residents of Crefield, Maryland, and the adjacent islands.

All these men are known for their size, their courage, their violent tempers, their endurance, and, especially, their strength—all, that is, except Thomas who, being a religious hero, leans heavily upon his miracles for fame. All are credited with lifting great weights—a dory, a wagonload of sand, an anvil. All come to their end by overexercise much after the fashion of Barney Beal who died picking up a loaded dory.

None of these men are remembered for their trickery, their dishonesty, their "gift of gab," or their alignment of the poor against the rich, and no emphasis is placed on their lack of "book larnin'" or their initial poverty. Indeed, their mental prowess is totally overlooked and their honesty implied. In short, they are in many ways antithetical to the character sketches of Crockett, Allen, and a host of others well known in storybooks.[4]

It could, of course, be argued that Crockett and Allen are not folk heroes because they were made in large part through the literary media and through calculated publicity. Even Allen had two writers to promote him—Jared Sparks and Herman Melville. Indeed, at the outset I called them popular legendary heroes. As the broadside has from time to time resuscitated the ballad, however, these men have become known to the folk, and stories are told orally about them derived largely through the media of the press. Both Crockett and Allen in their backgrounds are of the folk. Barney, on the other hand was not of the folk to begin with.

---

4 For references to Fred Carver and Barney Beal, see Richard M. Dorson, *Buying the Wind* (Chicago: University of Chicago Press, 1964); Horace Beck, *Folklore of Maine* (Philadelphia: J. B. Lippincott, 1957). For information about the Doan Brothers, I am indebted to Professor Don Yoder of the University of Pennsylvania and the late MacEdward Leach. Information on Joshua Thomas and Lickin' Billy Bradshaw was obtained from Dr. George Carey and the Folklore Archives of the University of Maryland.

Further, he was appointed to his military rank while the others were elected out of their own group—an indication that they loomed large in the eyes of their peers. This last argument, although valid, I do not feel draws as much water as the other aspects mentioned.

If the foregoing are the positive requirements for becoming a hero, there are a couple of things that one must never do if he would become famous. "God," "Mother," and "My Country" are sacred words in our country. The hero may butt his head against the monoliths created by our nation and achieve acclaim thereby, but if he puts another country first or suggests a national overthrow of power, he is in jeopardy of being called an unsuccessful patriot— a traitor. (In this regard I mean by "country," first a geographical area, then the people in the area, and finally their major institutions.) This may well have been Barney's greatest mistake— joining the French. It is, perhaps, permissible to change the form of worship, but it is never permissible to disclaim it. There is a place in our society, albeit small, for Joseph Smith but none for Tom Paine—"the dirty little atheist." It may well be that God has crawled into a test tube at this point in our career, but a pox will fall upon those who deny him. Allen could clear himself, partially, of the first charge but the second brought him low. Conversely, braying about these three things will not in themselves make one a hero, but inveighing against them will keep one from the hall of fame.

Of late there has been a demand to make folklore timely. Perhaps these few ideas will enable us to determine the heroes of tomorrow. Strict application to the rules may make popular heroes of some scholars in their own discipline.

Beanie Short: A Civil War Chronicle in Legend and Song

D. K. WILGUS, *University of California, Los Angeles*
LYNWOOD MONTELL, *Western Kentucky University*

This paper demonstrates the intrinsic value of a local fiddle song and a corpus of tenacious historical legends in reconstructing a century-old episode that could not have been written if the standard historiographical methods were the only means of articulation. Homer C. Hockett would have historians disregard the spoken word as something that is notoriously fallacious.[1] But the events that gave rise to the song and legends about Beanie Short, a rebel guerrilla, were never placed in writing—not in newspapers, for there were none, and not in the court records, for guerrilla bands during the Civil War seldom stood trial for their crimes.[2] We contend that studies that are based on oral traditional legends —the folk narratives that seem totally congruous at face value— demonstrate that, with due caution, the investigator can turn profitably to the folk themselves for their history. Despite strong counterforces, such as the constant interplay between fact and fabrication, it is still possible for the local historian, who has a thorough knowledge of the folklore properties of oral tradition, coupled with the methodology employed by the folklorist, to place the component parts of oral historical narratives in proper perspective.[3]

---

[1] Homer C. Hockett, *The Critical Method in Historical Research and Writing* (New York: MacMillan, 1955), p. 49.

[2] For a fuller consideration of the paucity of historical records in this area, consult William Lynwood Montell, *The Saga of Coe Ridge: A Study in Oral History* (Knoxville: University of Tennessee Press, 1970), pp. 3-7.

[3] Richard M. Dorson expresses similar views in his article entitled "Oral

The locale of the Beanie Short legend-song complex is in Monroe and Cumberland counties, located in the hill country of southern Kentucky at the point where the Cumberland River disappears into Clay County, Tennessee, just above Celina. These counties are not considered geographically a part of Southern Appalachia, but the folk culture as well as the physical terrain negates the truth— the casual observer would be hard put to make a distinction. Even with regard to verbal traditions, the area is closely linked with the mountains in a fairly rich survival of song and legend. The more ancient folk songs no longer flourish along the Cumberland, but are still recalled. Märchen have vanished from the memories of tale raconteurs, but "bear tales" are still told in the numerous country stores, and historical legends are amazingly persistent.

The rugged border country terrain was scarred during the war years by the constant passage of and numerous conflicts between Union and Confederate forces. The name of John Hunt Morgan is dropped frequently during conversations with older residents, and General Braxton Bragg, C.S.A., is commonly heard. The activities of the organized armies notwithstanding, this was guerrilla country during the Civil War. Much devastation was inflicted by the somewhat numerous renegade outfits who killed innocent persons and looted the countryside while operating under the guise of sectional loyalties to the North or the South. Jesse James is a household name throughout the area. Vivid tales are still recounted about Tinker Dave Beatty's Yankee guerrillas, whose base of operations was located in the environs of Byrdstown, Tennessee. Legends seem inexhaustible about Champ Ferguson, an elusive rebel from nearby Wayne County, Kentucky, who was pursued throughout the war years by his Union-sympathizing brother out to kill him. And Boney Pruitt and Burr Huddleston are still remembered as Yankee raiders who operated in the river areas of Monroe and Cumberland counties, where slaveholders were most densely located.[4] But of all the legendary guerrilla leaders along the Upper Cumberland, Beanie Short of Monroe County stands tallest in oral tradition.

Tradition and Written History: The Case for the United States," *JFI*, I:3 (Dec., 1964), 220–234.

   4 Our files are filled with accounts of guerrilla activities ascribed to Jesse and Frank James. Known collected tales of Beatty are scarce but nonetheless available to the field collector. Champ Ferguson has been studied by Thurman Sensing in *Champ Ferguson: Confederate Guerilla* (Nashville: Vanderbilt University Press, 1942), but numerous oral legends about the Ferguson brothers still exist, as is the case with the exploits of Huddleston and Pruitt.

The river area of Monroe County, with its fertile, fluvial bottom-
lands in the Turkey Neck Bend section, was the major seedbed of
Southern loyalty, while young men from the remainder of the
county swelled the Union ranks. Colonel Hiram "Hi" Biggerstaff,
one of the largest slaveholders and reputedly the richest man in
Turkey Neck Bend, was the subject of numerous anecdotes, one of
which relates that to the only one of his twelve sons who served in
the Union Army he willed all his slaves.[5] Many of the slaveholders
in Turkey Neck Bend were not secessionists, and according to tradition, these loyalists were the chief objects of Bean Short's activities
(13, 59), though his band is reported to have made a daily practice
of tracking down Union soldiers.

Beanie Short was from the Kettle Creek section of Turkey Neck
Bend, noted for its moonshining activities. He was the son of William Short. Of this point there is no doubt, for both oral tradition
and federal census schedules are in agreement. His real first name
is less certain, however. Three informants (30, 40, 55) claimed that
his name was George,[6] a claim that appears plausible when considered in light of census data.

The William Short clan had a reputation as troublemakers, yet
it was related by blood and marriage to some of the finest families
in the area, such as the Coes, Smiths, Kerrs, and Biggerstaffs. William Short himself "was always raising a ruckus with everybody."
One of his daughters, Fanny "Tump," is said to have been the
community prostitute who gave birth to one or more illegitimate
children. A son Albert was a heavy drinker who spent seven years
inside his house during an extended drunk (50). Beanie Short, another of William's sons, along with his band of "curillas," as they
were called by a Negro resident of Tompkinsville (56), is still a
subject of tenacious legendry and song in the area. The record of
Beanie Short, unpleasant as it is, will be allowed to speak for itself through a presentation of the numerous legends associated
with his name.

Some persons still search for the gold and silver Short supposedly
buried, and even those people whose families were victimized by
him and his rebel raiders talk profusely about those things. Some
of the stories have wandered to neighboring counties, where they
are told simply as cruel deeds committed by unidentified guerrilla

---

5 Louis Brownlow, *The Anatomy of the Anecdote* (Chicago: University of
Chicago Press, 1960), pp. 64–68.

6 Virtually every informant claimed that Ashlock's first name was Bill, and we
hold to this view. One informant, however, called him John Ashlock and
another referred to him as George.

bands. Certain tales now seem almost humorous, but in reality they relate wanton acts of murder. It would thus appear that the lapse of 106 years is sufficient to ascribe to Beanie Short the status of local folk hero. Many who tell of him seem almost proud that he injured or killed their ancestors, a fact that distinguishes them from those persons who cannot tell similar tales.

When the Civil War erupted, Short and his wife were living in the little community of Spearsville on Pea Ridge. It is said that he spent much time during those first few months talking about the war and pondering his role in the bloody fratricidal conflict. "He did not know which side was right and which one he would join. Eventually Beanie joined the South, but soon came home and got to raiding and robbing" (57). According to another source, Beanie and his wife moved into his father's home at Short's Chapel. There he began running around with Bill Ashlock, who "caused him to go bad" (3). From this simple beginning, Short organized a "rebel" group of about eight young men who were mainly from the Kettle Creek section of Monroe County. All their names are not known, but included in the group were some Murley boys (59), some Riley boys (59), Bill [7] Ashlock, and John Short (Beanie's brother) (40).[8] It is said that they never molested their home community of Kettle Creek (13, 26, 52, 54, 59), but otherwise "scattered and pilfered the whole country" and always managed to keep out of the way of the Union army which constantly sought their whereabouts (14, 56).

The motivation behind Beanie Short's guerrilla actions during the war years can only be conjectured. Some of the informants, but mainly those who are related to Short, claim that he was acting on behalf of the Southern army, but there is a fairly articulate belief expressed by the other informants that he was a rebel for his own cause. Here are some sample subjective commentaries concerning Short's activities during those stormy years:

> He was a real bad guerrilla, and you know how it is. He had a bad name and was blamed for many things (41).

> Beanie was just plain mean (10).

> He had dark black hair, black eyes and complexioned kindly. He was tall, heavy built enough—what you'd call robust. He was nice looking, but you could see the meanness in him. He was good to people, but what he wanted he took (30).

---

7 See n. 6.

8 John Short moved to Oklahoma during the post-Civil War years and was never heard from again, according to an informant (40).

Beanie Short would dist rob people. I never did hear of nobody he ever killed. Dist went around and robbed people—would steal what they had and take what they had. Beanie Short and Bill Ashlock would do that (45).

He jist slaughtered all the time. They couldn't have been much worse than Old Bean Short and his bunch. He ought to have been killed (38).

Short's virtual neutral position in the Civil War may be attested to by comments and narratives relating to his attitudes toward Negroes. On the one hand were the testimonies by four white informants (16, 20, 31, 51) and one Negro informant (15) that "he never mistreated the colored people," while on the other hand were the statements from two Negro women (32, 56) that Short hated all Negroes. In the paraphrased words of one (56):

Beanie Short and his men were riding toward the Moore house on the Cumberland River. They met an old colored man. Short stopped and drew his gun intending to kill him, but gave in to the old man's pleas and begs. Short let him go with the statement, "This is the last Nigger we will ever see." He hated them bitterly and was trying to get rid of them all.

Bill Ashlock probably shared Short's feelings toward the Negro race. The following account is now related in a humorous vein, but Negro Big Jim probably saw nothing funny about Ashlock's threat to cut off his head at the chop block. Price Kirkpatrick (35) recalled the episode, known also by three other informants (27, 36, 56), which involved his grandfather's slaves:

They got one of our slave Niggers; John Short was in that gang. And we had a meat log—flat top to it you know, in the yard. He got that Nigger—he was jist a boy, and they put him laid him down on that, you know, and got the axe to come down and cut his head off, you know, and he'd jump aside ways you know. That was John a-doin' that. But now Bill Ashlock and Bean wuz settin' back on their horses a-laughin' about it [chuckle]. When I was a boy workin' in my daddy's mill down there, John Short was a customer to the mill, you know. He was there most every week you know, with a turn of corn to have it ground. And the old Nigger was the one a-workin' for me, you know, that he had down on the log. And I said to him, we called him Big Jim; he was awful big Nigger. I said, "Big Jim do you ever think about John Short trying to cut your head off?" [laughter]. He said, "Yessir, I think of that ever time I see him." But he wouldn't say nothing. He'd wait on him just like he would any of the rest of them. Take his turn off and and take his turn out and put it on his horse.

A knowledge of the identity of Short's victims reinforces the notion that he was acting primarily on behalf of himself. Although Beanie may have concerned himself with getting food for the

Southern army by robbing Union sympathizers (35), he took cash,
valuables, livestock, and supplies from local slaveholders and non-
slaveholders alike (35). One informant, when asked whose side
Beanie was on, replied, "Side of the outlaw from what I've heard."
Another informant emphasized that although Short was a Southern
rebel, he most certainly was robbing slaveholders (59). And the fact
that his own brother-in-law helped to kill Beanie indicates that he
was robbing even his own relatives (30).

It is not possible to organize chronologically all the tales of
Short's atrocities and nefarious escapades. They simply "took place
during the Civil War." Instead of a chronological orientation, the
historical narratives revolving around the life of Beanie Short di-
vide themselves neatly into episodic cycles dealing with his raiding
activities, his treacherous death, his buried treasure—which apparently has successfully eluded all seekers—and, finally, a song whose
variant stanzas denigrate Beanie Short but confidently reiterate
that "he'll never be forgotten."

RAIDING ACTIVITIES

Accounts of Short's raiding activities bring into clear focus the
phenomena of oral traditional patterning in the oral tradition of
recent local historical events, legend displacement, and the migratory nature of certain legends and legend motifs. Johnny Killman
introduces an episode containing an example of displacement:
"Beanie and Ashlock came up to this house and they had a wild
horse with them. They took the man of the house out 'cause they
had something against him, and they cut off his arms and tied him
to the tail of this wild horse, and the last they saw of him he
was flopping up and down on the tail of this wild horse as it was
running off." During another interview, Killman (38) claimed,
"It run until it killed the man." This account is strikingly similar
to another that claims that Short "tied Stocky Dodson to a horse's
tail and run him up and down the road to try to get him to tell
where his money was" (31). Such an episode might have passed un-
noticed in those tense years had Stocky Dodson not been Beanie
Short's own brother-in-law (31). Short's tactics would involve a form
of torture at times. In the words of one informant, he "would take
a hot iron and stick it to your feet to make you tell where the
money was" (7, 8), or, to quote another, "He would pick people
up and make them walk barefoot and run them out of their house
in their nightclothes" (10).

It could be that the mention of nightclothes in the preceding quote was derived from the episode in which Short's gang attempted to rob Tom Wilson of Willow Shade in Metcalfe County. It seems that Wilson had much money cached away. Short and his guerrillas came and dragged Wilson out of the house, clad only in a nightshirt. They threatened him unless he revealed the hiding place of his money. When Wilson refused to tell them, Beanie and Ashlock pulled his nightshirt over his head, each grabbed a corner of it and, riding their horses, half dragged, half carried him between them. He was fully aware that they were headed for a tree, perhaps intending to bash his head in. But before they reached it, they dropped him (59).

Beanie Short was labeled as just a common horse thief (5), as a person who would steal meat (5), and as a prankster who would do things that at worst would be labeled ornery. For example, he was known to cut open feather beds and drag them through the houses strewing feathers everywhere (5), and to break into houses and cut woven cloth from looms (28, 38). Short and his gang would take any amount of money on any occasion (35).

There are no written records to corroborate the many murders supposedly committed by Short and his men, but to a great majority of people who still talk of Short, he is remembered basically as a killer. In all fairness to Short's name, it should be pointed out that some of the details of one or more murders ascribed to him tend to contain the same basic narrative elements, thus reiterating the possibility of a prolific interplay of the narrative elements in the traditional legends that evolve and revolve within the Beanie Short cycle. This has already been pointed out in the involuntary rider episode. Consider one more example of this phenomenon, which adequately illustrates the notion of folk association and the transfer of details from one situation to another. Beanie apparently killed both Sam Biggerstaff and John Martin, but under circumstances so similar that one is led to suspect that oral-traditional accounts of both murders rely heavily upon an event that happened in only one instance, but has been employed to give flavor and cohesiveness to the other account. The story of Biggerstaff's death goes like this:

Sam Biggerstaff lived in the hollow where Fred Coe lives. Biggerstaff looked down the hollow and saw Beanie. The people said he (Biggerstaff) had better leave or Beanie would kill him. Biggerstaff said he wouldn't leave! Beanie rode up and Biggerstaff shot his horse from under him, and the horse fell on the left hand of Beanie. And he got his gun with his right hand and killed Biggerstaff. Biggerstaff shot first; Beanie wasn't in the habit of missing (22).

Frank Biggerstaff (3) related how one of his Biggerstaff ancestors (probably Sam) was killed by Beanie, although there seems to be no connection with the above event.

> Biggerstaff started to get some bark to bottom chairs, or to hang meat. Beanie killed him down there before he started up the hollow. He killed him to get his money (48).

This fragmented account may indeed be a description of the way Biggerstaff actually died. The other testimonies claim that the person who wounded Short's horse was a Martin, either John or Jim. (The choice of the first name is not a clear-cut one.) Toll Dodson (21) almost a centenarian, had heard the story this way:

> John Martin shot his (Short's) horse in the neck and broke its neck, and the horse fell on him (Beanie Short). And he (Short) shot John and that horse a-layin' on him.
>
> They were fightin' cause that'us in time of the war, and he was jist a-killin' anything he could come up with. He was jist takin' all the money he could.
>
> Martin lived where Fred Coe lives. He was killed right at the corner of John Martin's house. They all (the Martin family) had peas and Irish potatoes for dinner. And Martin said that he'd not eat too many, for if Beanie 'ud come and shoot him that evening he'd be so heavy to carry.

A lifelong resident of that immediate portion of Turkey Neck Bend, told the story of the death of Martin in a manner that defended the action of Short:

> Beanie had ridden up to the house of John Martin and was threatening him when Martin spoke out and said, "Beanie, why are we arguing? We shouldn't have anything against each other."
>
> Beanie said, "Well, if you feel that way, I'll leave you alone."
>
> Beanie started to ride off and Martin then shot at Beanie but killed the horse instead. The horse fell and pinched Short beneath it. He then reached his left hand behind his back around to his gun on his right hip, then shot and killed Martin.
>
> It was a clear-cut case of self-defense, but on the tombstone of Martin on the Fred Coe place, it reads: "Assassinated by Southern Rebels." [9]

With the lapse of one hundred years plus, identity has been obscured to the extent that the real victim could not be identified were it not for the tombstone inscription that virtually points to Martin. One cannot explain the phenomenon of displacement or

---

[9] Informant identity withheld on request. Informant 25 felt that Martin's first name was Joe.

the transference of identity in the folk approach to history. It may be that a fallen warrior who, though pinned under a horse, could still fire a gun in self-defense formed a motif that was adaptable to similar situations. It may very well be that motifs are born in such a manner, then transmitted both horizontally, as was the Martin-Biggerstaff situation, and vertically across the years. We have on file examples of events dating from the early 1800's which contain narrative elements that were utilized to describe identical situations that occurred three-quarters of a century later to a descendant of the original person. It is our belief that the core of truth in a historical narrative is a constant factor surrounding an actual event, and that sensational episodes are interchanged to lend embellishment when needed to make a good story and to guarantee perpetuation through oral channels. This was and is a vital part of the folk historic process.

Sam Sartin and his daughter Louise of the Willow Shade community provide us with an excellent example of the tenacity and cohesiveness of certain oral traditions within family circles. Their accounts of one of Beanie Short's robberies were told eleven years apart in separate places and to different collectors, yet the similarities of content and narrative style are remarkable. In 1956 the daughter told it like this:

My grandmother, Mrs. Polly Jane Williams Sartin, used to tell this story of Bean Short, who was what she called a "rebel." He had a gang who, during the Civil War, went to the homes and robbed the people of everything they could find. Grandmother was five years old at the time and was sleeping on a trundle bed. One night her mother was alone in the house with the children, when she heard Bean Short's gang riding down the road. They jumped the yard fence with horses and rode up to the door, demanding that she let them in. She pretended that there was no one there, until Bean Short yelled," I know you are in there, and if you don't open up, I'm going to burn the house down." He promised he wouldn't harm them if she would let them come in. They ransacked the house and were unable to find any money. They told Great-grandmother if she didn't give them some money, they would burn the house. She insisted that there was no money, and one of the men took the shovel and got it full of coals and threw them under the beds. Grandmother had a new pair of shoes and she yelled, "Don't you burn my shoes."

My great-uncle was seven years old. A short while before he had been in the barn loft, where some guns were hidden, and had accidentally shot himself in the neck. He was seriously ill, and the doctor and all the friends and relatives had given him money. He told them where to find it, and they poured it down on the floor and scrambled after it just like dogs. He had thirty dollars, and Great-grandmother had some jewelry in the box. Great-grandmother begged them not to take her rings and brooch her mother had given her. They just laughed and took it all. She put out the fire, and after they had searched the house and had taken everything they wanted, they left. Later my great-grandmother saw Bean Short's wife wearing her brooch (48).

Sam Sartin's 1965 version was related in the following manner:

During the Civil War on Meshack Creek in Monroe County, the Bean Short gang come to the Lem Williams home, where his wife and small children were alone. They jumped the fences with their horses, and came to the door and knocked with their guns, and demanded Mrs. Williams to open the door. She at first pretended to be asleep, but when they started trying to tear down the door, she finally let them in. They demanded money and she told them they didn't have any. They shoved coals out of the fireplace onto the floor and threatened to burn the house. One small child about five years old was sleeping in a trundle bed. She had a new pair of fancy shoes and seeing the coals getting close to her shoes exclaimed, "You'd better not burn my shoes." The oldest child, an eight year old boy had accidentally shot himself in the neck. The wound was so painful that when the doctor dressed it, the doctor and all the boy's friends gave him money. He had saved about $40, which at that time was a small fortune. He had the money hidden in a small box along with his mother's jewelry. Believing that they were going to burn the house, the boy told the gang where the money was hidden. They poured it out on the floor along with the jewelry and fought over it like animals. Mrs. Williams begged them to give her a brooch that had been her mother's. They laughed at her pleadings. Years later she met Bean Short's wife on the street in Tompkinsville and she was wearing the brooch.

A bit of humor was added to the Beanie Short legend when he forced Isham Kidwell, resident of the Meshack community (53), to eat six or more hot puddings. In the words of Louise Sartin (48):

My grandmother's aunt and her husband lived alone during the war. And he was unable to fight. And she was expecting a lot of company one weekend, and had baked six or eight puddings. Bean Short's gang came by one day and they had ransacked the house for everything to eat, or money, or—and so forth. And they decided it was too many puddings to have at one time and probably she had poisoned them, and was hoping they'd come by and she could feed them to them. So they said that before they'd eat any of them they'd try them out on her husband; and if they didn't kill him, that they'd eat them. And they practically choked the poor man to death stuffing pudding down him before she could convince them that she was expecting company and that the puddings were really all right. And he was quite choked when the gang left.[10]

10 Lee Graves (25) claimed that the stuffing or poking was done with the barrel of a pistol. Informants 35, 37, 38, 42, 53, and 59 also told of the pudding episode. These accounts of forced eating are quite analogous with one in which

DEATH OF BEANIE SHORT

Hatred for Beanie Short grew as the war wore on and as his list of criminal acts mounted to an inconceivable proportion. Finally, in May, 1865, Short and men killed two, three, or four young men of the local area in rapid succession, perhaps within a two-day span, and many of the river occupants banded together to eliminate their common nemesis. The people relate the series of events leading to Short's death in the following manner:

> My grandfather Stockton was killed by Beanie Short. It was rumored that he was taken out with his hands tied in back and was killed by Beanie Short.
> Cloyd's Landing is the same graveyard my grandfather is buried in, in an unmarked grave. He was killed with Cary and Murray (41).

Another recalled this story:

> Beanie killed Marion Cary and Will Stockton about ten miles from the Cumberland River. He killed them under a big white oak tree about 400 yards from the house where my sister was born. The big tree is still there (11).

A high school student had heard her people talk of the cruel fate of Stockton and Cloyd:

> Two men, Stockton and Cloyd, were hiding out in 1865 in a house on the J. F. Butler place in the lower end of Noah Hollow. They had been there a week and were cooking their own meals.
> Beanie Short and Ashlock slipped over one night and captured them. They tied them up and cut off their ears, then took them across the river one mile away and killed them. The two are buried in the same grave in Salt Lick Bend (28).

A resident of Washes Bottom may have given a clue to the deaths of Stockton and the other when he called them spies:

> Mr. Stockton and Marion Cary and Murray were spies and Beanie found out about it and went hunting these men and found them in this house and took them across the river about Horace (Forest?) Biggerstaff's above the bluff and tied their hands and shot them and piled them up in the road.
> They cut their ears off before they ever took them out of the house, though, and the blood stain is still on the floor (7).

Jesse James forced a sheriff to eat a handbill advertising for James's arrest, then forced the residue down the lawman's throat with a pistol barrel. And Pancho Villa (or one of his men) used a similar weapon to poke horse manure down a captive's throat during the Mexican revolution. (Information about James and Villa was supplied by Rod Roberts, Cooperstown, N. Y.)

An occupant of Salt Lick Bend placed the death of Marion Cary at the same place but under different conditions:

> Cary and a bunch had ganged up at Hanse's grocery store [in Salt Lick Bend] at the head of the bluff, called Biggerstaff Bluff.
> Beanie and Ashlock seen two men and they followed them down the road to rob them. The people on the bluff heard the shots, and thought that both men were killed. But only one was killed when they went to see. Then they went down the bluff and there Cary hung. He had been shot, too, and hung to a mulberry tree. The tree was there 'til about ten years ago (3).[11]

On the morning that they were destined to die in their sleep that night, Short and Bill Ashlock [12] hid their stolen loot taken throughout the war years, somewhere near Kettle Creek—perhaps for all eternity—and rode toward Black's Ferry, located on the banks of the Cumberland River some four miles to the north. The date was May 4, 1865.[13] En route, the two desperadoes met an old colored man trudging down the road. Short stopped and pulled his gun intending to kill him but changed his mind when the old fellow pleaded and begged for his life. Either prophetically (18) [14] or out of anger, Short let him go free with the statement, "This is the last Nigger we will ever see" (56). Whether before or after, this encounter must pass unexplained, but during milking hours that morning Beanie and Ashlock reined up at the home of Aunt Margaret Richardson, who was still at her milking chores. She cautioned Beanie with the statement, "You are going to get killed the way you're a-doing" (58). Perhaps to chide Mrs. Richardson, Short "made the horse jump the draw bars of the fence," and rode away boasting:

---

11 Mrs. Isham Monday (38) corroborated this account: "They hung somebody right down there just north of Black's Ferry."

12 Of the twenty-one informants who discussed Short's death, twenty claimed that his partner was Ashlock; the other said that the companion was a Huff (57).

13 We cannot be absolutely certain when Short and Ashlock died, for there is no stone marker at their grave. On the basis of tradition, however, everything points to May 4 (or May 5 at the latest), for it seems safe to infer that Cary and Murray were killed by Short and Ashlock one day earlier. Cary and Murray were killed May 3, 1865 (tombstone inscription). Thus if telescoping and association have not clouded the legend—and we feel that such is not the case—then May 4 is the date Short and Ashlock died.

14 Mr. O. L. Coffey (18) said, "Beanie Short said that he knew that he was going to die because he had a premonition he could hear nails being driven into his coffin." This has the earmarks of a folk belief, but we found no recorded parallels.

I'll rosin my fiddle and draw my bow;
I'll make myself welcome wherever I go (58).[15]

It is claimed that Short and Ashlock had planned to spend the night at the home of Dr. Sam Moore in Black's Ferry,[16] and then "give the Judio community hell tomorrow" (7, 8).

The two guerrillas rode into Dr. Moore's place just before sundown that day. They fed their horses in his barn, ate supper with him (40), then went upstairs and went to sleep (30, 40, 59). In the words of Susie Taylor Moore, "Beanie was eating supper at the doctor's house, and some woman put something in his coffee which made him drowsy. Beanie went upstairs to bed and was killed" (35; also 30, 45).

Not long after the two men had fallen into a deep sleep, about sixty Union soldiers rode up, according to an informant who got his information from a man who was working for Dr. Moore at the time Short was killed (59). Others variously claim that the protagonists were home guardsmen (57), Union guerrillas, and bushwhackers (35), or a mob of all sorts (3, 7, 19, 21, 30, 41), who rode up and enquired for Short and Ashlock.

The killers-to-be were told by Dr. Moore that Short and Ashlock

[15] This episode seems to be a wandering anecdote. The Clay Co., Tenn., desperado Clure Williams on his way to his death in Tompkinsville, Monroe Co., Ky., Oct. 7, 1896, supposedly sang a stanza of "More Pretty Girls than One." (See D. K. Wilgus and Lynwood Montell, "Clure and Joe Williams: Legend and Blues Ballad," *JAF*, LXXXI [1968], 306.) Beanie Short was not singing a portion of "Rosin the Beau," but rather a stanza often found in the lyric variously titled "Jack o' Diamonds," "Drunkard's Hiccoughs," "Pretty Polly," "Rye Whiskey," etc. (See *The Frank C. Brown Collection of North Carolina Folklore*, ed. Newman Ivey White et al., III [Durham, N.C., 1952], 80–81; V [1962], 44–45.) Invariably set to the "Wagoner's Lad" form of the "Todlen Hame" tune family, the song has been collected throughout the United States and has even been taken up in "Cajun" tradition. "Travailler c'est trop dur" contains a translation of the stanza Short supposedly sang:

Je monte sur mon cheval et je prends mon violon,
Je prends mon archet et je joue ma vielle valse.

(*Sampler of Louisiana Folksongs*, Louisiana Folklore Society LSF 1201, 12″ LP, collected and edited by Harry Oster.) But the most significant reference for Beanie Short's performance is "The Bushwacker's Song," collected in North Carolina in 1922 (*Frank C. Brown Collection*, III, 458). The song is associated with Civil War deserters in Montgomery Co., N.C., and includes the "I'll tune up my fiddle" stanza. The report that the captain of the Owens' Fort bushwackers sang the song certainly strengthens its association with Short.

[16] Virtually all the testimonies indicated that Black's Ferry was the place where Short and Ashlock were killed, and specifically in the house belonging to Dr. Sam Moore. Four informants claimed that the incident occurred at a Dr. Black's. This is easily explained, however, for Dr. Black, after whom the community was named, had owned the house at an earlier date.

were asleep upstairs (22, 59). At gunpoint, they forced a member of the household to walk upstairs ahead of them, holding a lamp (22, 31, 35, 38) or lantern (5, 59) in his hand, to get the guns of the sleeping men (5, 11, 24, 51). Although most testimonies claim that the guide was Moore himself, there were three persons (30, 37, 59) who claimed that it was one of Moore's slaves. Beanie and Ashlock, who were sleeping with their pistols hung over the bedposts, did not awaken immediately. Some say that Short was shot and killed while asleep (21, 59),[17] but it is generally felt that he knew what was taking place. One informant claimed that "he raised up on bed when they shot him, then fell over in the floor" (58). Another said, "They shot Beanie in the temple, and he jumped up and crawled around the floor and died" (51). Still another informant testified, "Beanie was shot through the heart the first shot, but he managed to raise up. He got his gun from under his pillow and fired one wild shot. He immediately was riddled with bullets" (56). A fourth person said, "Bean Short jumped up in the bed and made for his pistol, and they shot him. They say blood's there 'til this day" (37; also 38).

It may be that Ashlock never moved when his brains were shot out and blood from the gaping wound splattered against the wall (51, 59). It is generally felt, however, that Ashlock awoke and grabbed for his pistol. One person claimed: "Ashlock run around the wall, and that streak of blood was on the wall that come out of him. And that blood was there as long as that house stood there; never did go away" (21). In the graphic words of Mrs. Myrtle Kerr (30):

His blood is in the corner whar he run across the floor and hunkered down over thar. Why it's on that wall down thar now when it rains.

---

17 There is an interesting although incongruous story that claimed Beanie's companion heard the men downstairs, then dressed as a woman in order to escape. Mrs. Leon Curtis (19) recalled it like this: "Well, Bean Short was killed in Cumberland County. And the men that came there to get him at night —he was upstairs. And the man that was there with him was afraid, and he came down and dressed in some women clothes. He was playing in the fire with a bonnet on to make them think that he was a woman. And when Beanie fired his pistol, the men saw him and killed him."

This is a good example of a local historical legend that has been garbed with a motif plucked from a migratory legend. A story found in Richard M. Dorson's *Negro Folktales in Michigan* (Cambridge, Mass.: Harvard University Press, 1956), pp. 98–99, contains the account of an escapee who disguises himself as a woman; Dorson lists additional occurrences on p. 218, n. 63. To that list add Montell, *The Saga of Coe Ridge*, p. 117n.

The oral accounts do not agree on the source of the ineradicable bloodstain. The fifteen accounts that mention the stubborn bloodstain are divided in opinion over whether it was Short's or Ashlock's blood that caused it. All testimonies claim that the stain could not be removed by repeated scrubbings nor by the passing of time. It became brighter each time it rained. Practically all informants claimed to have seen the stain and we personally saw the dark splotch allegedly the ineradicable bloodstain remaining from that day. It would be sheer folly to attempt to cite every recorded instance of the ineradicable bloodstain motif (Thompson number E422.1.11.5.1), but the three instances described in this paper, plus others uncovered by us in doing research for this work, tend to dwarf the references listed in both the Thompson and Baughman indexes. Generally speaking, the name of the person whose blood caused the stain is missing while other details are fairly complete. In still other cases, there is only a mention of the stubborn bloodstain.[18] The legend of Beanie Short places the bloodstain in proper historical perspective, however, and capably demonstrates how a folklore motif can be plucked from one narrative situation and easily transplanted into another one.

In light of the following story, there can be little doubt but that one or both men bled profusely:

> Mrs. Moore set by the children's bed that night. And they went up and went there to burn the doctor's house to kill them as they came out.
> Dr. Moore begged them not to do that. And they told him if he'd go in front of them and hold the light, why they wouldn't burn the house.
> Mrs. Moore set by the children's bed that night. They were downstairs in the room below where they were. And the doctor went in front and the men behind 'em would say, "Don't molest the doctor. Don't molest the doctor."
> And as they got in the room where Short was at he was asleep but he reached up overhead—and he had the pistol up there—reached for it, and they shot him just as he reached for it.
> And Mrs. Moore said she set by the bed all night. And at daylight she reached over in the bed to get some of the children's clothes and she put her hand in a puddle of blood where it had run down through the ceiling (12).

18 The already extensive bibliography of ineradicable bloodstain motifs (Thompson E422.1.11.5.1; Baughman E422.1.11.5.1(a) and E422.1.11.5.1(e)) may be extended by adding the fifteen additional references to printed materials on file in the Folklore Archives at the University of California, Los Angeles.

The bodies of Short and Ashlock were filled with bullets, then apparently abused by the killers. One informant claimed that he'd heard Old Shang Bill Cloyd boast, "Yeah, hot damn, we shot 'um 'til their hide wouldn't hold shucks" (35). In the words of another, "The men that killed them stripped the clothes off Beanie. One took his boots, and one his pistol—just divided up his clothes as souvenirs" (46). Still another told of the debauchery in these terms:

My grandma Dodson said that they beat their heads into a jelly up thar and then Dr. told them he was done dead. He begged them not to hit him anymore. "They're dead! They're dead!" he said.

Said they set the featherbed afire (with gunfire) and drug them out in the field and they burned up out there. Said you couldn't get your breath and the next morning because of the stench of the bodies (3; also 40).

Two additional testimonies state that the bodies were left in the house overnight. One informant claimed that his grandfather Richardson was selling groceries at Black's Ferry at the time Short was killed. He went over and spent the night with the two bodies (26). The other told how William Cain went to the house the following morning to get the bodies. Cain, it seems, had been told by a group of men to "have a wagon ready and wait at the gap; and when they had killed them, someone would come back and tell him" (33). Cain, a lad of about fourteen years, and a companion learned of the news and went to get the bodies. Cain "was afraid someone would shoot them while they were coming through the gap, so he got down on the tongue of the wagon between the two oxen that were pulling the wagon, and rode through. They went to the house and went upstairs and got Ashlock and Beanie" (33).

Ashlock and Short were taken to a small family graveyard located on the banks of the Crawford Branch of Kettle Creek by the barn on the present Wheeler Kerr farm.[19] There they were buried in the same grave, maybe even in the same homemade coffin (30). One is inclined to agree with Beanie's sister, who for years after his death would frequently utter: "Pore Beanie, he shore left this world in a mighty hard shape" (3).

The death of Beanie Short did not satisfy his assassins. After they had killed him, a group of the men led by Jack Pruitt and

---

19 Virtually every informant told that the two men were buried "on Kettle Creek." The real question is thus centered on the actual location of the graves, and we are satisfied, on the basis of oral testimonies and archaeological findings, that the burial site was on the present Wheeler Kerr farm.

B. Capps went on down to Kettle Creek and killed Beanie's dog, which, according to an informant, could tell all the guerrillas apart (30). Additionally, they forced the informant's grandparents to tell them where Beanie's fiddle and guns were (30). The lady of the house saw the men coming and hid the fiddle under the featherbed, but Pruitt forced entry into the house and found the fiddle anyway (51).[20]

It may be that the men who killed Short and Ashlock "died harder" when their time came than either of the two. At least B. Capps did, according to Myrtle Kerr (30):

> My mother laid Beanie's death on Old B. Capps. But when Capps died, we tried to keep her from goin' up there. But she said no; she wanted to hear what he had to say when he come to die for what he had done to Beanie.
>
> She went on up thar. Well, 'fore he died that evening, said he was a-rolling and a-turning. Said he said to her—my mother's name was Sarah—said, "Sarah, I see Beanie."
>
> She said, "Is he a-botherin' you?"
>
> (Oh, she didn't like him. That's what she was a-wantin' to hear, you know.)
>
> "Yeah, yes I see him. He's thar."
>
> "I can't help you none. That's between you and God!"
>
> "Right up thar hangs his pistol."
>
> "I know it, and right out yonder hangs his knife that you took off him." And says, "You left him with his shirttail hung over his face, naked to the world. Took all his clothes but his shirt turned over his face."
>
> Old Jack Pruitt tossed and all when he died, too. And he was mammy's brother-in-law! [21]

BURIED TREASURE

The actual extent of Short's stolen wealth is not known, but it was reputedly a goodly-sized fortune. A relative of Beanie Short com-

---

20 We wonder if the tale of Jack Pruitt's obtaining Short's fiddle is related to the story of how Franz Prewitt (the spelling in the report was phonetic) of neighboring Cumberland Co. obtained Joe Coleman's fiddle in 1847 by playing the condemned man's tune so well. (See Wilgus, "Fiddler's Farewell: The Legend of the Hanged Fiddler," *Studia Musicologica* (Academiae Scientiarum Hungaricae), VII (1965), 206.

21 The implied curse that was placed on the murderers of Beanie Short is reminiscent of the curse placed on the men who lynched the McDonald boys in Menominee, Mich., in 1891, and on those who lynched a half breed family of ruffians on Lookout Bridge in northeastern California in 1901. See Richard M. Dorson, "The Debate Over the Trustworthiness of Oral Traditional History," *Volksüberlieferung, Festschrift für Kurt Ranke* (Göttingen: Verlag Otto Schwartz, 1968), p. 33.

mented, "I am satisfied that he had thirty or forty thousand dollars. . . . You see, he was in that bunch that robbed the train up north of here . . .—somewhere I suppose in northern Kentucky. It was figured that that's where Beanie got his wealth" (16; also 33).[22] Other informants did not place an estimate on the amount of Short's wealth, preferring instead to quantify it in terms of bulk rather than actual amounts. One person claimed that Beanie Short's brother told him that "they had their saddle pockets full of money the morning before they got killed that night" (45). Another claimed that Short had "a half-bushel of gold"; (30) still others noted that the money was placed in a small tin trunk (5, 6) or fruit jar (20, 40, 46, 47, 51); and in the epitome of poetic descriptiveness, one lady called it "a pot of gold" (30). Whatever the amount, Beanie Short himself was best able to know. In his own words to his wife Missouri, Short said, "If I live 'til the war is over I'll have enough to take care of me" (30).

There is no question but that Short cached his stolen money, but the actual hiding place remains the big secret to this day. Two informants felt that it was stored in Wells Woods on Kettle Creek (16, 51), and a third said that the place was Sugar Camp Hollow on the Wells's place (30). Three others specified that a cave was the hiding place (33, 60, 57). Johnny Killman (33), for example, stated: "A day or two before they were killed, they came to this cave and got a blanket and tied it up and put their money in it. And the money was never found after that." And Beanie's own sister, Serilda Murley, was known to have stated that Beanie had told her that he "could stand on her porch on the banks of Kettle Creek and almost see the cave where his money was put" (25, 52).

There is nothing incongruous with the idea that perhaps the cave was located in Wells Woods. Yet, one must reckon with a body of traditions that indicates he hid the money near the William Short homeplace adjacent to Short's Chapel graveyard located on Coe Ridge about two miles from Kettle Creek. One of Beanie Short's great nieces claimed that "he had lots of money and hid it down yonder close to Short's Chapel. They's people who went

---

[22] Jesse James robbed virtually every bank and train in Kentucky, so claim the folk. One of the writers has personally heard it said on more than one occasion, "Jesse James robbed a bank up north of here." One is struck by the indefiniteness of such a statement. Yet, in another fine example of legend displacement, two informants said of Beanie Short, "He robbed a bank in northern Kentucky." There are no articulate legends to support the claim about Short. Most likely, Short was never in northern Kentucky, and he certainly robbed no trains, for, living in the heart of a fifteen-county area of Kentucky and Tennessee which has never boasted of iron horses, Short would have known nothing of their operation during his brief lifetime.

there and hunted and dug" (51; also 30, 40). Another informant interrupted, "Oh, my goodness! We used to couldn't keep shovels and grubbin' hoes around here. Somebody'ud come and carry'um off to the woods and dig for Beanie Short's money" (16).

Judging from the abundance of testimonials regarding the location of the now fabled treasure, it may be that Mrs. Edith Williams (58) was right when she stated, "It was claimed that he had lots of money and that it was buried at *different* places." Also, on the basis of the traditional accounts, it would appear that no one ever found Short's loot (60), regardless of its location. F. N. Williams (59), however, felt that Ike Short, Beanie's nephew, got all his money. Another informant, who prefers to remain anonymous, claimed that it was found by Hiram Wells, owner of Wells Woods. Even Short's own niece, plus a person who lives near Kettle Creek, cited evidence that indicates his money was found (30, 40).

THE BEANIE SHORT SONG

One might have expected that the legendary exploits of the rebel raider and his dramatic death would have given rise to a ballad. Such does not seem to have been the case. Instead Beanie Short is celebrated in a song, the variant stanzas of which can never have formed even so fluid a narrative as that of a blues ballad.[23] But the song is not unimportant in reflecting community memory of and attitude toward the guerrilla. Indeed the song was more than controversial in the area.

> My mother never did want nobody to sing that. Used to I reckon when she and other girls go to a dance, you know, have the music and they'd play that. And she never would want to hear it. I've dist heard her talk about it (20).

Another informant told of his brother's prank:

> My brother he done a feller worse one time about Beanie Short! And this feller was in the bunch that killed Beanie. And they's a tune, "Old Beanie Short," and this feller wuz a fiddler, and my brother asked him to play "Old Beanie Short."
> [Montell:] "Did he play it?"
> [Tim Coe:] "I don't suppose he did!" (16)

Reminiscent of the tale of a minstrel singing "Jesse James" being struck by Bob Ford's sister [24] is the account of a relative of Beanie

---

23 We have discussed to some extent the blues ballad form in Wilgus and Montell, "Clure and Joe Williams," pp. 295–315.
24 Vance Randolph, *Ozark Folksongs*, II (Columbia, Mo., 1948), 132.

Short offering a Negro performer twenty dollars to sing the song again, "fixin' to kill" him if he did (1).

"Beanie Short," at least as now performed, consists of one to three rigidly patterned stanzas, invariably set to the fiddle tune "Sally Goodin," [25] of which the following is an example (37):

With few and explicable exceptions, a stanza of "Beanie Short" consists of:

> Old Beanie Short,
> He'll never be forgotten,

followed by a comment on his activities or on not his death, but his status after death. A few examples:

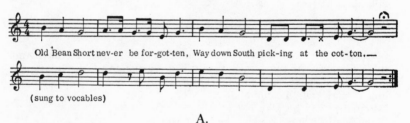

Old Bean Short nev-er be for-got-ten, Way down South pick-ing at the cot-ton.—

(sung to vocables)

A.

2. Old Bean Short,   3. Old Bean Short,
   Never be forgotten,   Never be forgotten,

---

25 *Frank C. Brown Collection,* III, 126–127; IV, 69–70. The tune is reported to have been played by Confederate fifers (*ibid.,* III, 127). It has been issued on innumerable commercial recordings.

Hole in his head	Buried down South
To hold a bale of cotton.	With his bones all rotten. (48)

On another occasion the informant recited the text as follows:

Old Bean-ie Short 'll nev - er be for-got-ten Hole, in his head 'n his brains all rot-ten.

B.

1. Old Bean Short
Ne'er be forgot,
Way down South
Pickin' out cotton.

2. Old Bean Short
Ne'er be forgot
Hole 'n his head
To hold a bale of
cotton

3. Old Bean Short,
Ne'er be forgot,
Way down South
With bones all
rott'n.

C.

Old Bean Short,
He'll never be forgotten,
He's gone South
On greenback a-trottin'. (14) [26]

If not the origin, at least the development of the Beanie Short song is clear. At square dances or play parties, the musicians or players improvised textual phrases to complete the stanza beginning "Old Bean Short/Never be forgotten." We have never been able to record such performances, but the evidence points rather to a fiddle-song or square dance setting than to a play-party development, as the textual material seems too limited to have suited the needs of the "singing-dancing throng." Indeed, in view of the legends of Short's activities, the paucity of comment in the song is surprising.

The insistence that Short will "never be forgotten" has quite possibly been restrictive through the tyranny of rhyme. Thus we find only *cotton, rotten,* and *trottin'*. Changes are rung on a few themes: Way down south Beanie picked or stole cotton; his brains or bones are rotten; he went to hell a-trottin'. The most specific reference to his death is that he had a "hole in his head/to hold a bale of cotton." And the only possible reference to his legendary treasure is that he was "on greenback a-trottin'," apparently referring to paper money. Rather than recounting his exploits, the song reflects the community attitude: "Damn his soul!" It is this attitude more than anything else that causes us to doubt the statement of an informant (30) that Beanie himself was responsible for

---

[26] Variants were also collected from informants 1, 2, 9, 12, 17, 20, 25, 27, 29, 30, 39, 40, 43, 45, 51, 53, 56, 61.

the ur-form of the song. Himself a fiddler, Short might well have created jocular derogatory stanzas on his activities, but the content of the surviving texts makes the conjecture unlikely.

The Beanie Short song is lyric, not epic. It depends for its meaning, its intelligibility, on the legend itself, though the song may stimulate the preservation of legend. If Beanie Short is not forgotten, his memory will depend on the survival of the *Sage*. Without them the song may live, but Beanie will join the shadowy figures of "Sally Goodin," "Marthis Campbell," and "Betty Larkin." [27]

CONCLUSION

The story of Beanie Short tells us something of the life in a small geographical portion of southern Kentucky where the tension of the war years was especially heavy because of the impact of fratricidal conflicts. It is not surprising to find divergent oral traditional accounts of the same events in Short's life. What is significant is that these narratives nonetheless *do tell* of the same events, even if in somewhat varying detail. Thus while the embellishments must be carefully and cautiously scrutinized, and while patterning, telescoping, and displacement may distort historical facts in oral traditions, there should be little doubting of the always present core of veracity.

The song of Beanie Short is a vital part of the story of Short's activities throughout the turbulent years of the American Civil War, but it cannot be considered as important as the legends associated with his name. Yet, without a song text uncovered during the 1950's, we would not be permitted a microscopic insight into the effect the Civil War had on the folk culture of the Upper Cumberland a century ago.

INDEX OF INFORMANTS

1. George Allred (Negro, 89), Meshack, Monroe County, Kentucky, August 12, 1961.
2. Hugh Bennett Bedford (ca. 80), Tompkinsville, Monroe County, February, 1958.
3. Frank Biggerstaff (62), Salt Lick Bend, Cumberland County, Kentucky, June 28, 1968; July 8, 1968.
4. Mrs. Maude Blythe (81), Judio, Cumberland County, July 8, 1968.

[27] For a possible identification of Betty Larkin, see Wilgus, "Fiddler's Farewell," pp. 200–201.

5. Keith Brewington (30), Judio, Cumberland County, July 8, 1968.
6. Mrs. Keith Brewington (30), Judio, Cumberland County, July 8, 1968.
7. J. F. Butler, Washes Bottom, Cumberland County, July 8, 1968.
8. Paul Butler, Washes Bottom, Cumberland County, July 8, 1968.
9. Mrs. W. F. Butler, Washes Bottom, Cumberland County, February, 1958.
10. Mrs. Capps (83), Ashlock, Cumberland County, July 8, 1968.
11. Frank Cary (70), Salt Lick Bend, Cumberland County, February, 1959.
12. Mrs. Frank Cary (ca. 70), Salt Lick Bend, Cumberland County, February, 1959.
13. Rebecca Cary (16), Temple Hill, Barren County, Kentucky, February, 1959.
14. T. K. Chism (ca. 85), Tompkinsville, Monroe County, February, 1958.
15. Lesie Coe, Jr. (Negro, 58), Kansas City, Kansas, June, 1962.
16. Tim Coe (74), Turkey Neck Bend, Monroe County, August 22, 1961.
17. Mrs. Tim Coe (72), Turkey Neck Bend, Monroe County, August 22, 1961.
18. O. L. Coffey (86), Burkesville, Cumberland County, July 15, 1968.
19. Mrs. Leon Curtis (65), Glasgow, Barren County, August 3, 1961.
20. Mrs. Mattie Davidson (79), Tanbark, Cumberland County, August 22, 1961; July 8, 1968.
21. Toll Dodson (100), Kettle, Cumberland County, July 8, 1968.
22. Cleo Finley (ca. 80), Turkey Neck Bend, Monroe County, July 8, 1968.
23. Deenie Glass (54), Judio, Cumberland County, July 15, 1968.
24. Joe Graves (ca. 45), Kettle, Monroe County, July 8; July 15, 1968.
25. Lee Graves (ca. 58), Tompkinsville, Monroe County, July 14, 1968.
26. Hascal Haile (55), Tompkinsville, Monroe County, August 22, 1961.
27. Eliza Kirkpatrick Hollingsworth (ca. 90), Meshack, Monroe County, July 8, 1968.
28. Jean Huddleston (16), Temple Hill, Barren County, February 17, 1959.
29. Porter A. Huddleston (ca. 85), Pea Ridge, Cumberland County, June 28, 1968.
30. Mrs. Myrtle Kerr (78), Judio, Cumberland County, August 15, 1961.
31. Tommie Kerr (ca. 40), Kettle, Cumberland County, July 15, 1968.
32. Willa Ann Kerr (Negro, ca. 78), Glasgow, Barren County, August, 1961.
33. Johnny Killman (74), Red Bank, Cumberland County, July 8, 1968; July 18, 1968.
34. Mrs. Johnny Killman (77), Red Bank, Cumberland County, July 8, 1968, July 18, 1968.
35. Price Kirkpatrick (88), Tompkinsville, Monroe County, August 21, 1961.
36. Robert "Bob" Kirkpatrick (89), Meshack, Monroe County, July 8, 1968.
37. Isham Monday (ca. 80), Cloyd's Ridge, Monroe County, November 27, 1959.
38. Mrs. Isham Monday (ca. 80), Cloyd's Ridge, Monroe County, November 27, 1959.
39. Mrs. Willie Montell (48), Rock Bridge, Monroe County, February 12, 1958.

40. Mrs. Susie Taylor Moore (78), Ashlock, Cumberland County, August 15, 1961; July 8, 1968.
41. Mrs. Ruth Stockton Murley (ca. 50), Washes Bottom, Cumberland County, July 8, 1968.
42. J. C. Newport (76), Tompkinsville, Monroe County, May 16, 1966.
43. Razzie Norris (ca. 60), Pea Ridge, Cumberland County, July 18, 1968.
44. Mrs. Eva Coe Peden (ca. 40), Glasgow, Barren County, August, 1961.
45. Bill Poindexter (77), Ashlock, Cumberland County, August 15, 1961.
46. Hunter Poindexter (61), Judio, Cumberland County, July 8, 1968.
47. Mrs. Hunter Poindexter (61), Judio, Cumberland County, July 8, 1968.
48. Mrs. Louise Sartin (31), Willow Shade, Metcalfe County, July 6, 1956.
49. Sam Sartin (ca. 65), Willow Shade, Metcalfe County, July, 1965.
50. Mrs. Jimmy Scott (Ab) (ca. 55), Kettle Creek, Monroe County, June 28, 1968.
51. Mrs. Etta Short (81), Tanbark, Cumberland County, August 22, 1961; July 8, 1968.
52. Fred Smith (ca. 75), Kettle Creek, Monroe County, June 28, 1968.
53. Mrs. Fred Smith (ca. 72), Kettle Creek, Monroe County, June 28, 1968.
54. Guy Spears (ca. 65), Kettle Creek, Monroe County, June 28, 1968.
55. Branceford Tooley (73), Meshack, Monroe County, June, 1964.
56. Mrs. Kate Tooley (Negro, 75), Tompkinsville, Monroe County, April 11, 1958.
57. Arnold Watson (68), Kettle, Cumberland County, July 15, 1968.
58. Mrs. Edith Williams (76), Black's Ferry, Monroe County, August 21, 1961; July 8, 1968.
59. Ferd N. Williams (80), Turkey Neck Bend, Monroe County, April 9, 1960; August 25, 1960.
60. Morris Williams (ca. 55), Black's Ferry, Monroe County, July 8, 1968.
61. Effie Wilson (43), Marrowbone, Cumberland County, May, 1957.

The Saint's Legend in the Pennsylvania German Folk-Culture

DON YODER, University of Pennsylvania

INTRODUCTION

The Pennsylvania German folk-culture, which was built up in the acculturation process between the emigrant cultures from the continent of Europe and the British Isles, was a mixed bag, a very mixed bag, a hybrid affair in which the elements that came into the culture from the "outside" were equally important with the elements that came with the German-speaking immigrants of the eighteenth century to colonial Pennsylvania. I have dealt at length with these aspects of hybridization in other papers,[1] and I am delighted to have the opportunity to present here my conclusions on one element in Pennsylvania German culture which can be almost wholly traced to the continent of Europe and to the German-language belt of Central Europe.

By saints' legends, I mean the specific knowledge of the legends of certain saints in and out of the traditional church year. Apart from specific legends, however, there was a partial survival and widespread reminiscence of the European saint system among the Pennsylvania Germans, in which names and days and functions of at least some of the European folk-saints continued in operation on American soil and, strangely enough, in a Protestant environment.

---

[1] "Pennsylvania German Folklore Research: An Historical Analysis," in Glenn G. Gilbert, ed., *The History of the German Language in America*, scheduled for publication in 1971 by the University of Texas Press. See also "Plain Dutch and Gay Dutch: Two Worlds in the Dutch Country," *The Pennsylvania Dutchman*, VIII:1 (Summer, 1956), 34–55.

The cult of the saints had developed in ancient Christianity
from the human need to have tangible, visible, human-scale patterns embodying the values central to one's society. When the saint
system flowered into full classic proportions in the Middle Ages,
not only were the saints individuals in which the values of medieval society were embodied, but they represented, especially for
the peasantry and lower strata of society, a manageable humanized
version of divinity. In the construction of the Christian plan of salvation by the early theologians, "the logic of popular piety," as
Mecklin puts it, "insisted that theology make central in its scheme
the work of the Savior-God Jesus, but the intellectuals demanded
that Jesus be raised to the level of the God of the universe, for
otherwise the Christian plan of salvation would lose its authori-
tativeness and its universal appeal" [2] The masses, however, were
unable to comprehend the Christian Myth as formulated by Au-
gustine, preferring and eventually getting a syncretistic "Christianity of the second rank." Hence they "gradually built their faith
around the cult of the saints. The cult of the Virgin in time came
to fill the gap left by Jesus, now remote and incomprehensible as a
member of the Trinity." This syncretism between theology, sacra-
mentarian cult, popular piety, and pagan survivals led to the universal popularity of the saint figure in the Middle Ages.

While the legendry of medieval sainthood was a creation largely
of the "Christianity of the second rank," it was legitimized and
used by the official Church. For the masses it expressed the aristocratic ideals of asceticism and world-denial and pointed here and
now to the paradisiacal world that was open to the common man
only after death. Also for the masses, the saints, as did the shrines
and holy places of pilgrimage and the church building itself, represented both a localization of divinity into tangible forms and a
concretizing of the divine and the holy which, according to Richard Weiss, is one of the marks of Catholic folk piety.[3] Where the
official Church could not keep pace with the human drive to create
usable local saint figures, the phenomenon of "folk-canonization"
operated.

---

[2] John M. Mecklin, *The Passing of the Saint: A Study of A Cultural Type*
(Chicago: University of Chicago Press, 1941), p. 15. The following quotation
in this paragraph is from pp. 13–15. For the ultimate origins of the saint in
ancient Christianity, see also the old standard works by the Bollandist Father
Delehaye, *Les Origines du culte des martyrs* (1912), *Les Légendes hagiographiques*
(1927), and *Sanctus* (1927).

[3] Richard Weiss, *Volkskunde der Schweiz: Grundriss* (Erlenbach-Zürich: Eugen
Rentsch Verlag, 1946), pp. 303–311.

At the time of the Protestant Reformation, the very nerve of the cult of the saints was cut by the reformers, and with it the veneration of the chief of saints, the kingpin of the system, the Virgin Mary. This retrenchment varied according to denomination, the Lutherans keeping much more of the official Catholic church year and its saints' days than the other Protestant groups, the Reformed churches and the Anabaptist sectarians. The canon for the purification of the church year of the Catholic saints' days was according to Albrecht Jobst, a pioneer German analyst of the relation between Protestantism and folk-culture, that "all specifically Catholic saints' days and festivals were set aside, because their pedigrees were not 'pure.' On the other hand, the festivals of the biblical saints, the apostles and the Virgin Mary were retained, in so far as they possessed 'pure' pedigrees, i.e., the gospel pericopes." [4]

This protestantizing of the church year was sharpened in the seventeenth century when an additional retrenchment came—in that period, for example, the Saint Nicholas cult of gift-bringer at Christmas was transferred to the *Christkind*. In the eighteenth century there was another cutback, when both Pietists and Rationalists, for different reasons, dropped other continuing aspects of medieval church life.

The Pennsylvania German folk-culture, which was built up in the eighteenth and early nineteenth century, reflects the passive continuance of much of the medieval Catholic world view and saint lore that marked the earlier European Protestantism, that is, the "Old" Protestantism before it was retreaded in the eighteenth century by Pietism and Rationalism. In the twentieth century, the specific knowledge of the saints' legends is of smaller consequence in Pennsylvania German culture than the general survival of bits and pieces of the European medieval saint complex that was so large a part of the pre-Reformation folk-mind. I shall organize my paper into three sections: (1) The Saint in Folk Medicine and Magic; (2) Transplanted European Saints' Legends; and (3) Native Analogues to the Saints' Legends.[5]

---

[4] Albrecht Jobst, *Evangelische Kirche und Volkstum: Ein Beitrag zur Geschichte der Volkskunde* (Stuttgart: Alfred Kröner Verlag, 1938), p. 64.

[5] Because of space limitations, I have omitted two additional sections of the original paper, (1) The Saint in the Pennsylvania German Calendar, which deals with the profusion of days, times, and customs associated with saint-lore in the Pennsylvania German folk-culture, and (2) The Saint in Pennsylvania German Onomastics, in which I discuss survivals of the European saint-complex in family names, personal names, place names, and church names. Both sections will be published as papers elsewhere.

THE SAINT IN FOLK MEDICINE AND MAGIC

In "powwowing" (*Brauchen, Braucherei*), Pennsylvania's continuing brand of occult folk-medicine, which uses charms in the attempt to heal the ills of man and beast, to quote the title of the
principal powwow book still in use,[6] the saints make a brief post-
Reformation appearance, occasionally trailing parts of their legends behind them.

Chief among the dramatis personae of the charm literature is
Saint Mary—*unsere liebe Jungfrau* or *die Mutter Gottes*—who
makes many appearances, sometimes alone, sometimes in company
with other New Testament figures. Principal among the latter is
Saint Peter, who seems to keep up a running conversation with
Mary in many of the formulas. Other biblical personages who serve
as saints in the folk-medical literature are *Tobit, Job, Pontius Pi-
late, "unsere liebe Sara,"* the *drey heilige Männer, Sadrach, Mesach*
and *Abednego, der liebe heilige Daniel, Annania, Azaria,* and
Misael, the four archangels (*Saint Michael, Saint Gabriel, Saint
Raphael,* and *Saint Uriel*), and last but not least, *Judas,* the anti-
saint. Above all stands the Blessed Trinity, *"die drei höchste Namen"* as the Pennsylvania powwower calls them, the Trinitarian
formula, without which terminal blessing, the powwow charm is
incomplete.

From the use of the saints, angels, archangels, Mary, and the
Trinity in the world of the folk-medical incantations and charms,
one gets a reminiscence, in Pennsylvania, across the Atlantic, and
four centuries after the Reformation, of the medieval *Weltbild* of
the heavenly hierarchies so frequently portrayed in Catholic art—
academic, popular, and folk.

Occasionally, too, bits of the saints' legends are imbedded within
the charm. For example, among the legends of Mary which are re-

---

6 John George Hohman, a Catholic emigrant who arrived in Philadelphia in
1802, published in 1819–1820 the single most influential volume of occult charms
in America, *Der Lang Verborgene Freund, oder Getreuer und Christlicher
Unterricht für Jedermann, enthaltend Wunderbare und probmässige Mittel
und Künste, sowohl für die Menschen, als das Vieh* (Reading, Pa., 1820). Translated into English in two separate translations as *The Long Lost Friend* (Harrisburg, 1846) and *The Long Hidden Friend* (Carlisle, 1863), the book has gone
through many editions in both English and German and has been used in occult
folk-medical practice far beyond the borders of the Pennsylvania German
counties. In my quotations from the book in this paper, I have used the third
German edition, published at Harrisburg, Pa., in 1840. The translations are
my own.

membered, at least in charm form, is that of the attempt to steal the baby Jesus. In a charm manuscript in my own collection,[7] dated 1816, from Berks County, Pennsylvania, appears the formula:

maria lig [lag] in Kindes banden da komen zwei Guden [Juden]
die wollen dass Kintlein Jesum ste[h]len
da schmach [sprach] Maria zu sangt petra Kind petra sprach
ich hab sie ge bunden wer mir her komt
mein guth zu ste[h]len der muss stehen wie Ein sack
und über sich sehen wie Ein bock und zehlen
alle sternen die an den himmel stehen und regen drapfen
und alle schneh flacken und stumbe und stecken
und muss stehen bis an den hellen Dag X X X

[Maria lay in childbed when two Jews came who wanted to steal the Baby Jesus. Maria said to Saint Peter, "Child." Peter said, "I have bound them. Whoever comes to me to steal my property must stand like a sack and look around like a buck and count all the stars that are in heaven and rain drops and all the snowflakes and stumps and sticks and must stand until daybreak. In the name of God the Father, the Son, and the Holy Ghost, Amen.]

To release the thief, in case one needs that detail of the procedure, one repeats the words:

Dieb leg ab was mein ist und was
dein ist und geh hin im Namen X X X

[Thief, lay down what is mine and [keep?] what is
thine and go forth in the name of God the Father,
the Son, and the Holy Ghost, Amen.]

Saint Peter, with his keys and powers of binding and loosing, was obviously a favorite saint in the charms relating to thieves and thievery. Another goes like this:

Ein Mittel, um zu machen, dass Diebe oder Diebinnen müssen stehen bleiben, und weder vor- noch rückwärts gehen können. * * *
O Petrus, o Petrus! nimm von Gott die Gewalt: Was ich binden werde mit dem Band der Christenhand, alle Diebe oder Diebinnen, sie mögen seyn gross oder klein, jung oder alt, so sollen sie von Gott gestellt seyn, und keiner keinen Tritt mehr vor oder hinter sich gehen [etc.].[8]

---

[7] This document, one of two purchased in Berks Co. in 1967, is signed by Peter Schles[s]man. The Schlessman family were immigrants of 1752, 1753, and 1773, from the county of Löwenstein-Wertheim in the Main valley up from Frankfurt. See Otto Langguth, "Pennsylvania German Pioneers from the County of Wertheim," trans. and ed. Don Yoder, in Pennsylvania German Folklore Society, XII (1947), 241–244, 262–266.

[8] Hohman, Der Lang Verborgene Freund (1840), p. 29.

[A formula for making thieves, male or female, to stand still, and not
to be able to move forwards or backwards. * * *

O Peter, O Peter! Take the power from God: What I bind with the
band of the Christian hand, all thieves, male or female, large or small,
young or old, thus shall they be stationed by God, and none shall move
a single step further forward or backward. etc.]

To loose the thief after this charm, two alternate methods are
listed, the first of which is: *"heiss ihm in Sanct Johannis Namen
fortgehen"*—"bid him depart in Saint John's name." So Saint John
has the power to loose what Peter binds.

One of the several postbiblical Catholic saints who appears in
the charm literature is Saint Laurence, appropriately on his grill.

Für das Verbrennen.
Unser lieber Herr Jesus Christ ging über Land, da sah er brennen
einen Brand; da lag St. Lorenz auf einem Rost. Kam ihm zu Hülf' und
Trost; Er hub auf seine göttliche Hand, und segnete ihn, den Brand;
Er hub, dass er nimmer tiefer grub und weiter um sich frass. So sey
der Brand gesegnet im Namen Gottes, des Vaters, des Sohnes und des
Heiligen Geistes. Amen.[9]

[For Burns.
Our dear Lord Jesus Christ went out walking, when he saw a fire
burning; there lay St. Laurence on a fire-grate. Came to help and
comfort him; He lifted up his divine hand and blessed it, the fire; He
signified that it must dig no deeper and eat no further round about.
So blessed be the fire in the name of God the Father, the Son, and
the Holy Ghost. Amen.]

The biblical figure Job appears in a charm versus sore mouth:

So ein Mensch die Mund' und Durchfäule hat, spreche man folgendes,
es hilft gewiss.
Job zog über Land, der hatt' den Stab in seiner Hand, da begegnete
ihm Gott der HErr, und sprach zu ihm: Job, warum traurest du so
sehr? Er sprach: Ach Gott, warum sollt ich nicht trauren? Mein Schlund
und mein Mund will mir abfaulen. Da sprach Gott zu Job: Dort in
jenem Thal, da fliesst ein Brunn, der heilet dir N.N. dein' Schlund
und dein' Mund im Namen Gottes des Vaters des Sohnes und des
heiligen Geistes. Amen.[10]

[When a person has a mouth and throat infection, say the following,
it will surely help.
Job went out walking, with his staff in his hand, when God the Lord
met him, and said to him: Job, why are you mourning so? He said: O
God, why should I not mourn? My mouth and my throat are rotting
away. Then God said to Job: There in that valley flows a spring which
heals you (here name the name of the patient) your mouth and your

---

[9] *Ibid.*, p. 53.
[10] *Ibid.*, p. 38.

throat in the name of God the Father, the Son, and the Holy Ghost. Amen.]

For burns and gangrene (*kalten und heissen Brand*), there is the curious formula that invokes "*Sanct Itorius.*"

Ein sehr gutes Mittel für den kalten und heissen Brand.
Sanct Itorius, res, ruf den Pest. Da kam die Mutter Gottes ihm zum Trost; sie reichte ihm ihre schneeweisse Hand, für den heissen und kalten Brand. X X X[11]

[A very good remedy for burns and gangrene.
St. Itorius, res, call the plague. Then the Mother of God came to comfort him; she offered him her snow-white hand, for burns and gangrene (literally, for the hot and the cold burning). In the name of God the Father, the Son, and the Holy Ghost. Amen.]

The anonymous "three holy men," probably Shadrach, Meshach, and Abednego of the Fiery Furnace incident in the book of Daniel, appear in a charm to stop burns:

Eine Cur, den Brand zu stillen.
Es giengen drey heiligen Männer über Land,
Sie segneten die Hitze und den Brand;
Sie segneten ihn, dass er nicht einfrisst;
Sie segneten ihn, dass er ihn ausfrisst. X X X[12]

[A cure to quiet a burn.
Three holy man went out walking. They blessed the heat and the burning. They blessed it to keep it from eating further. They blessed it that it would be consumed. In the name of God the Father, the Son, and the Holy Ghost. Amen.]

A curious picture is presented in the charm that contains the reference to "Sara": *Unsere liebe Sara zieht durch das land; sie hat einen feurigen, hitzigen Brand in ihrer Hand*[13] [Our dear Sara goes through the land; she has a glowing, fiery coal in her hand].

St. Cyprian is invoked in a charm against witchcraft:

So ein Mensch oder Vieh verhext, wie ihm zu helfen.
Drey falsche Zungen haben dich geschlossen, drey heilige Zungen haben für dich gesprochen. * * *
Hat dich überritten ein Mann, so segne dich Gott, und der heilige Cyprian; hat dich überschritten ein Weib, so segne dich Gott und Maria Leib; hat dich bemühet ein Knecht, so segne ich dich durch Gott und das Himmelrecht; hat dich geführet eine Magd oder Dirn, so segne dich Gott und das Himmelgestirn [etc.].

---

11 *Ibid.*, p. 15.
12 *Ibid.*, p. 26.
13 *Ibid.*, p. 46.

[When man or beast is bewitched, how to help him.
Three false tongues have locked you, three holy tongues have spoken
for you. (These are of course the Trinity). * * *
If a man has ridden over you, bless you God and St. Cyprian; if a
woman has stepped over you, bless you God and Mary's womb; if a
hired man has given you trouble, I bless you by God and the law of
Heaven; if a hired girl or maid has led you astray, bless you God and
the constellations of Heaven etc.] [14]

And finally all the supernatural powers are invoked in a charm
against thieves, and we get a Pennsylvania version of the medieval
hierarchical universe. This is the charm: *Einen Dieb zu bannen,
dass er still stehen muss* (To charm a thief, so that he has to stand
still). This charm, which is valid only on Thursday, invokes the
power of the Trinity, and for good measure, thirty-three angels,
Maria, "dear Saint Daniel" (*der liebe, heilige Daniel*), Saint Peter,
and finally "all angelic hosts and all God's saints" (*alle Engel-
schaar, alle Gottes Heiligen*). Again, to release the unfortunate
thief, who has just been ordered "to count all the stones that are
on earth, and all the stars that are in heaven," is relatively simple—
tell him to be on his way, in Saint John's name (*Willst du ihm
aber des Bannes entledigen, so heiss ihn in Sanct Johannis Namen
fortgehen*).[15]

TRANSPLANTED EUROPEAN SAINTS' LEGENDS

Of the medieval saints' legends that have been transplanted intact,
none is more widespread nor more popular among the Pennsylvania Germans than the story of *die heilige Genoveva* (Saint Genoveva of Brabant).[16]

Although her hagiographical authentication is not so sure as
that of her namesake, Saint Geneviève (Genoveva) of Paris, and
although German scholars are constantly in opposition to one another, as this crowd seems to be, attempting to determine to which
genre of folk literature the medieval story of Genoveva belongs,
there appears to have been a cult of Saint Genoveva in the lower
Rhineland, whence the story and possibly the devotion spread to
the areas from which came the seventeenth- and eighteenth-century
German and Swiss immigrants to Pennsylvania.[17]

---

14 *Ibid.*, p. 47.
15 *Ibid.*, pp. 50–51.
16 I am informed by Professor Américo Paredes of the University of Texas
that the story of "Genoveva de Brabante" is also popular among the Mexican-
Americans in the Southwest.
17 The literature on the legend of Genoveva of Brabant is extensive. In addition to the works cited in our notes (28–29), see F. Görres, "Neue Forschungen

The essential legend of the "Pfaltzgravine Genoveva" is that of the innocent wife, accused by her nobleman husband of infidelity and condemned to the forest, but vindicated at last. A version collected from oral tradition in Pennsylvania will give us the details; it calls the heroine "Genoeva":

Genoeva was a beautiful and a good woman, who was married to a prince, and who lived happily with him. The prince had many servants and among them was one—either the jester (Hofnarr) or the butler— who wanted to lead Genoeva into the path of sin. He tempted her, but she would not in the slightest way yield to his evil designs.

Then the butler—I know now, it was the butler and not the jester— became full of hatred toward Genoeva, and he went to her husband and told him that Genoeva was an unfaithful and a deceitful wife.

The husband believed the butler, and became infuriated at Genoeva. He drove her and her baby boy out of the palace into the dark forest.

Genoeva, carrying her baby in her arms, walked on and on through the forest, not knowing where to go for there were no homes among the dark trees.

Finally, she came to a bear cliff (Beregliffs) in which there was a bear den. Here she sought refuge, and here she made her home.

She lived on berries, herbs, bark, and roots, and every day there came to the cliff a doe from whom she got milk for her baby.

Thus she lived for many years. Her baby boy grew up into manhood and then he supplied her with food and clothing. She had often told him how she had been falsely accused by the butler and had been unjustly driven from the palace. When the boy was grown up and strong, he determined to go to his father, to defend his mother and to accuse the false butler.

After the father heard the son's story, he sent for the butler, who, when brought face to face with the son and hearing the accusation, broke down and confessed the evil which he had done.

Then, straightway, the prince went into the forest for Genoeva. He brought her back to the palace, where she lived happily with him the rest of her life.

As for the butler, the prince took four wild oxen and chained the butler to the oxen, one limb to each ox; and as the oxen sprang apart they tore the body of the butler to the four winds (ausnanner grisse noch di vier Wind).[18]

---

zur Genovefa Sage," *Annalen des Historischen Vereins für den Niederrhein*, 66 (1898), 1–39; *Die Religion in Geschichte und Gegenwart*, vol. II, cols. 1389–1390; *Lexikon für Theologie und Kirche*, vol. IV, cols. 384–385; and finally, Agnes B. C. Dunbar, *A Dictionary of Saintly Women* (London: George Bell & Sons, 1904–1905), I, 336–338, which retells the story in charming fashion, gives the saint's day as April 2, and at the end of her account admits that, as Cahier says, "Geneviève has no business among the saints [i.e., because she was never really canonized]. Local belief has it that she is still sitting spinning behind the altar in the church of Frauenkirchen, on the site of the famous Abbey of Lach, and that the hum of her wheel is heard there."

18 Thomas R. Brendle and William S. Troxell, *Pennsylvania German Folk Tales, Legends, Once-Upon-a-time Stories, Maxims and Sayings Spoken in the*

While the story is still obtainable in Pennsylvania in oral tradition, it was principally circulated in printed form and *nacherzählt* or told according to a printed original.[19] The earliest known American edition of the little *Volksbuch* or chapbook on Genoveva is: *Geschichte von der Pfaltz-Gräfin Genovefa* (Lancaster: Gedruckt bey F. Bailey, 1774), listed in *The American Bibliography of Charles Evans* (Worcester, Mass.: American Antiquarian Society, 1959) as No. 13297. A more elaborate edition appeared from the same press in 1790: *Historie von der unschuldigen Heiligen Pfalzgräfin Genoveva* (Lancaster: Gedruckt bey Jacob Bailey, 1790), Evans, No. 22524.[20]

The nineteenth-century editions are many. The most widespread, which turn up at country auctions and antique shops and book stores, are those published in the 1830's and later by Gustavus S. Peters[21] of Harrisburg, Pennsylvania's first color printer, and his successor, Theo. F. Scheffer. Typically, Peters and Scheffer issued and advertised together the Pennsylvania German chapbooks both of magic and of piety—*The Long Lost Friend, The Sixth and Seventh Books of Moses, The Heart of Man ('s Haerz-Buch*, as the Pennsylvania Germans called it), and the two medieval saints' legends, those of Saint Helena and of Saint Genoveva. The Peters and Scheffer presses were bilingual, and the English edition was entitled: *The thrilling history of Genovefa who by a villain was doomed to be executed* (Harrisburg: printed and sold by Theo. F.

---

dialect popularly known as *Pennsylvania Dutch* (Norristown, Pa., 1944), Pennsylvania German Society, vol. 50. The story was recorded from Mrs. Kate Moyer of Egypt, Lehigh Co., Pa. In the late 1940's when Professors Boyer and Buffington and I were gathering materials for *Songs Along the Mahantongo*, one of our informants, Mrs. William Beissel of Leck Kill, Northumberland Co., Pa., recited a spirited version of the story of Genoveva, but unfortunately since we were at the time genre-oriented and interested only in folk songs, we failed to record it. I have in the past year begun to sound out my present informants on the Genoveva tradition and will report my findings on Genoveva in oral tradition in a subsequent paper.

19 On the relation of printed text to oral transmission of folk legend material, see Linda Dégh, *Folktales and Society: Story-Telling in a Hungarian Peasant Community* (Bloomington: Indiana University Press, 1969), pp. 146–163. For the Genoveva legend in Hungary, see p. 159.

20 An additional eighteenth-century edition is entitled *Unschuldige Genovefa, Wie sie durch Verleumdung zum Tod verurtheilet, und nachdem sie 7 Jahr von Kräuter und Hirsch-milch gelebt hatte, wunderbarlich errettet worden* (Ephrata: Gedruckt bey Benjamin Meyer, 1796), 48 pp.

21 Gustav Sigismund Peters was born in Langebrück, Germany, in 1793, and died at Harrisburg, Pa., March 22, 1847. His name appears on Carlisle imprints from 1823 to 1827, after which he printed in Harrisburg. See Alfred L. Shoemaker, "Biographical Sketches of the Dauphin County Publishers," *The Pennsylvania Dutchman*, III:21 (April 1, 1952), 8.

Scheffer [1840?], 38 pp., cover-title, illustrations, and advertisements. The advertisements are of value for the light they shed on the popularity of other items in the German chapbook repertoire among the Pennsylvania Germans. An undated German copy of *Die Leidens-Geschichte der unschuldigen Genovefa, Welche sich 7 Jahre in einer Wildniss von Wurzeln und Kräutern ernährte, und wie ihr Kind durch einen Hirsch wunderbar am Leben erhalten wurde* (Harrisburg: Gedruckt und zu haben bei Theo. F. Scheffer, n.d.), 38 pp., advertises on the back cover: *Heinrich von Eichenfels, Oder das von einer Zigeunerin geraubte Kind; Die Leidens-Geschichte der Genovefa;* and *Die Trübsale der schönen Helena.*

The cover illustrations occasionally show Genoveva, as naked as her babe, seated at the entrance of her cave, with the friendly doe in attendance, as the wicked husband rides up on horseback. The nudity aspect has made Genoveva one of the three most popular motifs in "nude" or "topless" folk art, along with Sebastian and, of course, Adam and Eve. Like these worthies, she gave the folk artist his only chance to try his or her hand at a nude, which was otherwise forbidden in "Christian" art. This freedom of artistic expression reached even the closed world of the cloister, according to Robert Wildhaber, who recently sent me pictorial evidence in the form of three-dimensional wax figures of Genoveva and the other cast of characters, done as *Klosterarbeit* in the nunneries of the Catholic cantons of Switzerland.[22]

In fact it was the folk art produced by the Genoveva cult in Europe that first alerted me to the possibility of studying our homely old Genoveva comparatively. Reverse glass paintings in Czechoslovakia[23] and Sicilian cart panels[24] of the Genoveva story first showed me the wide influence of the Genoveva legend in Europe.

On higher cultural levels, too, Genoveva was a popular subject in the eighteenth and nineteenth centuries. There were several long poetic versions of her legend, several plays, and at least two operas.[25] And Richard Weiss refers to the countrified dramas that

---

[22] Thus far I have, unfortunately, found no similar development of the Genoveva cult into folk art forms in Pennsylvania, except for the crude woodcuts that embellished the chapbooks.

[23] Josef Vydra, *Die Hinterglasmalerei: Volkskunst aus tschechoslowakischen Sammlungen* (Prague: Artia, 1957), plates 59–64, 85, and XXIII.

[24] Noted on an autumn visit to Sicily during my 1961 sabbatical. For examples, see the plates in the book, Salvatore Lo Presti, *Il Carretto: Monografia sul Carretto Siciliano* (Palermo: S. F. Flaccovio, 1959).

[25] On the literary and artistic use of the Genoveva Legend, see B. Golz, *Pfalzgräfin Genoveva in der deutschen Dichtung* (1897); A. Müller, *Die*

were played on rural Swiss stages in the eighteenth and nineteenth
centuries, created from the chapbooks of Genoveva, Griselda of
Saluzzo, and other heroines whose unchanging loyalty is put to the
test by suspicious husbands.[26]

In addition to the legend books, the folk art, and the rural plays
about Genoveva, there were also songs, as for example the *Cantique de Ste Geneviève de Brabant* (Paris, 1766), which became
part of the Épinal repertoire in the nineteenth century as the
*Cantique Spiritual sur l'innocence de Geneviève, reconnue par son
mari* (Épinal, 1874).[27]

The most recent German scholarship on the background of the
Genoveva legend locates the beginnings of the cult in the middle
Rhineland, at Frauenkirch (Fraukirch) near Andernach. At Andernach there was a church dedicated to Saint Geneviève (Genoveva)
of Paris, from which her cult may have spread to the country regions adjacent. From this historical saint, the writer of the legend
of Genoveva of Brabant may have taken the name of his heroine.

At any rate, the legend is late medieval, and exists in two versions,
which differ only in inconsequential details. It is worthy of note
that the two copyists whose versions are the sources of the modern
legend both came from Andernach. The one version was copied
around 1500 by Johannes of Andernach from an older Latin original, whose editor is unknown. The other version, part of the collections of the Stadtbibliothek in Trier (Hs 1353) was produced
by Matthias von Emiych, also of Andernach, from an older version,
around 1472. Matthias von Emiych was later prior of the Carmelite

dramatische Bearbeitung der Genovefa-Legende (1902); and Albert Schneider,
Geneviève de Brabant dans la litterature Allemande ([1957]). The two operas
were those of Schumann (1848) and Scholz (1875).

26 Weiss, *Volkskunde der Schweiz*, pp. 205–206.

27 For parallel versions of these two editions of the French song, see Pierre
Brochon, *Le Livre de Colportage en France depuis le XVI* Siècle: Sa Littérature
—Ses Lecteurs* (Paris: Librairie Gründ, 1954), pp. 113–116. For an eight-verse
German *Moritat* with the Genoveva theme, published at Hamburg in 1867
in the chapbook *Genoveva, der frommen Pfalzgräfin Leiden und Errettung*,
see the facsimile reproduction in L. Petzoldt, ed., *Graue Thaten sind Geschehen:
31 Moritaten* (München: Heimeran, 1968). Dr. Petzoldt's notes on the text refer
to the earlier German version, *Eine erschröckliche Geschicht, welche sich hat
zugetragen mit einem Grafen* ([Oedenburg?], 1767), as well as to a Dutch ballad
entitled *Nieuw Liedeken van de deugdelyke Palsgravinne Genoveva*, published
in Antwerp in the first half of the nineteenth century by the printer, J. Thys
(1783–1854). For the texts and tunes of several of the ballads about Genoveva,
see Wilhelm Heiske, editor, with collaboration of Erich Seemann, Rolf Wilhelm
Brednich, and Wolfgang Suppan, *Deutsche Volkslieder mit ihren Melodien:
Balladen*, vol. 5, pt. 5 (Freiburg/Breisgau: Deutsches Volksliedarchiv, 1967), pp.
163–180, with bibliography on p. 180.

cloister at Boppard and died after being consecrated bishop of Mainz. From these medieval versions, the first printed version was drawn up; it was compiled by the French Jesuit Cerizier and appeared in 1638 as *L'innocence reconnue ou vie de Saint Geneviève de Brabant,* which was translated into German by 1685.[28] It is from the Cologne version of 1750 that the first American edition, that of Lancaster, Pennsylvania, in 1774, is derived.

In dealing with Genoveva of Brabant, Hermann Bausinger relates the legend on the one hand to the *Märchen,* and on the other to the *Schwank:*

> As a tale of many episodes of wondrous occurrences, the legend is above all close to the Märchen; a story like that of Genoveva of Brabant is related to the Märchen not only in individual motifs, but also in its entire course. This legend, composed in the late 15th Century by a Rhenish monk with reference to the Paris saint of the same name, received its characteristic form in the 17th Century at the hands of a French Jesuit and was then disseminated in Germany as a chapbook. Tieck produced a new version of it, Görres called attention to the chapbook, Christoph von Schmid wrote the popular sentimental version, and even to our own time the material has remained extraordinarily popular. To this popularity the Märchen-like character may have contributed; but it is especially in the oral narrative that the differences over against the Märchen clearly stand out. A short time ago an old woman in the Franconian area told me a variety of legends and Märchen. The only Märchen she told were those of the Grimm brothers. These she narrated matter-of-factly, almost indifferently, and even remarked on the inadequacies in the narrative, since Märchen are of course only for children. But the legend she took very seriously. In telling this latter her narration was directed toward the central miraculous events: these are accented, proved, attested; the story is true, and the miraculous events are immediate interventions of God. And there was still a second difference: while good fortune is the normal reward of the figures in the Märchen, in the legend the moral performance of the characters, their action, their perseverance, their patience are emphasized.

> Of course, this concern with the deeper aspects of man's nature is in constant tension with the cheerful certainty, indeed the triumphant certainty, which characterizes the frame of the legend. In this frame the legend can even approach the Schwank. The intimate connection between foolishness and sanctity (fool-ness and saint-ness, *Narrheit und Heiligkeit*) in the devaluation of worldly systems has already been pointed out in different ways; so it is no surprise when in the legend

---

[28] Nikolaus Kyll and Josef Räder, "Die Fraukirch in der Pellenz im Rheinlande und die Genovefalegende," *Rheinisches Jahrbuch für Volkskunde,* I (1950), 81 ff.; Heinrich Günter, *Psychologie der Legende: Studien zu einer wissenschaftlichen Heiligen-Geschichte* (Freiburg: Verlag Herder, 1949), p. 58. The latter work discusses the Genoveva legend's universal motifs of innocent-rejecting-seduction and animal-aiding-human (pp. 46, 58).

of St. Symeon of Emesa, for example, we encounter definite Eulenspie-
gel elements, and even the cunning deceits of Stricker's Pfaffe Amis
must be viewed in this light.[29]

In a sense the material involved is best approached via the chapbook, which after all is our immediate introduction to Genoveva.
Since the publication of the Cologne edition of 1750, Genoveva's
story has spread even more widely in Western Europe, until it has
become common knowledge among the masses. The Dutch author
Bilderdijk in a letter to a friend in 1786 mentions having seen old
women sitting by their market wagons absorbed in the stories of
Helena of Constantinople, Griselda of Saluzzo, and the like, books
that were made out of traditions from the span of time from the
last centuries of the Hellenistic period to the establishment of the
Frankish kingdom.[30]

In conclusion, I make no attempt at this point to analyze further
the reasons for the popularity of the story of Genoveva, or (heaven
forbid!) to psychoanalyze it, preferring to listen someday to Professor Dundas's version of that. Apart from its being a good story,
to rural Pennsylvanian audiences its didactic and moral character
kept it alive, with its pointed and simple message—virtue will be
rewarded, murder will out.

While the Genoveva legend is no longer read by the majority
of the Pennsylvania Germans (although it is still passively known
and occasionally told by older folk), among one segment of the
culture it is very much alive. The Old Order Amish of Lancaster
County, Pennsylvania, have recently established a press, and one of
the first items issued from it is a pamphlet, a modern-day chapbook, entitled *Genevieve: Or, God Does Not Forsake His Own*
(Gordonville, Pa.: A. S. Kinsinger, 1964), 44 pp. True to the ani-
conic character of Amish culture, there are no pictures, nude or
otherwise. But even the publishers' pitch in the brief preface reflects
to the older chapbook tradition:

> Generations come and go. Many books have been written and
> printed, thrown on the book market and then become a thing of the
> past; but not so with "Genevieve"—it was written to stay. Its contents
> are healthful, interesting and instructive, for children as well as their
> elders, and it is suited for all generations. It shows that also in the
> ancient times good and bad people lived, and that man, trusting in
> God, could, with perseverance, overcome privations, where otherwise
> in his misery he would have gone to ruin.

[29] Hermann Bausinger, *Formen der "Volkspoesie"* (Berlin: Erich Schmidt
Verlag, 1968), pp. 195–196.
[30] C. Kruyskamp, *Nederlandsche Volksboeken* (Leiden, 1942), p. 52.

This is a popular edition, and the price is such that even the poorest are able to buy it. This publication contains a great deal of reading matter, and good printing. May this little booklet find a welcome in every family.[31]

NATIVE ANALOGUES TO THE SAINT'S LEGEND

The Christian saint's legend proper belongs to the Middle Ages and to Catholic or Orthodox environments and cultures. It is difficult to deny the human drive to create saints, however, so even within the Protestant cultures we have native analogues to the saint's legend.

If the saint as ecclesiastically permitted mediator was exscinded from the Protestant realm of possibility by the reformers, the saint as model—of virtue, charity, forbearance, and universal love—has continued to appear, if somewhat sporadically, within the Protestant world. Protestant biography, especially the lives produced during the Puritan and Pietist centuries in Europe and America, bear the vestigial marks of at least the virtue aspects of the earlier saints' legends.[32] Full-length studies of the various sectarian varieties of spiritual biography—the Puritan lives, the Quaker journals, and the Methodist circuit-rider autobiographies—reveal striking resemblance in motif to the earlier saint's legend—resistance to the temptations of the "world," a radical conversion, which enables the subject to keep on a radarlike track direct toward salvation, in some cases the triumph of forbearance amid almost insurmountable difficulties, the detachment from personal love to universal charity,

---

31 The Preface contains also a P.S. signed by Ray S. Kinsinger, Springs, Pa., Star Route, representing the Amish community of Somerset Co., Pa., and Grant Co., Md. It reads as follows: "Having read this book over a few times I found it very interesting and impressive. I decided to get some more printed (as they are not to be gotten anymore) and believe most of them have passed through lots of hands to be read, as is the case with the one that I am rewriting this story from, which is getting very shabby. I do believe whoever reads it cannot help but take a liking to it." From the Kinsinger Press at Gordonville there also appeared, in 1966, *The Stolen Child: Or How Henry von Eichenfels Came to the Knowledge of God. A Narrative for Children and Children's Friends, Designed for reading classes in Sabbath schools, &c.*, as translated from German by J. Bachman and J. Miller and published by I. D. Rupp in 1836. This from my unpublished paper entitled, "Cultural Lag in Amish Reading Matter."

32 For the rationale of Protestant biography, see Kenneth B. Murdock, "Clio in the Wilderness: History and Biography in Puritan New England," *Church History* (Sept. 1955), pp. 221–238, which makes use of the theories in Romein's *De Biografie: Een Inleiding* (Amsterdam, 1946). Also useful is Daniel B. Shea, *Spiritual Autobiography in Early America* (Princeton, N.J.: Princeton University Press, 1968).

and detailed descriptions of the "holy dying" as well as the "holy living" of the saint.

Of the two foci, virtue and miracle, suggested by Professor Bausinger for the medieval saint's legend,[33] the Protestant versions normally accent virtue. The wondrous elements of the saint's legend are there, however, in some biographical cycles, although to a sharply decreased degree.[34] The Quaker journals, for instance, are full of guidance through dreams, visions, psychic leadings toward persons in need of spiritual counsel, and other hints of extrasensory phenomena.[35]

The Pennsylvania German materials are of interest in this connection. One form of charisma in the Dutch country involves a reputation achieved as a folk-medical practitioner. While most of the healers were laymen, occasionally a minister was connected with healing practices. One such case involves the story told of a very famous early Pennsylvania Lutheran minister, Dr. John George Schmucker (1771–1854) of York, Pennsylvania. His biographer tells of an incident where he almost became a charismatic healer:

> Though not superstitious, he was not entirely free from belief in supernatural influences. If his mind had not been well balanced, he was just the man to be wrought on by the presumed revelations of modern Spiritualism. I believe this infirmity was fostered by his high admiration of, and thorough acquaintance with, some of the mystic theologians of the last century, especially Jung Stilling.
>
> Quite unintentionally, and to his great annoyance, he once acquired the reputation of being a semi-miraculous healer of wens, warts, and similar ugly excrescences. On one occasion a plain countryman came to his study and complained of a wen on his head. "Let me see it," said the Doctor. He examined it, as a matter of curiosity, and touched it. The man declared that, from that moment, it began to diminish until it disappeared altogether. His neighbors heard of it, and, for miles around, all who were affected with similar unnatural protuberances, hastened to the "Pastor" to be healed by the magic touch; and it required some effort to convince the simple people that he possessed no supernatural powers, and he dismissed them to their deep chagrin.[36]

---

33 Bausinger, Formen der "Volkspoesie," p. 186.

34 See the discussion of American Puritan biography in Richard M. Dorson, American Folklore (Chicago: University of Chicago Press, 1959), chap. I.

35 Rufus M. Jones, The Later Periods of Quakerism (London, 1921), I, 92–103.

36 John G. Morris, Fifty Years in the Lutheran Ministry (Baltimore, 1878), pp. 13–14. Letter written April 14, 1861, for Sprague's Annals of the American Pulpit. The reference to the influence of Jung-Stilling is valuable. His Theorie der Geisterkunde, with its pioneer analysis of extrasensory perception, was so popular among the educated Germans in this country that it was reprinted here in 1816.

In this case the minister, whose education and world view differed from those of his parishioners, scotched the layman's drive to promote him into the role of charismatic healer.[37]

The principal Pennsylvania analogue to the European saint's legend that I wish to discuss is the story of Mountain Mary (*Die Berg-Maria*), a local Pennsylvania German hermitess who died in 1819 and about whom legends have arisen. So persistent are they that Mountain Mary is today one of the best known characters from early Pennsylvania history.[38]

Hermits, saintly and secular, abound in early American society. I am always amazed at the amount of material one comes upon in early American documentation on the nonconformists of this sort, whether voluntary or forced rejects of society. If our roads were crowded with offbeat "hawkers and walkers," tramps, religious itinerants, self-appointed messiahs, and utopia builders, Penn's woods seem to have had more than their share of hermits and hermitages. I recommend these as a special area of legend scholarship in America.

The life of Mountain Mary—whose name was Maria Jung (Young)—is today so shrouded in legend that it is difficult to cut back to what must have been her historical profile. A German immigrant of 1830 named Ludwig A. Wollenweber (1807–1888) published in 1880 a romanticized version of the life of Mary Young entitled *Treu bis in den Tod: Die Berg-Maria, oder Wer nur den lieben Gott lässt walten. Eine Geschichtliche Erzählung aus Pennsylvanien* (Philadelphia: Verlag von Ig.[natius] Kohler, 1880),

---

37 For a different assignation of charisma to a preacher, see Harry H. Hiller, "The Sleeping Preachers: An Historical Study of the Role of Charisma in Amish Society," *PF*, XVIII:2 (Winter, 1968–1969), 19–31; also Don Yoder, "Trance-Preaching in the United States," *ibid.*, 12–18.

38 Bibliography on Mountain Mary, in addition to the items cited in the following notes, include Rupp, *History of the Counties of Berks and Lebanon* (Lancaster, Pa., 1844); and Morton L. Montgomery, *History of Berks County in Pennsylvania* (Philadelphia, 1886). My editorial introduction to Frank Brown, "New Light on 'Mountain Mary,'" *PF*, XV:3 (Spring, 1966), 10, contains the basic general bibliography. The Sunday supplement versions of Mary's story, important for pictorial representation, include "Romances of Pennsylvania History No. XV—The Hermit Saint of Oley Valley," *The North American* (Philadelphia), May 31, 1914, showing a strong young Mary ax in hand, having just felled a tree in front of her one-story log hut. Wayne Homan's "Pennsylvania Heritage: Mountain Mary," *The Philadelphia Inquirer Magazine* (July 15, 1962), includes photographs of the Hill Lutheran Church, organized 1747, which Mary attended, and Mary's bake oven and springhouse, which many of the travelers' accounts mention. Some additional documentation on the Jung family appeared in the *Historical Review of Berks County*, Jan., 1939, and *The Pennsylvania Dutchman*, III:12 (Nov. 15, 1951).

which appears to be responsible for some of the legendary framework of Mountain Mary's life. Long a resident of Mary Young's home county of Berks, and with an interest in his adopted culture, which helped to stimulate its flowering into dialect literature,[39] Wollenweber may have gathered some of the legendary details in the neighborhood, but recast them into an historical novella, centering on the Revolutionary War period. The story as it appears on his pages is a highly romantic and sentimental one, a Dutch tearjerker from an era long before the television soap opera. According to Wollenweber, Maria Jung emigrated with her parents and two brothers from a village (he names it Feuerbach) in Württemberg shortly before the Revolution. Parents and brothers died of plague and were buried at sea, and Maria was left alone. Love came to the rescue, however, in the form of a young fellow passenger named Theodore Benz, from the city of Lahr in Baden. When they landed at Philadelphia after a voyage of ninety-two days, Maria generously paid Theodore's passage to avoid his being sold as a redemptioner, and the young orphans were befriended by Pastor Muhlenberg, Lutheran minister of Philadelphia, who got Maria a kitchen job at the Golden Swan Inn under a charitable (Lutheran) widow named Mrs. Kreuder, while Theodore the farm boy was sent to Oley to work on the Frederick Leinbach farm. After a year's work, Frederick Leinbach, who was growing old, gave Theodore a 175-acre farm in the Oley Hills, and Theodore hastened to Philadelphia to tell his prospective bride the good news. By this time the outbreak of the Revolution had Philadelphia in turmoil, and Theodore was prevailed upon to join the Berks County volunteers in Captain Hiester's company, and also finally to marry Maria. Pastor Muhlenberg tied the knot and Frau Kreuder gave a Swabian wedding party at the Golden Swan, but alas, Theodore was forced to leave his bride that very night, as his company was ordered across the Delaware to Trenton. They were never to see each other again. Theodore and his Berks County buddies were taken prisoner at the battle of Long Island and put on board the prison ship Jersey where they finally died of starvation. Heartbroken, Maria settled as a hermitess on the farm in the Oley Hills, where as a good neighbor and herbal healer she

---

[39] Ludwig A. Wollenweber's little book, *Gemälde aus dem Pennsylvanischen Volksleben. Schilderungen und Aufsätze in poetischer und prosaischer Form, in Mundart und Ausdrucksweise der Deutsch-Pennsylvanier.* Cyklus I. (Philadelphia und Leipzig: Verlag von Schäfer und Koradi, 1869), 140 pp., is actually the first volume of Pennsylvania German dialect prose published—as nearly as his acculturated *Pfälzisch* dialect could be called Pennsylvania German.

achieved a reputation for sanctity. When she died in 1819, Wollen-weber tells us, her funeral was the largest that had ever taken place in Pike Township. There was no house in Oley and the adjoining townships which had not sent its representative, and from far and wide the mourners came by wagon and on horseback to pay Maria their last respects.[40]

Fortunately there is some historical documentation preserved about Mary Young from which we can determine that she never married, and that while she lived as hermitess for at least thirty years in the Oley Hills, she had first settled there at least a decade previously, evidently during the Revolution, with her widowed mother and two sisters, who preceded her in death and are said to be buried in the private burial ground on Mary's farm. Mary's will, dated March 13, 1813, is on record at the courthouse in Reading—in it she describes herself as spinster, left legacies to two brothers-in-law, Matthias Motz and John George Schneider, and a niece, Maria Elizabeth Schneider, and names as executors her neighbors Daniel Joder and Thomas Lee. Mary died November 16, 1819, her will was probated November 20, and her forty-two-acre mountain farm sold to Martin Joder.[41]

Between the full-blown romance and this historical skeleton of fact, there was a body of legendry about Mountain Mary. As was the case with the classical European saint, her legend began to take shape while she was yet alive. Benjamin M. Hollinshead, a young Philadelphia Quaker, visited Mary Young in her mountain hermit-

---

[40] Wollenweber's *Gemälde* contains a short sketch of Die Berg Maria (pp. 125–127). Since he assigns her here a different European origin than in his novella of 1880, I quote his text in full: "In Pike Township, Berks County, hot vor Johre z'rick e wunnerbar Weibsmensch sich ufgehalte, ihr Name war *Maria Jung*, un sie hot über dreissig Johre lang ganz allenig in ener Art Hütt nächst zu Motz Mühl gewohnt. Sie hot während der lange Zeit bei Niemand gebettelt, Niemand nix böses, aber dorch ihre Kräuter un Medizin den Kranken arg viel Gutes gethan. —Mir ischt gesagt worre, in ihren Papieren hät gestande, sie wäre in Deux-ponts (Zweibrücken) in der Pfalz geboren, un sei anno 1769 in's Land komme mit em junge Mann, der sie gege ihr Vaters Wille fortgenomme. Wie sie e Zeitlang in dem Land gewese wärre, hät ihr Liebhaber sie verlosse in Philadelphia, un sie hät ihn dann lang gesucht, sei noch Reading kumme, un wie ihr Müh all umsonst wor, hot sie in die Berge verkroche, un e armselig Lebe geführt bis an ihr End. Sie isch im Johr 1819 gestorbe, un e Freund, der die Tugenden des armseligen verstossene Menschenkindes gekannt, un sie mit Leut oft besucht, die viele Meil geträwelt sind, for die *Berg Maria* zu sehne, hat folgende Verse uf sie gemacht (here follows the four-verse tribute by Daniel Bertolet, reproduced later in our text).

[41] Daniel Miller, "Maria Young, the Mountain Recluse of Oley," *Transactions of the Historical Society of Berks County*, III (1910–1916) (Reading, Pa., 1923), 209–220.

age in the summer of 1819. The account is a lengthy one, hence we shall digest it here.[42]

Upon his arrival in Oley Valley, Hollinshead's hosts proposed an ascent of the Oley Hills. Above all, they suggested paying "a visit to Mary Young, commonly known in the neighborhood as 'Mountain Mary.'" She received them with kindness, and "after an interchange of inquiries on the part of her and our friends, she commenced speaking in a religious strain, informing us through a lady of our party who acted as interpreter, that on serious subjects she was obliged to speak in her native language, the German." After a hike around the mountain farm they returned to say good-bye, and found "a table spread with delicious bread, butter, cream, milk and preserved fruits; and we were invited to partake in a manner so sincere and courteous, that we did not distrust our kind hostess when she assured us we were welcome." The account accents her unshaken faith and bright hope "that nothing would be permitted to happen to her that was not for her good." From her neighbors in Oley and acquaintances in Reading and Philadelphia, Hollinshead collected anecdotes revealing her character, and all his informants "concurred in bearing testimony to her great worth." Her industry, they reported, was prodigious. Living alone, she kept several cows and did all her haying; she marketed butter; she kept bees. The paths on the mountain she graded to make the ascent easier. Her benevolence extended even to "animals of a noxious kind." When marmots invaded her walled garden, she set traps and caught them, but "instead of putting them to death, which she might have done as sole lady of the garden, she took them to the neighboring hills, telling them to go and trespass no more." [43]

---

[42] Benjamin M. Hollinshead, "Mountain Mary. (Die Berg Maria)," *The Pennsylvania German*, III (1902), 133–142. The account was made available to the present generation of readers by Dr. Preston A. Barba in his column, "'S Pennsylvaanisch Deitsch Eck," *The Morning Call* (Allentown, Pa.), Nov. 20 and 27, 1965.

[43] Mrs. Mayer Sprague of Germantown, Pa., in connection with the publication of the Hollinshead account in 1902, added to the Mountain Mary legend the following extrasensory incident from family tradition: "The friend spoken of by Mr. Hollinshead was an ancestor of mine (Mrs. Susanna de Benneville Keim, wife of John Keim, and daughter of Dr. George de Benneville), who, upon awakening from a vivid dream, in which she saw Mountain Mary in dire distress, was so impressed that she made immediate preparations to see Mary. The lady's son tried to dissuade her from going, saying the distance was great, through roads almost impassable, the weather inclement, and the lady herself neither young nor robust. 'My son' said she, 'Mary needs me. My Master has bidden me seek her. I dare not disobey His call.' With the early morning light the old

From the period immediately after her death, there came two tributes in verse which increased the veneration. In 1822 there appeared in Philadelphia a small volume of verse entitled *The Phantom Barge, and other Poems,* by an unidentified poet (possibly Hollinshead himself), who called himself "The Limner." The book contains a poem called "Mary Young," who according to the author was "an old German lady, of a remarkably pious character, residing among the Oley Hills, near Reading, in the State of Pennsylvania." [44] While Mary had died in 1819, it is clear from the poem that she was living when the verses were written.

The second poetic tribute to Mountain Mary was written in 1819, a poem that John Joseph Stoudt in his recent collection of Pennsylvania German verse calls "Mountain Mary's Epitaph" and ascribed to "A Gentleman of Oley." [45]

MOUNTAIN MARY'S EPITAPH

Hier unter diesem Steine
Sanft ruhen die Gebeine,
Der frommen Maria:
Ihr Herz und ganzes Leben
War ihrem Gott ergeben,
Dass man's an ihrem Wandel sah.

Sie hat ganz unverdrossen,
Bis dreis[s]ig Jahr verflossen,
In Einsamkeit gewohnt:
Ihr Angesichtes Zügen
Verriethen Gottes Lieb,
Damit der Herr sie hat belohnt.

Nachdem sie schon verschieden,
Sah man den Süssen Frieden
In ihrem Angesicht;
Es war voll Lieb und Wonn

---

lady, with her grandson, started, taking such comforts as she thought might be needed. Upon arriving there she found her vision confirmed—Mary confined to her bed, and the creatures dependent upon her care in bad need. Great-grandmother stayed with Mary until the end. Mrs. Keim was frequently heard to say, that she counted among her earthly blessings the privilege of being with this sainted woman in her last hour, to witness her loving faith and confidence in her Heavenly Father, who has promised He will never leave or forsake His children who seek Him in spirit and in truth."

44 The poem was republished in Barba, " 'S Pennsylvaanisch Deitsch Eck," *The Morning Call,* Nov. 27, 1965.

45 John Joseph Stoudt, *Pennsylvania German Poetry, 1685–1830* (Allentown, Pa., 1956), Pennsylvania German Folklore Society, XX (1956), 266. The poem had earlier appeared in print in Rupp, *History of the Counties of Berks and Lebanon,* p. 260; and Wollenweber, *Gemälde,* pp. 126–127.

Als zur Gnaden-sonn,
Noch immer hingericht.

Nun ist sie weggenommen;
Gott hies[s] sie zu sich kommen,
Aus diesem Jammerthal:
Wo auf den Himmels-Auen,
Sie Jesum wird anschauen,
Mit seiner auserwählten Zahl.

[Here under this stone rest in peace the remains of the pious Maria, her heart and her entire life were dedicated to God, as any could see from her conduct. In solitude she lived without complaint for thirty years, the lines of her face betraying God's love with which the Lord rewarded her. Even after death sweet peace was visible in her countenance, it was full of love and bliss, as if still directed toward the sun of grace. Now she is taken away, God bade her come to Him out of this vale of tears, where on the meadows of Heaven she will look upon Jesus amid his elect number.]

The poem actually was written by a neighbor of Mary's, Daniel Bertolet (1781–1868), poet, hymnist, farmer, and local preacher whose work in folk hymnody I have described in detail elsewhere.[46] In his German Journal for 1819 he describes his neighbor's death and funeral, and includes as a tribute the lines above.[47]

The legend of Mountain Mary continued to grow in the nineteenth century. At the end of the century, a Reading newspaperman named Frank Brown, one of the first active folklorists to deal with Berks County's own traditions, wrote a sketch of Mountain Mary for the *Sunday Eagle*, based principally upon Wollenweber, but to which he appended materials he gathered by interview in the Oley Valley.[48]

---

[46] *Pennsylvania Spirituals* (Lancaster: Pennsylvania Folklife Society, 1961), pp. 356–357, *passim*. For translations of his German poetry, see Raymond W. Albright, "Daniel Bertolet of Oley," *Historical Review of Berks County* (April, 1945), pp. 74–79.

[47] The German Journals of Daniel Bertolet for 1819–1820, Bertolet Collection, Pennsylvania Folklife Society, contain three references to Mountain Mary: (1) "Sam Feb 6 1819 Heute war ich bey der Berg Maria" [Saturday, Feb. 6, 1819: Today I was at Mountain Mary's]; (2) "Den 18 November 1819 Heute war die Maria auf dem Berge begraben—'Hilf Herr die Heiligen haben abgenomen' Der tode Leuchnam sehe gans liebreich und schön und ohn zweifel ist sie in die Ruhe eingegangen" [Nov. 18, 1819: Today Mary of the Mountain was buried— "Help, Lord, the saints have decreased." The dead corpse looked quite lovely and beautiful and without doubt she has entered into rest]; (3) On Tuesday, Jan. 25, 1820, he inscribed in his journal the four-verse poem and headed it with the words: "Grab-Schrift vor Maria Jungin die am 18ten Novem 1819 begraben siehe Blad 719" [Epitaph for Maria Jung who was buried Nov. 18, 1819, see p. 719].

[48] I republished these materials with an introduction on sources of the life and legend of Mountain Mary, in Frank Brown, "New Light on 'Mountain Mary,' "

Among the information that he collected is that she grafted apples, known among her neighbors as the "Mammy," "Weiss," and "Good Mary" apples, that she carried her cheese to the huckster's down the mountain on a tray on her head, and that she made her own paths over the mountain in every direction, lightening the grade in some spots to enable her to move with ease even at all hours of the night, since her services as a healer were required as much at night as in the daytime. But we are also enlightened by this writer about Mary's belief in and use of occult powers:

> She was a great believer in witchcraft. She frequently related that for a time an owl came and drank out of her milk pail every evening while she was milking. She could not prevent the bird from getting near the pail except by catching it, since it was so tame that it couldn't be scared away. So one night she caught the owl and burned its feet by slightly holding it over her fire. The next morning a neighboring woman, whom she took to be the witch, couldn't put on her shoes on account of burned feet. "Die Berg Maria" was known not only in every corner of this county, but all over eastern Pennsylvania. She was sometimes called as far as Philadelphia to practice medicine in her novel way.

The importance of this evidence is that while the contemporary accounts accented the virtue and holiness of the mountain recluse, these later traditions, gathered from old folk who remembered seeing Mary sixty or more years previously, accent Mary the apple-grafter, Mary the road-grading engineer, and what is more significant, Mary the healer, even, it appears, Mary the powwower, the practitioner not of the rational herbal medicine encouraged, according to Wollenweber, by Pastor Muhlenberg, but what is much more likely, a healer by traditional means in which religion, prayer, and even magico-religious charms played a great part.[49]

Actually the best historical account of Mountain Mary was Daniel Miller's "Maria Young, the Mountain Recluse of Oley," a paper read before the Historical Society of Berks County, December 10, 1912. Miller noted that "all the older people are familiar

---

PF, XV:3 (Spring, 1966), 10–15. The materials quoted in this paper are found on pp. 14–15.

49 I am here interpreting the folktale of the owl-witch, which of course involved counter-witchcraft rather than folk medicine proper, to mean that by this period Mary's reputation as healer involved the occult as well as the herbal approach. In nineteenth century Pennsylvania, belief in both witchcraft and the efficacy of powwowing were part of the common folk religion of the layman, and Mary's reputation may have been based on her actual use of magico-religious formulas in her comfort and care of the sick and dying. On the negative side is of course the fact that none of the earlier accounts mention the occult element.

with the story and love to recite it, but these are rapidly passing away. For the benefit of the younger people and future generations it has been thought well to put into proper form and on record a sketch of the life of this interesting character, before the flight of time shall bury her in oblivion." He thought it especially urgent to get the story straight since Wollenweber's booklet of 1880—"an interesting and touching story written in fascinating style"—unfortunately "contains many errors, and is therefore unreliable. It is evidently far more legendary and imaginary than authentic." [50] Miller's account, drawn from Hollinshead, Rupp, and other early sources, emphasized Mary's industry (a Pennsylvania Dutch virtue), her role in the community as spiritual adviser, and her work as healer. He mentions nothing of an occult side to her practice.

> Mary Young was also a physician, of course not in the modern sense. She gathered many kinds of medicinal herbs and prepared remedies for various ailments. In this employment she was successful. Her intelligence served her well in this line of usefulness. People came to her from near and far for help in sickness, and in this way she came to be widely known as "Mountain Mary." She used mostly so-called household remedies in the treatment of the sick and rendered the community a great service in the absence of regular physicians. She not only relieved the sick, but gave Christian comfort to the dying. It is said that she spent much time at the bedside of those departing this life and gave them such instruction and comfort as were at her disposal.

In the twentieth century a kind of local cult of Mountain Mary developed. In 1934 the Berks County chapter of the D.A.R. erected a marker to her memory which described her as "a pioneer nurse, comforter of body and soul, benevolent, pious, brave and charitable," closing its tribute with the biblical verse, "She hath done what she could." [51]

From 1945 until 1962 pilgrimages to Mountain Mary's grave were annual affairs in November. Responsible for this development was a local dialect poet, Ralph W. Berky. Among the speakers on one of these cold, shivering occasions in the November woods that

---

[50] Miller, "Maria Young," p. 209. Miller (1834–1913) was a native of Lebanon County who established the *Republikaner von Berks* in Reading in 1869 and also published and helped to edit the *Reformirter Hausfreund*. He was himself a well-known dialect writer and published two volumes of Pennsylvania German dialect poetry and prose. For his biography, see Harry Hess Reichard, *Pennsylvania-German Dialect Writings and Their Writers* (Lancaster, Pa., 1918), Pennsylvania German Society, XXVI (1915), 158–161.

[51] Cited in Barba, " 'S Pennsylvaanisch Deitsch Eck," *The Morning Call*, Nov. 27, 1965.

I myself remember attending were Dr. Preston A. Barba of Muhlenberg College and Dr. Elmer E. S. Johnson, Schwenkfelder historian and retired professor at the Hartford Theological Foundation.[52] Also involved in stimulation of contemporary interest in Mountain Mary is Dr. Barba, who republished earlier accounts of the mountain saint in his column in the Allentown Morning Call.

In conclusion, the legend of Mountain Mary has some of the same general appeal as the legends of the classic medieval saints. To her neighbors as well as to a wider circle of admirers including some representatives of Philadelphia Quakerdom, Mary's renunciation of the world showed an inward strength that most of them admired, even envied in their dealing with everyday interpersonal crises. Her saintliness had an appeal in the early stages of Pennsylvania German culture when frontier crudities were found everywhere—it offered a glimpse of the unworldly in a world of confusion. But with all her high and holy qualities that make this Protestant saint different from and yet a model for her common neighbors, she was obviously one of them in her human sympathies and in her folk-medical beliefs.

Where does it go from here? Mountain Mary is of course not a saint complete with cult, either ecclesiastical or folk-religious, in the European sense of the word. But somehow through the century and a half since her death, her story and her memory, complete with minimal but significant legendary framework, have continued to minister to some need in the local culture of Berks and adjoining counties and to a certain extent to the entire Pennsylvania German area.

CONCLUSION

Our brief study of the saint's legend in the Pennsylvania German folk-culture points to the following conclusions.

1. American legendry must be studied in relation to the stratigraphy of the cultures that produced and used it. In addition to the obvious values of comparative legend studies, we need more and not fewer historical studies, more documentation on the shifts and trends in the use of myths and legend in our American regional folk-cultures as well as our national culture. Applying Pro-

---

[52] The memorial meeting described was on Nov. 16, 1946. See ibid., for John Birmelin's dialect poem, "An der Baerrig Maria Ihrm Grab" [At Mountain Mary's Grave], which was read on the occasion.

fessor Dorson's three-century framework [53] to such regional folk-cultures as the Pennsylvania German culture, we can ask, what types of stories were dominant in the culture of the eighteenth, the nineteenth, and the twentieth century? Since the myths and legends of one epoch are never completely replaced by those of the new, what happened, for instance, to the oldest stratum of legend in the culture, the European saint's legend, in the American experience? Old materials inherited from earlier stages of a culture are often reshaped, retreaded, combined, syncretized with the new. When an earlier form does disappear (or is relegated to an ultra-conservative or sectarian remnant culture, for example, the last gasp of the Genoveva legend among the Amish), what substitutes has the majority culture found for the lost trait?

2. Cross-genre and cross-media studies of American legendry are also called for. As in European settings, American legendry was presented in multigenre and multimedia approaches. Iconography (folk and popular prints, for example) as well as balladry and popular imprints, (chapbook and broadside materials) have to be studied together for American legend subjects, to see whether the same values are not expressed in all the media. When the fraktur symbols of the eighteenth century, the Lilies and Tulips and Flat Dutch Hearts, were replaced by the popular culture symbol of the American Eagle,[54] what happened at the same time to the legends of the Genovevas and the Mountain Marys? Pictorial evidence is particularly important. In some cultures, portraits of holy men—paintings of Zen masters in Japanese Zen Buddhism, framed portraits of favorite preachers in Protestant areas—served as foci of lay devotion, a kind of devotional shorthand, a substitute for the biography or the legend, but calling forth the same emotional reaction.[55] This is even more apparent in European Catholic cultures, where the simplest peasant recognizes his favorite saints by the crude almanac woodcut, or the starkest *ex voto* on the walls of a healing chapel.

3. Shifts or trends in the concept of sainthood itself need study in the United States.[56] We have mentioned the obvious difference

---

53 See Richard M. Dorson's paper in this symposium.

54 See Don Yoder, Introduction, *Pennsylvania German Fraktur and Color Drawings* (Lancaster: Pennsylvania Farm Museum of Landis Valley, 1969).

55 Martin Scharfe's valuable book, *Evangelische Andachtsbilder: Studien zur Intention und Funktion des Bildes in der Frömmigkeitsgeschichte vornehmlich des schwäbischen Raumes* (Stuttgart: Verlag Müller und Graf, 1968), suggests the relationship of the ikon and portrait to devotional literature.

56 Here again I recommend to my folklorist colleagues Mecklin's book, *The Passing of the Saint.*

between Roman Catholic and Protestant attitudes toward the "saint," and the development of Protestant substitutes for the forbidden items after the Reformation, as for example the substitution of Old Testament stories for earlier saints' legends. The ethos of American Catholicism also has produced a new syncretism in regard to traditional saints. Not all the favorite saints of all the ethnic groups that make up the American Catholic church were portable. Flying nuns, for example, who have recently made an appalling reappearance in television, belong in places like Calabria, where they should have been left.[57] If there has been an obvious shift from the miraculous to the virtue pole of the saint's legend, there are some other questions that need to be studied. What is the reason, for instance, for the continuance in popularity of so many of the traditional women saints in the twentieth century, while the number of favorite male saints has sharply dwindled? What effect will the downgrading of so many of the popular saints in the wake of Vatican II have on everyday Catholic piety? Will there be Catholic substitutes, intellectual or biblical, for the Philomenas and the Christophers? These are some of the many questions that can and should be asked about the concept of the saint, as one studies the surviving legends of the saints in our twentieth-century world.

One closing thought. Perhaps we can remind ourselves after looking over the vast range of human personality represented in the saints' legends, that as one of the great students of medieval sainthood put it, "goodness admits more variety in type than wickedness, and produces more interesting characters." [58]

---

[57] For some of the more unusual aspects of South Italian folk religiosity, see Ernesto de Martino, *Sud e Magia* (Milano: Feltrinelli Editore, 1959); also Phyllis Williams, *South Italian Folkways in Italy and America* (New Haven: Yale University Press, 1934), especially chaps. VII–VIII.

[58] Vida Scudder, trans. and ed., *Saint Catherine of Siena as Seen in Her Letters* (London: J. M. Dent, 1906), p. 2.

Modern Legends of Mormondom, or, Supernaturalism is Alive and Well in Salt Lake City

JAN HAROLD BRUNVAND, *University of Utah*

The Latter-Day Saints, compared to other American minority religious groups, are peculiarly susceptible to the growth and dissemination of supernatural folk legends. Founded on the basis of a new revelation, Mormonism encourages its adherents to seek divine guidance directly. Persecuted by nonbelievers (termed "Gentiles") in the early days, the first Mormons seized eagerly on providential rescues and fateful setbacks as evidences of the Almighty's pleasure or displeasure with his chosen people. Converts as they all were, they brought with them into Mormonism any magic and mysticism known from their native regions or faiths; and, of course, people with a mystical slant were most strongly attracted to latter-day revelations. Modern saints, settled as they are in regional enclaves and organized in a tight system of social and religious duties, like their forebears treasure their past legends and tell ever new ones in order to "bolster group solidarity . . . indoctrinate the children, and establish in them a group consciousness."[1] Probably no characteristic American religious group since the seventeenth-century New England Puritans has sustained and explored its faith so much by means of oral legends of the supernatural as have the Mormons.

Not only does Mormonism encourage the growth of folk legendry, but Mormons—and in particular ex-Mormons—are often

---

[1] Wilfred Bailey, "Folklore Aspects in Mormon Culture," *WF*, X (1951), 225.

185

attracted to the study of quasi-historical wonder tales. The Mormon emphasis on education has a bearing on this. Although the founders of the faith were middle-class, small-town men, they valued learning highly and supported it vigorously.[2] Present-day Mormons are encouraged by their leaders to get all the education they can, to read, compare, and inquire about their beliefs and others'. The importance of genealogy in Mormonism is also significant, because it makes virtually every active adult member into a part-time research scholar, developing in him respect for the past and some acquaintance with the problems of distinguishing historical fact from tradition. Ex-Mormon scholars share the background of in-group consciousness, but they may also turn a scientist's or a liberal humanist's eye, or a debunker's eye, upon the past. The result of all this is that we have abundant collectanea of Mormon legendry, albeit some of it gathered to propagandize for or against the church. And we have, if not *complete* studies, at least some good partial studies of the major traditions. One need only list names like Austin and Alta Fife, Hector Lee, Thomas Cheney, and Juanita Brooks to recall their scholarly works in Mormon folklore to the student of general American folklore, even if that student's acquaintance may not go much beyond Dorson's samples of their work in *American Folklore* and *Buying the Wind.*

Folklorists should not make the mistake, however, of assuming that the legendry of Mormondom is a closed account and that the past studies are definitive for all time. Not only does this run counter to our very definition of folklore, but also the best authorities on Mormon folklore have cautioned us as to the incompleteness of their work.[3] It is too easy to snap off the kind of judgment that is attributed to Stith Thompson in an interview published recently in the journal *Asian Folklore Studies,* although it must be realized that Thompson was speaking casually and his words were transcribed and edited by a foreigner. Thompson's quoted generalization was, "Austin Fife and his wife Alta . . . issued a com-

---

2 Austin E. Fife stresses the Mormon "commitment to health, education, and recreation" in his article "Folk Elements in the Formation of the Mormon Personality," *Brigham Young University Studies,* I–II (1959–60), 1–17.

3 Even the mere quantity of solid professional published research turns out to be surprisingly small when we begin to look for it beyond the well-known summaries. I can list only about fifteen items concerned with supernatural legends. Besides the studies specifically cited in this paper, the following should be noted: Fife, "Popular Legends of the Mormons," *CFQ,* I (1942), 105–125; Hector Lee, "The Three Nephites: A Disappearing Legend," *American Notes and Queries,* II:3 (June, 1942), 35–38; and a response to the last item by Wayland D. Hand in the same journal, II:4 (July, 1942), 56–57.

mon volume several years ago called *Knights of the Sage and Saddle*. Now they have pretty well cleaned up this Mormon folklore and are specializing on the cowboy material." [4] Concerning their book *SAINTS of Sage and Saddle*, the Fifes have been more modest; they admit that such a work "cannot be absolutely typical, absolutely representative, and certainly not comprehensive." [5]

Dorson is right, of course, in *Buying the Wind*, when he describes the Fifes' book (1956) and Hector Lee's *The Three Nephites* (1949) as "admirable analytical works based on extensive field recordings." [6] But we must also notice their dates—one and two decades ago—as well as their obvious limitations. Lee's dissertation, for instance, contained 150 variants, of which only 33 were printed in the published version, and Austin Fife has written very frankly recently of his editorial work in converting field transcripts into publishable texts. It involved, he says, "sorting the essential from the trivial . . . condensing, summarizing, [and] intensifying." [7] In contrast, the work-in-progress of a current student of the Three Nephite material—Bert Wilson of Brigham Young University—presently embraces about 450 texts and already suggests some major revisions in the interpretations of this legend cycle. Wilson, an Indiana University doctoral candidate in folklore, has recently written me as follows: "Two facts are quite clear: 1) Lee's view that new stories are no longer being generated is not true; 2) Fife's view that believing Mormons will accept without question such supernatural stories is not true." [8]

It must be understood at this point that there is no dispute raging between past and present students or theories of Mormon folklore, or even between Mormon and Gentile or Mormon and Jack Mormon scholars. What disagreement there has been in the past among students of Mormon folklore has concerned basic attitudes toward the folk group itself. For instance, in 1945 M. Hamlin Cannon, writing in *California Folklore Quarterly* on "Angels and Spirits in Mormon Doctrine," suggested that the belief in evil spirits had waned with the growing sophistication of the average

4 *Reminiscences of an Octogenarian Folklorists* [sic] (*Stith Thompson*) by Hari S. Upadhyaya, reprinted from *Asian Folklore Studies*, XXVII:2 (1968), 58.

5 Fife, "Myth Formation in the Creative Process," *WF*, XXIII (1964), 234.

6 Page 499; Lee, *The Three Nephites*, University of New Mexico Publications in Language and Literature, no. 2 (Albuquerque, 1949).

7 Fife, "Myth Formation," pp. 236–237.

8 Letter from Bert Wilson dated 9 May 1969. Hereafter cited as "Wilson letter." See Professor Wilson's recent article "Mormon Legends of the Three Nephites Collected at Indiana University," *IF*, II:1 (1969), 3–35.

church member. Cannon stated, "This article is but a historical summary . . . though the membership believes in all the manifestations of a preternatural nature that befell the founding fathers, it would put little credence in modern-day miracles." [9] Compare this assessment with Austin Fife's words on the same subject published in 1948: "The integrity of the philosopher and the objectivity of the man of science are in Utah as a thin crust over a pie of spiritualism and propitiatory ritual still hot from the oven." [10]

The fact is, even in 1969, that supernaturalism *is* alive and well in Salt Lake City, as elsewhere in Mormon country. The faith of the founding fathers has altered but little since the church was organized in Palmyra, New York, in 1830. The scriptures are the same, and only some aspects of interpretation and ritual have varied. Eight presidents of the church have served since Joseph Smith's martyrdom in 1844, and new revelations have been announced, but only in a few details of behavior has Mormon group life changed noticeably—most noticeably in response to the Manifesto against Polygamy announced in 1890. Another quite visible change is the growing emphasis dating from the late 1860's on the Word of Wisdom taboos concerning use of certain foods and tobacco, taboos that were actually a part of the *official* faith from 1833 and loosely followed for many years.[11]

Studies of the legends of Mormondom may continue in the directions they have had since 1938 when the first article on Mormon folklore appeared in a scholarly journal.[12] Such a continuation would certainly be fruitful. Texts collected twenty and more years ago remain unpublished and unanalyzed in such depositories as Hector Lee's doctoral dissertation, the Fife Collection,[13] and the WPA Writers' Project files at the Utah State Historical Society. Only one cycle of Mormon legends—the Three Nephites—has received special attention so far, and this needs to be brought up to date. Other legend cycles have been only randomly discussed. New fieldwork is needed to supplement the sometimes very scanty coverage of earlier projects.[14] Revisiting earlier informants or their de-

---

9 M. Hamlin Cannon, "Angels and Spirits in Mormon Doctrine," *CFQ*, IV (1945), 350.

10 Fife, "Folk Belief and Mormon Cultural Autonomy," *JAF*, LXI (1948), 30.

11 See Leonard J. Arrington, "An Economic Interpretation of the 'Word of Wisdom,'" *Brigham Young University Studies*, I (1959), 37–49.

12 Hand, "The Three Nephites in Popular Tradition," *SFQ*, II (1938), 123–129.

13 Part of the old Utah Humanities Research Foundation at the University of Utah.

14 For example, Fife published a major article in *JAF* from the results of a two-week collecting project carried out in 1939, mostly in the neighborhood of

scendants to study changes in their texts would be another useful project.

To approach the subject this way, however, would *not* be to study fully or most meaningfully the modern legends of Mormondom. There were aspects of the subject not considered by former students; there are new influences at work among the Mormons; there is constant bombardment upon Mormons from outside cycles of legends; and, verily, there are even some *new* Mormon legends.

One aspect that has been insufficiently studied is the influence of printed material. Both official and unofficial Mormon publications as well as anti-Mormon literature abound with supernaturalism—signs, wonders, judgments, blessings, warnings, omens, miracles, messages, and the like. Previous students of Mormon folklore have drawn on this,[15] but there are many gaps in the study of printed sources. No one has been systematically through *all* the relevant publications—the general church periodicals like *The Improvement Era* and the *Relief Society Magazine,* the Daughters of Utah Pioneers publications, county and community histories, *The Deseret News,* and the like. Nor has anyone tried to assesss what I call the apocryphal allusions to printed sources—when an informant (as some of Fife's did) says "I read that in the *Juvenile Instructor* when I was a little girl." Such remarks are analogous to the non-Mormon informant of Urban Belief Tales who feels sure he read the "true story" about the Solid Cement Cadillac in *The Reader's Digest* last year. Nor has anyone sufficiently recognized that even recent publications from Mormon-owned publishers like Bookcraft or Deseret Book Company, may be mines of folklike tradition, not only for scholars to collect, but also for informants to learn from. Such books are popular inspirational reading among Mormons and undoubtedly feed into oral tradition. Consider, for example, an anthology not mentioned in the Fifes' book and concerning a topic barely touched on there. This is a work published privately by its compiler, N. B. Lundwall, in 1952, titled *The Fate*

St. George, Utah. This is hardly enough coverage in time and space to be representative of all Mormons, but still the article has served as the background for many later generalizations about the Nephite tradition by readers of Fife. See "The Legend of the Three Nephites Among the Mormons," *JAF,* LIII (1940), 1–49.

15 Fife, for example, refers to the section in the *Doctrine and Covenants* that gives directions for identifying good and evil spirits; see Fife, "Folk Belief," p. 27. Cannon emphasizes the importance of Parley P. Pratt's 1855 book *Key to the Science of Theology* as well as to early columns of missionary miracles printed in church periodicals; see Cannon, "Angels and Spirits," pp. 343, 349. Hector Lee studied printed and even literary versions of the Three Nephites.

of the Persecutors of the Prophet Joseph Smith, and its long subtitle suggests the kind of grab bag that it is:

> Being a compilation of historical data on the personal testimony of
> Joseph Smith, his greatness, his persecutions and prosecutions, conspiracies against his life, his imprisonments, his martyrdom, his funeral and
> burial, the trial of his murderers, the sorrow and mourning of his followers, the fate of those who persecuted and killed him, and the attitude of his followers who also endured and passed through many of
> these experiences.

Lundwall's book draws upon all kinds of sources, including personal interviews, and it uncritically combines history and tradition in much the same manner as the New England Puritans gathered their "remarkable providences." The fate of the persecutors described in the book was to suffer a variety of exquisite tortures by disease, accident, and degradation brought down on every single "mobocrat" by what the Gentiles called the "Mormon curse."

Another seldom discussed aspect is the occasions for telling stories that Mormonism fosters, along with the effects of these different contexts upon narrators. It is one thing to tell a Nephite story to a folklore collector, and quite another to tell it in a Testimony Meeting; it makes a difference whether a returned missionary is chatting about his experiences in a college dormitory or is giving his formal testimony at a Sacrament meeting back in his home ward in Utah. (It also makes a difference whether the missionary returns to study at Brigham Young University or at that supposed hotbed of radicalism the University of Utah.) Mormon social life has numerous occasions, formal and informal, for exchanging legends. These have provided folklorists with some excellent texts, but seldom have the contexts been fully noted along with the words of the informants. We need collecting that records the actual language and behavior of tale-telling in Sacrament and Testimony meetings, at church conferences, in meetings of the Mutual Improvement Association (MIA), Relief Society, Boy Scouts, Beehive Girls, and Primary. We should collect tellings from family groups, school and college bull sessions, firesides, missionary reunions, and from the radio "talk programs," which are sometimes entirely given over for hours at a time to telling of experiences with the supernatural or speculating about the truth of wondrous stories the callers say they have heard.

A third new direction should be to distinguish more clearly between what I will call the "folk Mormon" versus the "liberal," "emancipated," or "Jack" Mormon. My Mormon colleagues at the

University of Utah do not regard the faith identically with most Morman faculty at BYU; nor do all the BYU or UU faculty think alike, and nor do our students. Different neighborhoods and suburbs of Salt Lake City shelter varying shades of Mormonism, and characteristic Salt Lake City Mormonism is not the same as that in Manti, Levan, Nephi, Bountiful, Salina, Panguitch, St. George, Logan—or, for that matter, Los Angeles. In a Mormon family there may be bishops, missionaries, and gleaner girls as well as a few black sheep. Every Mormon may tell a folk legend for a different reason or tell it differently in other contexts. We should get deeper inside the Mormon personality that Austin Fife has so well described for us in broad outlines,[16] down to the individuals and their specific needs and uses for folk legends in different situations.

A typical encounter that occurred just one month ago demonstrates all three of my points—the influence of printed material, the significance of context, and the distinction between varieties of attitude among informants. The place is Salt Lake City; scene, my living room; time, Sunday night May 18; cast of characters, my wife and me with a young Mormon couple, LaVerne and his wife Patty. They are devout members of the church, married in the Temple, in their late twenties, both sometime-students at Brigham Young University. They would not have wanted coffee or liquor if we had offered it, and we are polite enough not to suggest it; everyone sips lemonade. Patty graduated with a major in geology, taught school last year, is now pregnant, tends to be the more orthodox of the two. LaVerne, a senior in Library Science, working full time as a library assistant, is finishing his degree with night classes at the Salt Lake extension center of BYU. He served a mission in Austria from 1962 to 1965, and values the experience, but speaks with undisguised irony about some aspects of the church. LaVerne's and Patty's attitudes are suggested by remarks about BYU. LaVerne declares, "After I graduate, if I work for my Master's, I'll come up to 'The U' for a *real* education." Patty cries out, loyally, "Oh, you shouldn't say that!"

The very fact that they are here with us—Gentiles—on Sunday night enjoying themselves (hopefully) instead of hearing "testimonies" at a church meeting seems indicative of a certain looseness of practice. But then the conversation reveals that Patty did go to her Sacrament meeting earlier in the evening while LaVerne was at work. When I mention sermons in other churches, LaVerne

---

16 See Fife, "Folk Elements," cited above.

remarks, "Sometimes I think *we* should have preachers, because
we have to listen to some terribly dull things from our members."
Patty rushes to the defense again: "One woman gave a very interesting talk tonight on some work she's doing . . . they aren't always so dull." LaVerne, who has done a little creative writing himself, also scoffs at the kind of moralistic drivel that too often passes
for fiction in *The Improvement Era,* but Patty remembers a particularly good sad story she read there once which brought tears
to her eyes.

Asked what I am doing with local folklore, I describe my interest
in jokes and legends of Mormonism. We exchange a few jokes, and
as the talk turns to legends, LaVerne and Patty quickly recognize
the genre and refer me to Lundwall's book which they regard (correctly) as a tangle of quasi-historical semilegendary traditions. They
remember that they have heard it said that John the Revelator
spoke at the dedication of the Los Angeles temple in 1956, and
they know another book of Lundwall's to check for that.[17]

Thus the context has begun to be sketched out, now for the
text. I mention the Three Nephites, and our guests furnish my
wife with a succinct, orthodox account of the scriptural basis for
the stories. I mention the updating of Nephite stories, especially
the combination with the Vanishing Hitchhiker, and the allusion
to automobiles triggers a recollection.

"Would you like to hear *my* experience with the Three Nephites," LaVerne asks. Naturally. During his mission LaVerne and
his companion found themselves late one summer night walking
up a mountain path to an Austrian resort hotel. Villagers in the
valley below had warned them in which direction to turn when
the trail forked, but the two young men, though proficient in
German, disagreed about which way they had been told to go.
Perhaps the atmosphere had boggled their memories, for LaVerne
says that it was quite dark, fireflies were twinkling about, and owls
were hooting. Hiking along, they disputed the problem—should
they turn right or left at the trail's fork? All of a sudden, down
this mountain trail, quite improbably, comes a white Volkswagen
carrying three old Austrian farmers dressed in fine national cos-
tumes. In beautiful German accents, they ask, "What are you doing out here in the middle of the night?" "Walking back to the

---

17 The book was Lundwall's *Temples of the Most High* (12th print., Salt
Lake City,: N. B. Lundwall 1960); although there was a detailed description of
the dedication of the Los Angeles temple, there was no mention of a miracle
occurring.

hotel," the Americans answer. "Oh, then you must be sure to turn *right* when you get to the fork in the trail." The VW putts on down, the young men walk on up, and LaVerne's companion turns to him and says, "Those were the three Nephites!"

LaVerne has told us this story in a dramatic serious manner, holding our attention throughout and skillfully sustaining the suspense. He chooses his words carefully, and he paces the timing expertly; he has told it again and again, but likely not to many Gentiles or folklorists—certainly not to a Gentile folklorist who knows a bit about Mormonism. The text is a folklorist's dream, but if we stop there we miss what LaVerne wants to illustrate with the story. He doesn't believe that he has seen the Three Nephites. He knows that they very seldom appear all three together, and that their special territory is the New World. He also senses that this bit of helpful advice was probably too trivial to have been divine aid. He shakes his head and smiles as he describes the many times that his missionary companion repeated the story as his personal "testimony." Then LeVerne adds a comment that quite possibly he has never articulated to anyone else before—not even to his wife, judging from her wide-eyed silence. He says, "I lied when I came home; I told the people just what they wanted to hear. I just said what I had heard other guys say after their missions."

I have paraphrased both text and context here, but I hope my point is clear. Namely, that this kind of collecting in Mormon legendry would allow new dimensions of analysis to reach far beyond the tallying of motifs or the comparisons of variants. We would have the materials, for example, to study the development of memorates into legends—perhaps to draw a "flow chart" of legend formation such as Lauri Honko made in the *Journal of the Folklore Institute* with Finnish data.[18] A functional analysis would be inviting, along the lines of determining the relative values that are ascribed to the missionary or other "faith-promoting" experience at different levels of the church and in different individuals. A rhetorical approach, such as Roger Abrahams recommends,[19] would be fascinating—to analyze how the threads of conversation in my example eventually wound themselves around to the mo-

---

[18] Lauri Honko, "Memorates and the Study of Folk Beliefs," *JFI*, I (1964), 5–19.

[19] Roger Abrahams, "Introductory Remarks to a Rhetorical Theory of Folklore," *JAF*, LXXXI (1968), 143–158; Abrahams, "A Rhetoric of Everyday Life: Traditional Conversational Genres," *SFQ*, XXXII (1968), 44–59.

ment of self-revelation. Another obvious approach might be psychological, and next, perhaps, how related legends have stemmed from similar experiences.

This brings us to the subject of modern legends that belong to the contemporary practice of Mormonism among its most sophisticated practitioners. These legends offer a fascinating area for new research, because they vividly combine the old traditional capacity for belief in supernaturalism inherent in the faith with the current desire to "tell it like it is."

In my three years at the University of Utah, I have had several hundred young Mormons like LaVerne and Patty, as well as nonpracticing Mormons and Gentiles in my folklore classes, and most of them (in response to my queries) have put items pertaining to Mormonism into their term papers. Many have tape-recorded their texts, and most use themselves, close friends, and family as major informants. Little of this material has been surrounded by full contextual data, but the texts are reliable and informants have been identified; there is usually at least as much context provided as in the average published folklore study. These collections (and Bert Wilson's BYU student papers are similar) demonstrate what kind of legends are still vital in Utah Mormonism. In them we can see how older legend themes have been updated and what new legend types are emerging. Presently the two to three hundred legends on file suggest that modern supernatural legends of Mormondom might conveniently be put into seven classes before further analysis.

First in any survey of Mormon legends must come *The Three Nephites;* and, although I have actually met Utah students who have never heard of them, most have had some personal acquaintance with the appearing-Nephite tradition. There is no doubt that the old Nephite motifs linger on—the sudden disappearances, dispensing of advice, asking for or bringing food, and so forth—but, as Bert Wilson's studies verify,[20] not every Mormon who repeats one of these old stories really believes it. In fact, most second-hand accounts seem to be told as something *someone else* believes; the informant himself is never quite sure, hasn't enough information to tell, and so forth. Often there is a rationalization or other comment at the end of a narration; after telling a Nephite tale into a small portable tape recorder in the hallway of the Bountiful 33rd Ward Church House, one informant commented, "Of course, maybe you hear a lot of things like that. I try to shy away from

---

[20] The Wilson letter quotes from a thirty-page article accepted for publication in *IF.*

them . . . because they can become old family tales that have
more imagination in them than—uh—reality."

A cycle of Nephite hoax and mistaken identifications also circu-
lates.[21] Some supposed Nephite appearances are perpetrated deliberately to fool people, while other times the chance arrival of
a stranger is at first interpreted as a Nephite visitation. First-person
accounts (memorates) tend to be set in completely modern contexts: "In Layton [Utah] in back of J. C. Penney's, there's only one
entrance and one exit to the parking lot . . . a man came up to
the side of the car and told my daughter some things about her
baby. . . . My daughter said, 'One of three Nephites,' and her
husband said it almost at the same time." Or: "And then the hitchhiker wants out right in the middle of nowhere . . . along the
freeway [between Provo and Salt Lake City]." The following
slightly shortened but otherwise verbatim transcript from a student's tape recording is a good example of a recent tale containing
hints of context and some allusions to contemporary themes:

> [Collector asks for a Nephite tale.]
> *Informant:* This was told to me by one of the boy scouts in our ward,
> since I am the scoutmaster; he and I were having an interview as to
> what he wanted to do in life. . . . He told me this story was related
> to him by his older brother who had been straying from the church.
> He was attending the University of Utah and had begun to believe
> some doctrines that were in opposition to the church. He met a fellow
> on campus one day who walked up to him and told him exactly what
> was on his mind, and exactly some of the problems that this fellow
> had been encountering . . . and he told him that he had better start
> living the commandments of the Lord which he had been taught in
> his youth. And the man turned around and left. Now he did not dis-
> appear in any way, but he did seem to know all about this young fellow
> and what was happening in his life.
> *Collector:* Does the boy scout believe this story?
> *Informant:* Oh yes, yes, he does.
> *Collector:* Do you?
> *Informant:* Well, I'm not sure it was a Nephite, but the fellow did
> shape up and started coming out to church more regularly.

My second category, rather miscellaneous, is *Other Spiritual Visi-
tations,* and as in the Nephite stories we find a contemporary overlay on older traditions. Here, too, cluster some legendary motifs
common in non-Mormon folklore, but provided with LDS touches.
A ghostly warning of death, a mysterious stroke of luck, a pro-
phetic disembodied voice,[22] all may be regarded as "testimonies"
or "faith-promoting" experiences. Such stories are told from gen-

---

21 Hand mentioned Nephite hoaxes in "The Three Nephites," p. 126 n. 20.
22 In Mormon usage this is the "wee small" or "still small" voice.

eration to generation, eventually sometimes being written into a family's genealogy. Often a person who knows a legend feels that someone else—a grandfather or uncle or sister-in-law—knows it more correctly; *that* relative, of course, thinks someone else knows it properly, until we get back to a deceased member, who knew it best of all. Many of these stories, I suspect, derive from official church narrations—oral or written—and are repeated almost ritualistically, more as a duty of membership than as a matter of belief. The following short text seems to support this view:

> One time this guy was out climbing by himself in the Uintahs [mountain range]. He was climbing up this quite steep ledge, and he was almost to the top when he slipped and fell. He caught on to a branch of a bush there on the side of the cliff, and he heard a voice say, "Do you believe in me?" The guy was pretty scared, and said, "Yes." The voice told him to let go of the limb. The guy let go of the limb and a gust of wind took hold of him and blew him to the top. (This was told in church in Orem, Utah, as a true experience.)

A third category is stories concerning *Evil Spirits*. Contrary to Cannon's supposition in 1945 that belief in evil spirits declined as sophistication increased, I still find that numerous accounts of evil spirit attacks circulate, while there are very few stories about angels or other good spirits. Joseph Smith from the earliest days of his ministry was challenged by powers of the Devil determined to deny the ministry to other men, and modern Mormons have continued to feel themselves come under vicious attack from invisible spirits, spirits inhabiting human forms, or monstrous spirits. The victims are likely to be new missionaries, or people suffering doubts about the church. Right triumphs over evil only after a fierce struggle that may be concluded abruptly when the sufferer invokes his power of the priesthood or rebukes the evil spirit in the name of Christ. Dogs and other domestic animals may detect the presence of spirits before humans do. Sometimes a person sensing the activity of spirits may call on them to come out for a direct confrontation; heroic battles may ensue with sulphurous smells and smokes, scorched walls and furnishings (sometimes, instead, intense cold), screams and groans of defiance and despair. Many stories concern the presence of evil spirits when a group tries to read the future with a ouija board.[23] These ouija board stories—often personal experiences told as memorates—are especially popular among high school and college students, as, indeed, are the ouija boards

---

23 Fife mentioned a ouija board belief in "Folk Belief," p. 27.

themselves.[24] Evil spirits may manifest themselves anywhere, but frequently they seize on a person alone in his bedroom, perhaps sitting or lying heavily upon him in his bed or pinning him to the wall. If the spirits come in human form, they are often Negroid, exceptionally ugly, birthmarked, or with a fire-red complexion, wearing dark clothes, or possibly looking like the Devil himself. Someone offering to shake hands with an evil spirit in human form will be refused or will feel nothing at all when the hands come together. Evil spirits may possess the bodies of ordinary humans, sometimes good Mormons, but usually either of likely converts or staunch members of another religious sect that is opposing the Mormons in an area.[25]

Two examples of these legends suggest some approaches to analyzing them. The first was taken down verbatim from a twenty-year old junior at the University of Utah. She was raised in Salt Lake City by devout parents, but at the time of the experience described had backslidden from the faith, much to her parents' dismay. The informant offered the guess that the event she described was a subconscious attempt on the part of her mother to warn her away from sin, or perhaps it was to rationalize the daughter's faltering faith as the result of evil outside influences rather than any failure in her upbringing.

> I came home one night very late and found my mother in the bathroom crying. When I finally wrung it out of her what was the matter, she said that she had been walking past my room and something had reached out and grabbed her and she'd fallen to her knees. She said when she looked in my room she saw these horribly ugly beings— really grotesque. So she said, "In the name of Jesus Christ I command you to leave." Then she went downstairs and got my dad, because he had the priesthood and he came and said, "In the name of Jesus Christ I command you to leave," and they did. This occurred in the spring of 1966.

Another example was heard by a student at a Stake Conference a couple of years ago; it was told by a missionary just returned from Brazil. It is a form of story that crops up repeatedly in the archive, usually attributed to a missionary in a Catholic country and sometimes told to explain why missionaries are required to work and travel in pairs. Clearly, I think, we can recognize here one effect of cutting young men off from normal female compan-

---

24 Wilson has some 140 ouija board legends in one student collection.
25 Thomas E. Cheney has one story of possession by an evil spirit in "Mormons and Miracles," *Proceedings: Utah Academy of Science, Arts, and Letters*, XXXIX (1961–62), 30–39.

ionship for two years at a time in a foreign country; where reality
is lacking, fantasy enters:

> My companion and I were walking through a town one day when
> we decided to knock on one door, and a beautiful nude woman ap-
> peared at the door. We got out of there as quick as possible, but this
> woman kept calling up my missionary companion to come over and
> see her. [In some versions she locks them in with her and pursues them
> around the apartment until they manage to escape.] He became very
> upset about it, and we decided to go back there and see if this woman
> was possessed by evil spirits. My companion and I commanded the
> evil spirits to leave her body. Her body became limp and she fell on
> the floor. She came back to consciousness, but she almost seemed to
> be an imbecile. So we took her to the police to find out her identity,
> and later it was discovered that she had escaped from a mental hos-
> pital and her family had been searching for her for two weeks. We
> told our mission president and he told us that many evil spirits took
> possession of the bodies of the mentally ill.

The fourth group of legends will only be mentioned here, since
it is the subject of a continuing study by Professor Ray R. Canning
of the Sociology Department at the University of Utah. These are
the *Return-From-the-Dead Stories*—accounts by "apparently normal and reliable Mormons who died and lived to tell about it." [26]
Canning has published a description of his detailed interview transcripts with seven first-hand subjects, and he has references to
many second-hand accounts. The experiences usually involve a
sense of painless, peaceful levitation of the spirit out of the body
and a transport to some celestial realm where angels and souls are
living in happy harmony. The spiritual traveler then is returned,
sometimes unwillingly, to his earthly state to fulfill his mission
here before going to heaven permanently. My texts are all second-
hand, not as detailed as Canning's, and often blurred by modern-
ized or confused details, as, for instance, the informant who explained that the doors to heaven opened automatically, "just like
those doors when you go to Safeway." Canning is continuing the
study of these texts and enlarging his research into cross-cultural
comparisons, so I shall leave the field to him.

In the fifth grouping, I have placed all legends that are concerned with *Religious Duties and Regulations,* such as the patri-
archal blessings, genealogy work, the wearing of the sacred under-
garments, and "Temple Work" (i.e., "sealings" and "vicarious bap-
tisms for the dead"). These topics lead to both a positive, reinforc-

---

26 See Ray R. Canning, "Mormon Return-from-the-Dead Stories, Fact or
Folklore," *Proceedings: Utah Academy of Science, Arts, and Letters,* XLII (1965),
29–37.

ing lore that stresses the importance of correct behavior, and a negative body of folklore suggesting that the religious requirements are pointless. Most of the supernatural legends fall into the first category and are told by Mormons themselves, while jokes rather than legends are told by non-Mormons to debunk church work. There are exceptions, however. Genealogy being the complicated and often exasperating task that it is, Mormons working for the various genealogical societies and libraries collect "funny files" of ludicrous answers that supposedly have been filled in on the Family Group Sheets submitted for verification:

> "I found my Grandmother crossing the plains in the library yesterday."
>
> "The information was acquired partially orally. Child number three was received by letter."
>
> "Number seven child died as a child turning somersaults and did not show up at the census."

The serious legends about religious duties and regulations may emphasize the futility or impossibility of performing certain tasks if conditions are not propitious. A patriarch finds that he is unable to deliver the traditional blessing to a boy, and the very next day the boy dies in an automobile accident or is arrested for a crime. A spirit that was improperly sealed to his family in a temple rite returns to haunt his descendants until they look up the records and repeat the work correctly. A temple marriage is halted when divine inspiration reveals to the presiding official that the groom's genealogy contains undisclosed Negro blood several generations back. Legends about genealogical work usually deal with providential reception of needed information by a dream, a vision, or a mysterious stranger, usually identified as a Nephite. The following treatment of this theme collected in 1967 from a Mormon boy is interesting because the informant used the word "imaginary," perhaps unconsciously. Also, it seems to demonstrate how serendipity may become interpreted as supernaturalism:

> This one fellow had to go down to L.A. on business. He had always been interested in genealogy, but too busy to do anything. After he'd finished his business, he had a free afternoon and decided to go to the Genealogical Research Library. Of course, everything being new, he didn't know where to go or to start. As he walked into the library he saw an arrow; it wasn't painted or anything, it was imaginary. And he followed it down some stairs and down an aisle. It pointed at a book. He picked up the book and found pertinent and necessary information that he needed in filling out his genealogy sheets.

Legends concerning the temple rituals may contain secret information, thus they are harder for Gentiles to collect; nevertheless,
I have several texts of two particular stories. The first concerns a
temple sealing or baptism that is halted just before its conclusion
by an official who insists that he sees another person (invisible
to the rest) not yet accounted for. Eventually one of the participants remembers a child that died at birth or discovers a name
that was overlooked in the work sheets, and the vision fades.
A second common story takes various forms, but always contains
a new baby-sitter who has luckily been found just when a mother
was scheduled to do temple work. Upon her return, she learns that
the baby-sitter has disappeared a moment before, sometimes after
having saved her baby from drowning in an irrigation ditch. When
the baby-sitter cannot be located, and her phone number is reported as having been disconnected for years, the mother recalls
that a woman she had been doing work for in the temple that day
had the same name as the baby-sitter. In another version the baby's
rescuer answers to the description of a person the mother saw in
the temple that day just as she felt a vague premonition of danger
and started to go home; the mysterious stranger advised her to
finish her temple work first, for everything would be all right at
home.

Temple garments legends have two modes—a Mormon one that
stresses the power of the garments to protect the wearer, and the
Gentile one that pictures the Mormons as fanatics. Bert Wilson
has a collection of about sixty of the former, which I have not yet
seen but which probably are like my own. Pioneers wearing their
garments, though slain in an Indian massacre, were not scalped,
presumably because the Indians ("Lamanites") recognized the religious symbols sewn into the garments as signs of the one true
God. Accident victims wearing their garments are free of wounds
or burns wherever the garment touched their bodies. Lightning
strikes but does not harm the garment wearer, and so forth. The
Gentile mode is more a joke or anecdote than legend: a Mormon
woman insists on her baby being delivered through the garments; [27] a girl sleeps with her boyfriend, so long as she may keep
her garments on; a Protestant minister or Catholic priest wears the
garments simply because he thinks they are a comfortable kind of
underwear.

---

27 I have also heard the term "Smith's Garment Dystocia" for a pseudo-
complication known to Utah obstetricians referring to difficulties of emergency
deliveries performed for garment wearers.

My last two categories of Mormon legend have just begun to show up in my collections and need be mentioned only briefly. First, there seems to be a considerable variety of fantastic tales told concerning *Ancient American Archaeology* and how it supports the *Book of Mormon* account of pre-Columbian history, a subject too vast and baroque to be gone into here. Suffice it to say that much of this probably derives from certain widely read books by one Dewey Farnsworth,[28] an amateur archaeologist. His works are large, lavishly illustrated compendia of quotations and homemade conjectures about archaelogical finds in South and Central America. The folk mind, I believe, revises Farnsworth ever more in the direction of fantasy, so that for every example in legend of something like an unsupported spiral stairway discovered in a jungle clearing which baffles modern science, there is an illustration in Farnsworth of a well-wrought, but quite explainable, Mayan or Aztec staircase. Such wonders as unknown metals and alloys, cryptic echoes of Hebraic or Egyptian culture, medical skills, and use of Christian symbols, all supposedly present before Columbus, crop up in the oral tales, as in Farnsworth's and others' books.

The last category of legends is one that I also include in another context among Mormon jokes,[29] but that overlaps here too. These are the *Famous Church Members* stories, known by many Mormons but seldom believed. Show business personalities and other notables are said to be LDS members in secret—Walt Disney, Roy Rogers, Pat Boone, Howard Hughes, and others. One of these that has acquired a supernatural motif is appropriate to conclude a paper read in California. Cecil B. De Mille is said to have come very close to the Mormon church in his later years—speaking at a BYU commencement, meeting David O. McKay, using a Utah artist to design sets for his film *The Ten Commandments*. A returned missionary asks, "Do you know how Cecil B. DeMille died?" The collector replies that he cannot recall what it was that was wrong with him. "No, that's not what I mean," the missionary says, "I heard that he was getting so close to the church that after he finished *The Ten Commandments* he wanted to make a movie of the *Book of Mormon;* but he would have had to change too many parts of it, so the Lord took him away."

---

28 These include *The Americas Before Columbus* (El Paso, Tex.: Farnsworth Publishing, 1947) and *Book of Mormon Evidences in Ancient America* (Salt Lake City: Deseret Book, 1953).

29 The reference is to my paper "As the Saints Go Marching By: Modern Jokelore Concerning Mormons" read at the annual meeting of the American Folklore Society in Bloomington, Indiana, Nov. 8–10, 1968.

These groupings that I have suggested for the modern legends of Mormondom are necessarily tentative at this point, and new categories will have to be created as both the collecting of legends and the legendry itself grow. For instance, a place must be found for stories concerning curses that fall upon those who defile and profane church rituals; another niche must be reserved for the anecdotal tradition concerning mistakes in church services, a consequence of the Mormon use of a lay clergy. New insights for the study of Mormon legends will doubtless appear as the work of collecting and classifying continue. For example, the better understanding of the relationships between memorate, legend, anedote, and joke among Mormons must probably await more and better collecting efforts as well as further theoretical advances in American legend study generally. For the present, it might be well to close with a recent quotation from a folklorist who is a member of the Church of Jesus Christ of Latter-Day Saints and whose words reflect both an awareness of the legendary aspects of such material and a sensitive regard for its psychological and religious aspects. The following is from Professor Thomas E. Cheney's Faculty Lecture delivered at Brigham Young University on March 26, 1969, titled "Imagination and the Soul's Immensity":

> the spiritual eyes of church folk are not always clear, and some have been too quick to see miracles, too prone to see the diabolical devil himself operating a ouija board, too ready to interpret a peregrination of the mind as a possession of the devil, or too eager to call a stranger who does a kindness an ancient Nephite of supernatural power, too much inclined to hear the voice of the dead or to die and experience a few hours of celestial living, or even to embark into wild fantasy in the name of religion which is little short of schizophrenia.

Ma'i Joldloshi: Legendary Styles and Navaho Myth

BARRE TOELKEN, *University of Oregon*

At the outset let me make it clear that I am neither an anthropologist nor a specialist in Navaho language and culture. My knowledge of the Navaho comes primarily from having lived with them on and off for thirteen years and having been adopted by an old Navaho raconteur, Tsinaabaas Yazhi (Little Wagon). During the year 1954–55 I lived almost exclusively with Little Wagon's family (his wife, his daughter, his son-in-law, and his grandchildren) in then-remote Aneth Extension in southern Utah, and heard English chiefly at the trading posts. On at least two occasions I have owed my life to the ministrations and actions of this family, and I came very close to staying with them permanently. Nowadays I visit them about twice a year, and most of what I am about to say is drawn from conversations with them over the years.

Little Wagon died about three years ago, well over ninety, but my first exposure to his legends and stories came during the winter of 1954, during which he continually recited Coyote tales, origin stories, anecdotes, and personal reminiscences. Many of these, especially those in the etiological category, began to puzzle me. It became clear that although a story might be told to explain the origin of some phenomenon (like snow) on a very local level, as soon as anyone questioned it in the slightest, Little Wagon would quip, "You'd better make up your own story about the matter." That is, even though a story might be told like an explanatory myth or legend, no one, including the narrator, seemed to take it very seriously as really explanatory. Yet, when Little Wagon's grandchildren are reminded of such incidents today, they are quite certain that the old man was *not* serious when he told people to make up their own stories. Clearly, then, while "fact" may not have been central, neither does fiction quite represent what was happening. It will emerge from my discussion that those elements we normally connect with legend (both textual variation and alleged factuality) are used stylistically by the Navaho for varying purposes. The same stories, same characters, same motifs, will be used here in tale, here in anecdote, here in ritual, sometimes by the same narrator.

It is important to note, however, that while I want to avoid the limitations of our categories, I must use our words. Although I know of no clear Navaho equivalents to such generic terms as "myth," "legend," "märchen," and so on, they are necessary means of dealing in English with recognizable aspects of Navaho narrative. It will become clear, however, that such terms, since they are based in our own generic biases, can be used properly and with clarity only when applied to our own cultural output. The Navaho expressions that we might construe in terms of legend and myth are for the Navaho actually closer to matters of style and modes of conceptualization than they are to our genre categories.

If we view the Navaho legendary narratives closely, we find nearly all our favorite distinctions blurred. Short of inventing an entirely new set of terms, we find we must cope with such dilemmas as the following:

1. Navaho Coyote tales, for example, which are usually dealt with by whites as fictional, secular narratives, are believed in as factual in many central respects (Coyote is real and exists in real life; he has actually done those things attributed to him in the stories, and continues to do them). While the narrator is free to embellish his literary style while telling the stories, the narratives themselves are held to be of considerable moral and religious import and indispensable to participation in, and understanding of, myth.[1]

2. The concept of "fact" is in itself quite different to the Navaho (or to us, depending on whose premise one starts from). There is no possible distinction between Ma'i, the animal we recognize as a coyote in the fields, and Ma'i, the personification of Coyote power in all coyotes, and Ma'i, the character (trickster, creator, and buffoon) in legends and tales, and Ma'i, the symbolic character of disorder in the myths. Ma'i is not a composite but a complex; a Navaho would see no reason to distinguish separate aspects.

---

[1] I take up this topic in some detail in "The 'Pretty Language' of Yellowman: Genre, Mode, and Texture in Navaho Coyote Narratives," *Genre*, II:3 (Sept., 1969), 211–235.

3. These stories, while considered factual, and often local in origin, also carry recognized traditional moral applications that are seldom if ever stated (making them both like and unlike that body of narratives we often classify as "fable").

4. In contrast to our usual definition of a legend, even the most legendary Navaho legends usually will have more than one motif.

5. Navaho legends often feature etiological details that do not, in the final analysis, have anything to do with the reasons for telling the story.

6. In most cases I am familiar with, both myths and tales are told in what I would call legendary style, with myths using the factual, localized assertions parenthetically and intrusively, while legendary tales use the same references centrally and prominently —even when the main point of the tale has absolutely nothing to do with the stated legendary "fact."

An incident one hears recounted in a legendary tale will be encountered on another occasion in a myth. Something alluded to in a myth will come out in rationalized, local form in legend. There are legends of witches and werewolves told constantly, and there are corresponding rituals, complete with myths, to counteract the effects of witches. There are separate stories about place names and plant names which can also be heard in the myths. Etiological stories will appear here in complex form in a myth, there in a humorous anecdote or tale. For example, in one myth, Coyote, in stealing fire, ties a torch to his tail and scorches the tip black; in one humorous tale, Coyote, in a burst of typical egotism, seeks to show how rapidly he runs and ties a smoking torch to his tail and scorches the tip black. Both "versions" are considered factual and not mutually exclusive with respect to the question of Coyote's black-tipped tail.

I refer here chiefly to the Coyote materials because they are particularly striking examples of the way myth and legendary tale utilize the same characters and attitudes. Ma'i is the exponent of all possibilities. According to my informants it is through his actions that we are enabled to conceive of, and experience, all things. He still operates in the world (else how could new things come about?) and is very much believed in. He is at once symbolic and mythically important (brings fire, creates death), unprincipled, oversexed and underfed, a threat to all normalcy, a taboo breaker, a laughingstock (the ultimate in Navaho punishment), and a poignantly consummate idiot.[2]

---

[2] For a more detailed and devastating character reference, see Gladys A. Reichard, *Navaho Religion* (New York: Pantheon Books, 1950), pp. 422–426.

When Coyote appears in the myths, the style of narration begins to feature local place names, authenticating formulas (not unlike those of the urban tales), factual assertions, as if suddenly in the midst of celebrating mass a priest were to relate an interesting factual anecdote concerning a funny trick played by the pope on the archbishop of Canterbury. For example, in the myths and ceremonies concerning creation, while the stars are being carefully placed, each one for a particular reason, Coyote comes along and by mistake or by whim scatters an entire pouch full of stars indiscriminately across the sky.[3] In the midst of Red Antway, a very serious chant used to cure abdominal distress and sometimes pneumonia, Coyote begs lizards to let him play games with them. In an exciting sequence of Emergence myth, Coyote, pursued by beings bent on revenge for incest, pauses to yell at the spider people, "You don't even know how to screw!" [4]

Many such stories are told separately as place-name legends. In addition, there are numerous stories about nature spirits, witches, and so on, which allege within their own narrations the factuality of the occurrence. Although these and other Ma'i tales are classed as secular tales by such people as Thompson and Kluckhohn, my informants assure me that they are heavy in religious and moral implication. Yellowman, my best informant, feels that *all* narratives are religious in nature and function. Further, he has reacted to my description of generic distinctions with the reply that they are meaningless as far as he can see.

I find the following observation important, however. In the myths, on one hand, Coyote usually comes in as part of an explanation of how disorder came to be possible in the natural world. In the legendary tales, on the other hand, his actions are usually those that Navahos connect with one's conscious morality; that is, in these tales Coyote exemplifies moral excesses and taboos that one would not normally experience, and the audience is caused—partially through narrative style—to laugh at Ma'i.[5] Disorder is dealt with through ritual; excess is a private moral matter, but it may *lead* to disorder.

A quick glance at Navaho religion here, though unfairly superficial, may help to orient the non-Navaho. To begin with, there

---

[3] One brief account of this episode is given in Berard Haile, O.F.M., *Starlore Among the Navaho* (Santa Fe: Museum of Navajo Ceremonial Art, 1947), p. 4; it appears with minor variation in a number of myths.

[4] These episodes are encountered in several myths, and usually feature local references (names of canyons and mountains, for example).

[5] See "The 'Pretty Language' of Yellowman," pp. 227-231.

is no supreme being, and nothing that can fairly be called gods; nothing, in short, is worshiped. By the way, there is not even a Navaho equivalent for the word "God"; thus, when the Bible people came to translate into Navaho, they retained *God*, which, pronounced "gahd," means "juniper tree" in Navaho (hence, "In the beginning, a juniper tree created heaven and earth"). Instead of worshiping, the Navaho participates reciprocally in the process of nature. Participation is primarily ritualistic, and extends to nearly all features of life.[6]

The main concern of Navaho religion is the attainment and maintenance of health, which is construed as including not only one's personal physical and mental health, but that of one's family, herds, and crops, and, in addition, well-being in a rather broad area we might call luck. For the natural world to function properly, all segments must be healthy and ordered. One's ill health thus disrupts not only his own life but troubles the entire natural world. Almost everything one does, then, can be (and usually is) considered as a religious act. Excess of *any* sort is avoided, for it causes ill health (or it may be construed as a symptom of serious disorder); thus avoidance and repression are justifiable as religious acts equal to gestures of participation.

The myths are primarily narratives that are actual *parts* of healing ceremonies (called "sings"); that is, much more than explanations of the rites, they are themselves narrative symbols of the very kind of order the ceremony seeks to reimpose on the ritual life of the patient. Order is stressed (one might even say created) throughout the entire ceremony in the form of visual symbols (sandpainting), sound symbols (the bull roarer), musical/poetic symbols (the chants), anatomical and geographical symbols (certain postures, cardinal directions of human movement, positions of seating), celestial symbols (astronomical referents for beginning the ceremony), and narrative symbols (the ordering of events in ritual time and in relation to other ritually important "facts")—to mention a few—in company with the application of medicines. The medicine is for the body; all the rest are devices that are consciously employed to reinstate the patient in his proper reciprocating relationships with the ordered, rhythmic patterns of nature. Within the ceremony, man *becomes* "supernatural," by walking on pollen paths, by sitting on the sandpaintings, by being enveloped by myth and rhythmic

---

[6] A refreshingly brief and up-to-date discussion of this concept may be found in David F. Aberle, *The Peyote Religion Among the Navaho* (Chicago: Aldine Publishing, 1966), pp. 47–49.

chant. He is, in short, magically saturated with order. Nothing is propitiated (in the Christian sense) or worshiped; for the Navaho, his is a direct interaction with important aspects of the real, factual world, but in this case those that exist on a plane reached only through the magic of ritual. The spirits and oneself are brought into a common order indispensable to both, and are magically caused to behave harmoniously together.

Myths can be recited without the ceremony, of course, but in my experience they seldom are. One who knows a myth but cannot perform the entire ceremony is considered simply to be knowledgeable. It is the myth, along with the ceremonial it informs and orders, which is considered by Navahos to be "the real thing."

An expansion of these comparisons between myth and legend may be revealing here. Because of the position of myth in the healing ceremony, one normally would not hear a myth unless at least the basic requirements and ingredients of a ceremony are present: a patient, a singer, medicines; a fee must be paid the singer, and the ceremony usually must take place in a hoghan. The legendary tales, conversely, require no patient, no fee, no particular surroundings; they are not magical, and they are not designed to "do" anything. The usual context in which myth is heard, then, is impregnated with sacredness, and the group of participants will be friends, neighbors, singers, and a wide spectrum of relatives. The legendary tales occur in a smaller, less magical (though not to the Navaho less religious) situation, mostly within the immediate family group. In the myth context, the audience is participating actively in a ritual system that involves relations with the supernatural; in the legend context, the audience is involved with a factual-sounding drama, with entertainment and instruction, with personal aesthetic reactions rather than magical participation. The myth and its ritual provide depth involvement with nature through magical use of words, while the legendary tales bring about a breadth of involvement with the visible, immediate, practical and moral life context. Art of a striking quality appears in both areas, of course, but in the recitation of myths and ceremonies the ideal is exacting repetition according to traditional codes, while the narrator of the legendary tales is quite free to supply his own textural variations.

Obviously, then, the differences between materials we might call myth and legend are, for the Navaho, primarily based on matters of function and context, not on differences of content and genre. Further, the variety of their expression seems similarly to be stylistic and modal in nature; that is to say, with much identical material being used in a variety of contexts, the talent of a Navaho narrator seems to lie largely in his ability to conceptualize and use a style appropriate to the immediate social and religious context.

Both myth and legendary tale concern the way one operates in the real world. For this reason, I think, the singers of magical cere-monies have found it quite appropriate to use legendary style in order to maintain at certain intervals a solid connection with the personal, local world in which the patient and his people live—the immediate context for which they seek harmony. Ritual health *requires* magical contact with powers that operate in a somewhat different mode, however, and so the bulk of the ceremony will necessarily be that which *must* be performed for magical efficacy. The legendary references therein, then, are subordinated to this end.

The legendary tales, as I have mentioned above, concern them-selves with matters about which the individual must form his own opinion, but which, nonetheless, are of considerable religious im-port. This is the area of conscious relationships to one's fellow man, to one's local geography, to one's family, and, most important, to the idiosyncrasies of one's own body and mind. Here are ideas *about* oneself, his clan, his tribe, his religion; here, in short, are the immediate rational concerns of the individual in his own social and historical contexts. While the ritual myths are obligatory and com-plicated (thus known in detail only by specialists), the legendary tales concern every man's everyday life insofar as they expose him to a great amount of cultural information that he ought to know. Ex-posure to a maximum amount of legends may thus keep his needs for myth at a minimum. From this view, the two fields are quite distinct to the Navaho: tales of local witches keep a person in mind of how he ought to act with respect to the reality of witch-craft; the *effects* of witchcraft, once contracted, are matters of health, and are thus the concern of myth and ritual. Witches, when detected, are usually murdered, often for very practical rational reasons (out of political expediency, Chiefs Manuelito and Ganado Mucho had some forty witches murdered in 1879; and just about three years ago a whole family of witches was murdered near Farm-ington, New Mexico). But the sickness and disorder brought about by the witch can *only* be cured through the magic of ritual—regard-less of the witch's death. Both the existence of the witch and the effect of the witch are considered real, and factual, but must be dealt with differently.

Thus, for the Navaho, the worlds of morality and ritual—or, if you will, the subscription to social patterns and behavior, and the obligation to ritual patterns and natural order—interpenetrate. They are not construed as opposed areas of: reality versus imagination; or this world versus the Otherworld; or custom versus faith (though this last comes closest). Instead, these are two planes of real existence in the real world which intersect in every individual. The characters, motifs, attitudes, and morals are all geared to one broad religious view of the ways in which one must confront his entire environment. What differs is the mode, the approach, to a manipulation and an understanding of each plane.

Public and personal morality are not supernaturally enforced or ritually controlled—even though they are considered areas of religious concern. Health and natural order, however, are ritually controlled. For the Navaho, then, legend is an indispensable, rational, personal, voluntary counterpart to myth and ritual, and it exists therefore on the level of rational persuasion, social pressure, local and ascertainable "fact." Its style is productive of credibility, which anchors the legendary tales to the real and local world, preventing them—for all their spirit animals and magical motifs—from becoming fictive escapes from immediate concerns. The myths use the same styles, selectively, using the credibility to remind the participants of the real-world aspects of the ceremony without disturbing its magical processes.

Thus, *belief*, per se, is not at question, for both tale and myth assume a context of belief. Rather, the aura of credibility, administered stylistically, proclaims a feeling of comfortable certainty, an immediacy and application of cultural values in those processes of life—personal and ritual health—which are most likely to be associated with tension and anxiety.

Since most Navahos do not consider themselves *bilagaana* (American), we need not trouble ourselves about rationalizing this mass of terminological puzzles into the corpus of American Legend—the topic of our conference. Ironically, what most of us mean by American legend is essentially nonnative in its origins and development. Thus, this paper is not in any way a plea for the inclusion of Navaho materials in our deliberations, but rather a consideration for ourselves—in the way of a folk remedy for the scholar, perhaps, a specific for constipation and for arthritis of the category. Looking at our own critical distinctions, as they may or may not apply to the traditional output of another culture, can afford us some views not easily obtainable on home ground, and should bring us to realize that our categories are not natural but are themselves an outgrowth of our own cultural myopia (as would be Navaho categories if applied to our materials).

While perspective is my real aim here, cultural shock of a sort may also attend the process, as it did when I showed Little Wagon a photograph of the Empire State Building. He asked, "Dikwii dibe bihi'niil sha' bigha?" ("How many sheep will it hold"); when I declined an answer, he obviously felt I had missed the point. On a later occasion, when my Navaho was somewhat more advanced, I showed him a picture of the latest jet bomber. "Dikwii dibe beegeela sha' bigha?" ("How many sheep can it carry?"), he asked. By now I knew what he really meant: "What's it good for?" And I began explaining the varied uses of jet bombers, feeling very much like Gulliver in Brobdingnag. Finally, Little Wagon stopped me; he was unwilling to have his mind enlarged in such a shocking way. Such perspectives as my culture was likely to afford him were in the nature of ideas he would rather have done without. I hope the effect of this paper will not be so extreme, and that its suggestions will hold at least a few sheep.

The Index of
American Folk Legends

WAYLAND D. HAND, *University of California, Los Angeles*

If the old axiom of folklore study is valid that the investigation of any genre of folklore must rest on as complete a survey of variant texts as possible, then indexes and finding lists must still retain the prime importance assigned to them by the systematizers of folklore early in the twentieth century. With members of my own generation of workers, I have never doubted this basic working principle. It has helped explain, among other things, why the study of folk legends has been so badly neglected until our own time. Scholars have either found the legend unattractive as a basic form, or they have shied away from the wearying tasks of locating and classifying the vast material involved as a preliminary step to more meaningful researches. It is easier to use a ready-made scholarly apparatus than to create one, and scholars in this country, like their confrères in Europe have, I fear, not disdained folk legend as a field of study —they have simply been bewildered by the vast and scattered material involved, and have preferred to work in certain convenient areas rather than to compile surveys cutting across this whole diverse field. As an important first step to help open up the field of legend study in this country, the Center for the Study of Comparative Folklore and Mythology announced plans in 1961 to compile an Index of American Folk Legends. My paper today will chart the progress that has been made since that time.

The present UCLA Conference on American Folk Legend was conceived as a primary step in mobilizing the country's scholarly resources for the important work at hand. The work in our country is a direct outgrowth of a worldwide effort to concentrate on legend study, which was begun in Kiel and Copenhagen in 1959 as part of the first meeting of the International Society for Folk-Narrative Research. The previous year had seen the publication of Christiansen's survey of migratory legends,[1] and Simonsuuri's type-and motif-index of Finnish mythic legends was being readied for publication.[2] A third venture talked about at the Kiel and Copenhagen conference was the proposed Pan-Scandinavian index of legends that was to be prepared by the Nordisk Institut for Folkedigtning in Copenhagen. All these enterprises were discussed against a backdrop of earlier efforts to compile national legend indexes throughout Scandinavia and in the Baltic states, dating back to 1912,[3] and Sinninghe's catalog of Dutch legends, compiled in 1943, which had become the most generally serviceable legend index in Europe.[4] Johannes Künzig was present at the Kiel and Copenhagen conference and reminded workers that he had begun an index of German legends as early as 1928. This index was never published.[5]

The fear that the proposed Pan-Scandinavian legend index might be adopted as a more or less standard legend index, just as the Aarne Index of folktales had become a canonical finding list in 1910, led delegates to forestall its compilation. It did not take much persuasion to show that a regional compilation would suffer from the same cardinal weakness that beset Aarne's index, namely, too narrow a base. The Scandinavian legend index would have lacked the breadth even of the Aarne finding list, which, after all, was based on Grimm, on Grundtvig's Danish collection, and on Aarne's own unpublished collection in the Finnish Literary Society.

Once these strictures were voiced, it was an easy step to adopt a more reasonable plan, and I had the pleasure of introducing a sense motion that individual countries proceed to compile their own national legend indexes, with an attempt, much later on, to create some sort of international legend index. In retrospect, I must admit

---

[1] Reidar Th. Christiansen, *The Migratory Legends. A Proposed List of Types With a Systematic Catalogue of the Norwegian Variants* (Folklore Fellows Communications, No. 175, Helsinki, 1958).

[2] Lauri Simonsuuri, *Typen- und Motivverzeichnis der Finnischen mythischen Sagen* (Folklore Fellows Communications, No. 182, Helsinki, 1961).

[3] Antti Aarne, *Verzeichnis der Finnischen Ursprungssagen und ihrer Varianten* (Folklore Fellows Communications, No. 8, Hamina, 1912).

[4] J. R. W. Sinninghe, *Katalog der niederländischen Märchen- Ursprungssagen- Sagen- und Legendenvarianten* (Folklore Fellows Communications, No. 132, Helsinki, 1943).

[5] For bibliographical details, see Wayland D. Hand, "Status of European and American Legend Study," *Current Anthropology*, VI (1965), 441 n. 1.

that this hope seems much more difficult to attain now than it did then. As a direct outgrowth of the Copenhagen resolution, the International Society for Folk Narrative Research called two special working conferences on folk legend, namely, those at Antwerp, 1962, and Budapest, 1963. Plans for the American Index were made soon after the Kiel and Copenhagen conference and were formally announced in 1961. A preliminary report and prospect were made at the Antwerp conference the following year.[6]

I had long been interested in the relationship of legend to folk belief, and had had the wit, soon after beginning work on the Brown Collection in 1944, to stamp any and all folk beliefs found in folktales and legends with the term "Folk Narrative." Later on, this broad designation gave way to the more precise labels of "Folk Tale Matrix" and "Legend." Later still, provenance was noted with stamps reading, "Custom," "Ballad Source," "Proverb Source," "News Account," and the like.

Ideally, I should have made extracts of legends as the data on folk belief were compiled, but I did not have the manpower. It will be a relatively easy matter, however, to go back to the original sources and excerpt the needed material. We are already investigating the Xeroxing costs. While this joint folk belief and legend project places the bulk of so-called belief legends immediately at our disposal, it naturally leaves out of account many categories of so-called local legends and historical legends. As we pursue these legends by resort to compilations of legends per se, to books and journals on local history and antiquities, to biographical writings, to family accounts and day books, to ballads, and to works of literature, we constantly enrich not only the stock-in-trade of legends, which now is our main concern, but add to holdings of folk belief and superstition all along the line.

In the search of these non-folklore sources, we have included folk customs along with legends and folk beliefs, which, for purposes of related research, and as time wears on, I am coming to think of as the complex of belief, legend, and custom. The idea of folk belief as being basic to both legend and custom is certainly not new with me. Several modern workers, and Peuckert in an earlier generation,[7] have been struck with the basic affinities among these

---

6 K. C. Peeters, ed., *Tagung der "International Society for Folk-Narrative Research" in Antwerp, 6.–8. Sept. 1962* (Antwerpen: Centrum voor Studie en Documentatie, 1963).

7 Will-Erich Peuckert and Otto Laufer, *Volkskunde: Quellen und Forschungen seit 1930* (Bern: A Francke AG. Verlag, 1951), "Volksglaube" (pp. 50–80); "Sitte und Brauch" (pp. 81–122); "Sage" (pp. 180–225).

three genres, and some of the European folklore archives, including the Folkemindesamling in Copenhagen, reflect these interrelationships in their classificatory systems. It will be of interest to this group here at the UCLA Conference that Linda Dégh and I are doing a joint paper at the forthcoming Bucharest Conference on the interrelationship of folk belief, custom, and legend.[8]

Although these connections of legend with other genres of folklore are most instructive, particularly with regard to function and a broader social matrix, I must come to the main purpose of this paper, namely, a charting of the subject fields of legend, and the specific problems encountered in the making of the legend index. To date the work has centered almost entirely on the search for legends in published sources. Beginning with the collections of folk legends themselves, which are certainly not numerous, the search has broadened to include smaller collections of legends, or even single items, in standard folklore sources: books, monographs, and journals. Much of the best material has come from these scattered sources. Not a little of it has been analyzed in a folkloric context, particularly legends dealing with occupations. Within the last three years, the search has included works dealing largely with local and regional history. In this way, careful gleanings have been made from complete runs of the American Guide Series, the American Country Series, the American River Series, the American Mountain Series, the American Lake Series, and the American Custom Series. Scores of legends not found in folklore literature at all have come to light in this way. A search for legends has also been made in representative runs of almanacs dating back, in some cases, to the late eighteenth century. The findings in these sources have hardly repaid the effort, but the material turned up can at least be accurately dated. The early historical records of several state and county historical societies in New England, Pennsylvania, and along the Eastern Seaboard have been carefully searched, as have historical society journals and other records in another part of the country, namely, Arkansas, Oklahoma, and Texas. Work in other states has been less systematic. For over twenty-five years, the UCLA library has bought freely books on local history all over the United States that in any way have the words "legend" or "lore" in the titles. Some of these really do have legends of the sort that are useful to

---

8 "The Interrelationship of Folk Belief, Legend, and Custom in Modern American Folk Tradition." I plan to enlarge a paper later on that I gave before the second UCLA Conference on Latin-American Folklore in 1967 on this same general subject.

the student of folk legend; many of these nostalgic volumes, however, are useless to the scholar, since they are little more than reminiscences of local events set down in a highly personal and sentimental way.

Little of nothing has been done with biographies, diaries, commonplace books, and family papers. These sources have a high potential, and particularly so when dealing with occupational pursuits, as the systematic work of Jerry Foster has shown for accounts dealing with the life of sailors.

Perhaps the potentially richest source of legends in the country still remains largely unexploited. I am referring to the unpublished legends in folklore archives all over the country. Only Indiana University, I believe, has started to work through this material with a view to getting the corpus into print. The richness of the first samplings gives a fair adumbration of what must exist in archive after archive across the country. After obtaining from each of you at this conference informal reports on the archives that you know, I propose to solicit reports on legend holdings in folklore archives across the country, and also to urge publication of material in convenient groupings. Such publication should notably widen the scope of holdings.

For a group of specialists as versatile as the one that has been assembled for this conference, it might be instructive to survey American folk legend from the point of view of the European carry-over, on the one hand, and the development of relatively new bodies of native American material, on the other. I shall await in the discussion following this paper a filling out of some of the information only sketched in the presentation itself.

To start with one of the most universal fields of folk legend, namely, the creatures of lower mythology, one can say that the belief in certain categories of creatures has been kept alive in some cases, and that it has either rapidly dwindled or died out in others. Whereas there are still stories to be gathered in America about werewolves and vampires, and whereas in many parts of the country there are still reminiscences of fairy folk, either in the well-known traditions of the British Isles, or in those countries that have given us *Zwerge, lutins, duendes, tomtars,* and *nissen,* I do not know of any active tradition having to do with either dragons or giants. The Wild Hunt is encountered in the French-American tradition, but I have not come upon the nightmare in legend, even though this creature, or this phenomenon, is otherwise well known in folk belief, and particularly so in folk medicine. Belief in witchcraft and

devil lore has persisted to our own time, as has a belief in the evil
eye and in magic and conjury, generally speaking.[9]

Ghostlore and the realm of the dead remain a persistent and
inexhaustible source of folk legend, and there have been in recent
years many modern innovations on old themes. A few banshee
legends have come down to us in different parts of the country, but
stories about ladies in black, or ladies in white are perhaps more
common. In Spanish-speaking parts of the country *La Llorona*
stories seem to persist, as do those of *El mal Hijo,* which also deals
with the realm of the dead. Belief in vampirism and the living dead
has not entirely died out, as indicated earlier, but in addition there
is a special development of this phenomenon in the Caribbean
in zombies and similar creatures. Some of the phantom creatures
of the swamps, as well as the more classical figures such as the will-
o'-the-wisp, are connected with the dead, as are the fabled boundary-
mark-removers of the Pennsylvania German country. Sixth-sense
stories or the so-called death tokens are perhaps modern manifestations of the belief in wraiths. These stories can still be collected
from college students as memorats.

Religious lore is a fruitful field of legend study, over and above
the field of saints' legends, per se. To be found in this category of
belief and legend are stories dealing with divine providences of
all kinds, and the intervening of other-worldly ministrants in human affairs. Legends dealing with God's house, including bells and
other holy utensils, and with the piety of the church's servants and
the Lord's flock are to be found both in the established places of
worship and the missionary life on the frontier. To be treated
in this general field also, of course, are legends dealing with sin
and blasphemy. The fate of sinners and mockers has always been
held up as a warning to the unfaithful, and every religious community has preserved stories of what has happened to those who
do the devil's bidding. Devil lore, insofar as it does not concern
witchcraft, should be taken up, in my opinion, not with the creatures of mythology, but rather with religious lore. Where the Devil
prevails upon witches to destroy the church, even witchcraft may be
treated within the realm of religious lore. Many European collections devote a special section to the Devil. Legends dealing with
so-called restless souls are often treated in a religious context rather
than as a part of ghostlore.

I have not come to any final decision with regard to saints'

---

[9] In addition to various recent books and articles, the reader should consult
Harry Middleton Hyatt, *Hoodoo, Conjuration, Witchcraft, Rootwork,* 2 vols.
(New York: The Alma Egan Hyatt Foundation, 1970).

legends, but I believe they should be treated at some appropriate place in the index. Sinninghe, as you will recall, has worked saints' legends into his index, and the folklore people in Belgium have come to think of the *légendes chrétiennes* as belonging side by side with the *légendes profanes*.[10]

Treasure legends constitute an important field in American legendry, as the studies of Hurley and Granger show, and legends dealing with lost mines amount to a major legendary tradition. The Granger dissertation has charted this field in minute detail.

Etiological legends constitute a body of important material. Whether physiographic features of the land are described in terms of their origin, or flora and fauna, they all represent an attempt to account for the physical character of the land and the plant and animal life that it sustains, as well as the watery and airy expanse. Stress, of course, is usually upon striking or unusual features. I doubt that etiological accounts of the early colonists and those who have come to live here from various parts of Europe and elsewhere can be strictly segregated from the Indian origin myths. This is a problem that must be faced in connection with how much Indian material should be used, and what kinds.

There are many kinds of legends that defy easy classification. Among these are legends about unusual characters, all the way from charlatans, peddlers, hermits, and desert rats, to heroes and darlings in the various trades and occupations, to public figures in the professions, in sports, in the entertainment industry, and even in public life and politics. To include or not to include this material is a question that will have to be decided when more of it is in hand. Guidance in these marginal areas will be sought from specialists at a later date.

Historical legends dealing with people, places, and events constitute an important body of material. This material will come partly, I suppose, from history books; more of it will no doubt come from local historical and traditional accounts dealing with such diverse subjects as wars, skirmishes with the Indians, Gypsy curses, natural prodigies, cyclones, floods, earthquakes, and other natural disasters, and with explosions, wrecks, the sinking of ships, and other kinds of calamities associated with travel, industry, or commerce. Whether the beliefs and customs that have grown with the electronic and space age ultimately will yield legends of the general kind with which we are accustomed to deal remains to be seen.

There are many problems of policy and numerous technical matters that will have to be faced in the compiling of data, and in

10 Peeters, *Tagung*, pp. 19–21 *passim*.

the actual editing of the material that will go into the Index. Although in most matters I have learned, in the words of the old proverb, not to take off my shoes before I reach the river, there are some decisions that cannot be put off much longer. To what extent should American Indian material be utilized in the Index? Up until now in researches related to the finding lists of legends, I have made use of American Indian folk materials only as they relate to interaction between our native American peoples and the colonists from Europe. Fields of folklore in which such intimate contact is reflected include animal and plant husbandry, weather lore, hunting and fishing, and folk medicine. During the last 350 years the exchange of folk material, while not completely reciprocal, has easily demonstrated a two-way flow. In mythology and religion there has been no such ready exchange, and in many individual areas of human thought and action there is really not enough common ground, in my opinion, to warrant an attempt at a common classification. No one forecloses the possibility, I guess, of an eventual narrowing of this gap as more workers undertake to specialize in American Indian folklore as well as in European and American folklore. In this connection, one might fervently hope that anthropologists themselves would organize and systematize their study of American Indian folklore and mythology so that at least common points of departure can be plotted. In addition to the basic reasons stated, I am disinclined to include American Indian legends in the index for reasons of space. Everyone would welcome, I am sure, someone's undertaking to make a special collection of American Indian Legends. Whether myths should also be included, I would leave to the judgment of people who know more about the connections between these two genres than I. Certain kinds of American Indian material that have been assimilated into the Spanish tradition of the Southwest might well find their way into the Index, just as certain Indian traditions early got mixed up in the traditions of the earliest European settlers. In addition to the Spanish explorations in the southwestern part of the United States, and the incursions of Mexicans into the United States in more recent times, we must take into account French exploration and colonization, not only in the Mississippi and St. Lawrence river basins, but elsewhere in the country. Similarly, the settlement of different parts of the country by German, Dutch, and Scandinavian immigrants should be taken into account, and an attempt made to record the legends that may have been brought here and transplanted. This goes also for Slavic and Finno-Ugric peoples, as well as for other groups that may have come to our shores.

Skinner did not hesitate to include the Caribbean area in his surveys, nor Mexico and adjacent countries to the South,[11] and, if the Index is to use the term "American" in the title in any meaningful way, neither should we. Separate special indexes, of course, would be a better solution, if people could be enlisted to prepare them.

The scheme of classification and numbering of the Index will be along lines of existing legend indexes in other countries. Whether open numbers will be left for addenda is a decision that can be reached later when the extent of coverage can be foreseen more properly than now.

Within reasonable limitations of space, I should favor the inclusion of as reasonably full a set of references for legend type numbers as can be mustered. I have always thought of type numbers per se as ineffective unless there is a good backup of references to start the researcher on his way. The early indexes failed notably to do this, and thus their usefulness has always been greatly impaired.

A basic question of policy involves the inclusion of legend index numbers when there is only a rudimentary idea, and not a legend in full narrative trappings. Perhaps legend fragments and nuclear beliefs should be carried in the index with proper endorsement as to what they are. In that way, these numbers may serve the function of a jury text in bringing in full narrative examples over the years.

Years ago when the Index was first started, we had all Legend indexes translated into English on 5-by-8-inch cards for interfiling with American material. In that way one can easily supply European legend index numbers for any and all American legend types that happen to have foreign analogues. The section on "Death" in the new German Legend Index has already been clipped up, pasted to cards, and translations of legend index captions made so that it can be integrated in the same way as the other indexes. From the preliminary work trying to pattern American material after this notable European research effort, one can easily foresee, I believe, that The Index of American Legends will have a special character of its own. That is how it should be, and those of us who are connected with this important enterprise will spare no effort to see that it will marshal and classify American stocks of folk legends to their best advantage.

---

11 Charles M. Skinner, *Myths and Legends Beyond Our Borders* (Philadelphia and London, 1899), "Mexico" (pp. 213–319); *idem., Myths and Legends of Our New Possessions and Protectorate* (Philadelphia and London, 1900), "The Caribbean" (pp. 23–174).

Index